Masculinities in the Gospel of Matthew

Masculinities in the Gospel of Matthew

Joseph, John, Peter, and Judas

Kendra A. Mohn

LEXINGTON BOOKS/FORTRESS ACADEMIC
Lanham • Boulder • New York • London

Published by Lexington Books/Fortress Academic
Lexington Books is an imprint of The Rowman & Littlefield Publishing Group, Inc.
4501 Forbes Boulevard, Suite 200, Lanham, Maryland 20706
www.rowman.com

86-90 Paul Street, London EC2A 4NE, United Kingdom

Copyright © 2024 by The Rowman & Littlefield Publishing Group, Inc.

All rights reserved. No part of this book may be reproduced in any form or by any electronic or mechanical means, including information storage and retrieval systems, without written permission from the publisher, except by a reviewer who may quote passages in a review.

British Library Cataloguing in Publication Information Available

Library of Congress Cataloging-in-Publication Data

Names: Mohn, Kendra A., 1977– author.
Title: Masculinities in the Gospel of Matthew : Joseph, John, Peter, and Judas / Kendra A. Mohn.
Other titles: Real men
Description: Lanham : Lexington Books/Fortress Academic, [2024] | Revision of the author's thesis (doctoral)—Brite Divinity School, 2018, under the title: Real men : masculinities in the Gospel of Matthew. | Includes bibliographical references and index. | Summary: "Kendra A. Mohn traces how the constructions of nonelite men in the Gospel of Matthew negotiate expectations of elite Roman masculinity. Highlighting wealth, divine service, and dominating control, Mohn shows how the depictions of Joseph, John, Peter, and Judas shape expectations of men in terms of discipleship, power, and leadership"—Provided by publisher.
Identifiers: LCCN 2023045061 (print) | LCCN 2023045062 (ebook) | ISBN 9781978709485 (cloth) | ISBN 9781978709492 (epub)
Subjects: LCSH: Bible. Matthew—Criticism, interpretation, etc. | Masculinity—Biblical teaching. | Masculinity in the Bible. | Elite (Social sciences) in the Bible.
Classification: LCC BS2575.6.M34 M64 2024 (print) | LCC BS2575.6.M34 (ebook) | DDC 226.2/0830531—dc23/eng/20231117
LC record available at https://lccn.loc.gov/2023045061
LC ebook record available at https://lccn.loc.gov/2023045062

♾️ The paper used in this publication meets the minimum requirements of American National Standard for Information Sciences—Permanence of Paper for Printed Library Materials, ANSI/NISO Z39.48-1992.

To my grandparents, Eitel and Frieda Mohn and Clarence and Helen Alquist, whose love and hard work made so much possible

Contents

Acknowledgments	ix
Chapter 1: Introduction and Methodology	1
Chapter 2: Joseph and King Herod	49
Chapter 3: John the Baptist and Herod Antipas	89
Chapter 4: Peter	127
Chapter 5: Judas	169
Conclusion	203
Bibliography	209
Index	223
About the Author	233

Acknowledgments

I wish to acknowledge the following people for their assistance in bringing this book to fruition. First, I am deeply grateful to Warren Carter, my advisor and the director of this project when it was a dissertation at Brite Divinity School, for his consistent advocacy, clarifying feedback, academic rigor, patience, high expectations, and encouragement. I also extend gratitude to Francisco Lozada and Shelly Matthews, who gave their time to sit on the committee.

A number of colleagues and friends have offered helpful conversations and essential feedback, specifically Jillian Engelhardt, Zhenya Gurina-Rodriguez, Annelies Moeser, Stephanie McFarland, and Amanda Nance. Tasha McGhie (Bend Your Lens Coaching) was a most excellent coach and editor, without whom I doubt this project would have been completed. Those at Fortress Academic have been wonderful collaborators, especially Gayla Freeman. Additionally, the staff and congregation of Trinity Lutheran Church, Fort Worth, TX, have been enormously patient and encouraging, especially Diana Smith and Beth Gomez.

Finally, I wish to thank my family: my parents, Jim and Connie Mohn; my sister and brother-in-law, Alicia Mohn and Eric Boudreau; my spouse, Erik Gronberg; and my children, Annika, Greta, and Axel Gronberg, who have provided inspiration, beneficial distraction, and motivation to persevere.

Chapter 1

Introduction and Methodology

In her now-classic work on feminist theory, Mary Daly declares, "if God is male, then the male is God."[1] This provocative statement not only highlights the exclusion and devaluing of women, but also emphasizes the problematic association of masculinity with divinity, which is often equated with virtue, power, and privilege. These associations, however, prove troubling in the context of the Gospel of Matthew, which highlights sacrifice, self-denial, suffering, and death as expectations of the male disciples of Jesus. What does masculinity mean in the context of a Gospel where John the Baptist is beheaded at the request of a woman, Joseph obediently protects the life of a vulnerable baby boy who is not his own son, Peter is known as much for denying Jesus as he is for outspoken leadership, and Jesus is handed over by Judas, one of his own disciples? And what, if anything, do these varied masculinities have to do with God?

The complex masculinities in Matthew introduce challenging questions about gender, power, and divinity. In this book I engage these issues, exploring the masculinities of several figures in Matthew's Gospel—Joseph, John the Baptist, Peter, and Judas—in light of Greco-Roman constructions of masculinity, the imperial narrative of the ancient world that surrounds and shapes the New Testament. I also consider the masculinities of contrasting figures King Herod and Herod Antipas in the context of these discussions. I argue that the pictures of masculinity in Matthew's Gospel involve ambivalence, inscribing certain aspects of the dominant construction of the ancient world while seeking to create distance from others.

For example, the Gospel's privileging of obedient discipleship challenges the dominant cultural emphasis on wealth and the societal control of elites by valuing submission to God, but it clearly approves of other expressions of dominating control over self and others that serve divine purposes. Thus, even as some aspects of ancient masculinity are challenged, the essential problematic relationship between masculinity and power remains intact, ultimately reinscribing the pattern of divine sanction of the imperial status quo.

The central question that guides this project is, "How does the Gospel of Matthew construct masculinity and how do those constructions relate to Greco-Roman constructions of masculinity that dominate the world of the Gospel?" In this book, I provide possible answers to these questions by discussing the characterizations of individual male characters in Matthew in light of the characteristics of the dominant construction of ancient masculinity that support and communicate assumptions and values of the Empire. I focus on where and how the Gospel's constructions intersect with this dominant construction by means of mimicry, resistance, redefinition, and negotiation.

This kind of contextualization is potentially fruitful particularly because of the social location of the New Testament as a non-elite text. Because of the fundamental relationship between masculinity and power in the Roman Empire, it is not difficult to find examples of Roman thought originating from and largely concerned with elite males.[2] Indeed, Roman masculinity itself was an ideal, a perfect storm of factors enabling the flawless performance of a man. This ideal occupied one end of a gender spectrum that categorized males according to behaviors and characteristics; the remainder of the spectrum was occupied by those who did not meet the expectations of masculinity for various reasons. Movement along the spectrum was assumed, both toward and away from the ideal, creating a climate where performance and competition were integral to the assertion of identity. It is not surprising, then, that much of the ancient discourse on masculinity points to men who either exemplify or fail to meet the ideal standard in key ways, underscoring the qualities of masculinity that matter most to elites.[3]

The hegemonic masculinity characteristic of the ancient world was effective because its emphasis on valor and domination kept elite males occupied with competitive rhetoric and actions, and because most non-elite men either couldn't compete for honor and power, therefore supporting it by default, or chose not to compete by removing themselves from public competitive environments focused on demonstrating masculinity. Hegemonic masculinity's dominance means it is not always easy to determine other forms of masculinity that would have functioned in the lived experience of human beings, especially those whose lives were less than ideal.

Because of their non-elite origins, the New Testament texts provide a unique and potentially important example of a different kind of literature from a different kind of people.[4] But what, precisely, is the difference? In what ways do the presentations of masculinity in the New Testament diverge from or replicate dominant constructions? And, if the former, what is the nature of the divergence? Is it simply a change of clothing, emphasizing different qualities while downplaying others? Or are these constructions fundamental?

From this research, what emerges is a complex picture of the way that masculinities in the Gospel of Matthew relate to the masculinities of their imperial context. In particular, three ideas emerge consistently from the discourse in the Gospel as sites for negotiation of masculine status: divine service, dominating control over self and over others, and wealth.[5] While these are not the only possible themes that could emerge from such an analysis, they can be considered as particularly important and helpful themes when addressing constructs of masculinity in the Gospel of Matthew as they relate to those of Greco-Romans.

I contend that constructions of masculinity in the Gospel of Matthew attempt to challenge conventional elite masculine norms in antiquity, which are shaped by the Roman Empire, and to redefine them in terms of the story of Jesus of Nazareth and the social location of his followers. This attempted challenge is primarily visible in the Gospel's rejection of wealth as an aspect of discipleship; the Gospel does not understand wealth to be a source of power or evidence of divine favor for men in divine service. This attempt, however, is ultimately limited by the same emphasis on discipleship, which sanctions dominating control over self and others as an aspect of divine service and retains a hegemonic understanding of God's power.

Engaging these Matthean figures through the lens of divine service, dominating control over self and over others, and wealth illuminates these issues in a variety of ways. By rejecting wealth and emphasizing obedient service, the Gospel challenges, undermines, and redefines several key aspects of masculinity from ancient conventional constructions. At the same time, it appropriates and imitates others, namely the presumed relationship between masculinity and divine service and the demonstration or execution of masculinity by control over self and over others when it serves divine purposes.

The resulting concepts of masculinity in Matthew display an inherent tension both for original and contemporary interpreters. On the one hand, the Gospel makes a strong case for an alternative masculinity that eschews the role of status defined by wealth so prized by other ancient writers and emphasizes self-denial and discipleship oriented toward submission to God and service to others. This construction is potentially a powerful challenge to the Empire, resisting and rejecting its values. On the other hand, this challenge is undercut by the persistence of a fundamental relationship between masculinity and dominating power that connects masculinity both with divine service and with control over self and over others. This connection to control produces an understanding of masculinity that is problematic for both ancient and contemporary hearers and readers of the Gospel who would consider its concept of masculinity to carry authoritative weight or to portray a model to be emulated.

METHODOLOGY: MASCULINITY STUDIES

My conversation partners for this project come primarily from those engaged in work investigating the function of masculinity in the Gospels: Colleen Conway,[6] Susanna Asikainen,[7] Brittany Wilson,[8] Eric Thurman,[9] Tat-siong Benny Liew,[10] Stephen Moore, and Janice Capel Anderson.[11] My study utilizes similar methodology and asks similar questions. However, I turn my attention to exploring aspects of masculinity in the Gospels that differ from what others have done thus far, notably applying consistent themes of divine service, dominating control over self and over others, and wealth to multiple characters within the Gospel of Matthew.

Broadly conceived, the discipline of masculinity studies foregrounds questions of masculinity in the interpretation of biblical texts. My particular approach to this methodology employs questions that seek to identify (1) where masculinity is present in the text, (2) how it is variously constructed and represented, and (3) how those constructions function with respect to power. This last task is interested in tracing and exposing the relationship between masculinity and power, problematizing facile interpretations, and working through the implications of this relationship for the use of Gospel texts in faith communities.

In order to put this methodology into practice, I utilize scholarship on ancient masculinity to construct a context within which to consider the Gospel text. This constructed context highlights important aspects of ancient masculinity, such as a focus on elites, competition, a continuum of masculine status, a culture of outside interpretation, and exhibition and evaluation of behaviors and traits. To provide language for the interpretation of this constructed context, I draw on theories and concepts from contemporary studies of masculinity, which in turn are influenced by disciplines such as feminist theory and gender studies.

One important concept for this study is "hegemonic masculinity." Coined by Connell, the term refers to a particular kind of masculinity that emphasizes power and dominance over women, as well as men who do not meet its standards.[12] Connell defines hegemonic masculinity as "the configuration of gender practice which embodies the currently accepted answer to the problem of legitimacy of patriarchy, which guarantees (or is taken to guarantee) the dominant position of men and the subordination of women."[13]

Connell's compelling concept has been used widely by scholars in many different fields. It has also undergone some revision and challenge, notably by Demetrakis Demetriou. Demetriou's critique draws attention to the social forces at work in hegemonic masculinity, highlighting what he calls the "internal" and "external" dynamics that exist both between masculinity and femininity, and among different expressions of masculinity.[14] Demetriou problematizes Connell's categories and argues for a more nuanced understanding of the ways that alternative masculinities not only are oppressed by hegemonic masculinity, but also contribute to it.

New Testament scholars interested in masculinity have also critiqued the term, particularly in its usage. For Wilson, the concept has become too closely aligned with "imperial masculinity," and so is understood more in terms of its content than its function.[15] Asikainen emphasizes this same point, critiquing the reduction of the concept to a list of traits, and preferring to talk about the way that different masculinities (including subordinate or marginalized forms) compete for ideal hegemony.[16]

I concur that such usage misses a critical element of power dynamics present in Connell's concept. However, while the term may be contested and imperfect, the concept of hegemonic masculinity remains important because, in the words of Connell, "we still require a way of theorizing gendered power relations among men, and understanding the effectiveness of masculinities in the legitimation of the gendered order." Hegemonic masculinity does not simply refer to one type of masculinity. Rather, it recognizes various constructions of masculinity and refers to the process by which masculine power is asserted, shifted, and reasserted in order to maintain the desired structure of privileging some kinds of men and oppressing women. Connell considers this dynamic (what Demetriou calls the "external" dimension of hegemony) to be the context within which the construction of gender plays out.

Therefore, while some types of masculinity may exhibit traits more obviously associated with power, all expressions of masculinity contribute to a system that perpetuates male privilege. And the relationships among the different kinds of masculinity (what Demetriou calls the "internal" dimension) are critically important for examining the ways masculine power is executed and upheld. For Connell, "'hegemonic masculinity' is always constructed in relation to various subordinated masculinities as well as in relation to women. The interplay between different forms of masculinity is an important part of how a patriarchal social order works."[17] Studying New Testament texts, then, is not just a window into alternative masculinities. It is an examination of hegemonic masculinity itself. Therefore, I continue to make use of the term with its modifications and critiques in view.[18]

An integral part of the assertion of hegemonic masculinity is an awareness of sexuality and the wider conceptualization of the social construction of gender.[19] Connell argues that because of the way hegemonic masculinity has asserted itself in the last few centuries, marked by dominance of self and oppression of others, homosexuality was an obvious and immediate casualty.[20] Likewise, Butler and Foucault both identify the force of the heterosexual paradigm on the negotiation and performance of gender.[21]

These perspectives come out of a contemporary Western paradigm, so their conclusions cannot be assumed to be immediately applicable to a discussion of gender in the ancient world. But the larger question of the role of sexuality in a conversation about masculinity remains important, especially because the construction of masculinity is played out in a variety of arenas, including sexual experience.

Using a nuanced concept of hegemonic masculinity as a hermeneutical filter for the New Testament texts is helpful, therefore, as it focuses the interpreter's attention on (1) manifestations of ideal masculinity, (2) forms of alternative masculinity, and (3) the hegemonic system upheld by the construction and interplay between these various constructions. The concept provides an indispensable framework for asking questions and grasping the complex dynamics at work.

Moreover, I share Conway's conviction that masculinity studies from a feminist perspective is critically important.[22] Not only does this approach de-center masculinity as a social construct, opening it up to critique and possible reconstruction, but it is interested in the ways that normative assumptions about masculinity in the past have done significant damage to men and women, creating a context in which gendered oppression remains possible and perhaps inevitable.

Ancient Masculinity: Overview

I next provide a discussion of ancient masculinity as context for applying this methodology to the New Testament. A comprehensive description of ancient masculinity is a full-length project in itself, so I do not attempt one here. Rather, the next discussion is tailored to the questions I consider in this project, naming important concepts in how masculinity was constructed and understood, and focusing on its relationship to power and how that relationship functioned in the imperial world. After an introduction to ancient masculinity, I introduce my three themes of dominating control over self and others, wealth, and divine service, and then discuss arenas where these issues are negotiated.[23] I return to these same themes and relationships to provide points of entry and comparison as I engage the male characters in Matthew.

Ancient masculinity was an ideal focused on elites, and consequently reflects elite realities and concerns. Ancient masculinity was so tied to status that to be "masculine" was to be "elite."[24] Even the conversation about masculinity was elite. Ancient thought on masculinity is found primarily in the writings of elite males comparing themselves to one another, which would not have been part of public discourse available to other classes.[25] Because of this exclusive focus on elites, there is no such thing as a "real man" from the lower classes. Some elements or aspects of masculinity might be present in some individuals from those classes, and perhaps even recognized as such, but the absence of elite status meant that those men could never truly compete.

In contemporary terms, non-elite men might be categorized as R. W. Connell's "marginalized" masculinities.[26] In the ancient world, they were "less masculine" than other men. Contemporary understanding of gender stresses a binary opposition based in biology. Ancient understandings of gender suggest more fluidity along a continuum or spectrum. Movement along that spectrum had powerful consequences, including the possibility that "male and female bodies were considered not so much different in kind as in degree."[27] Male bodies, then, occupied positions along a spectrum of gender, and, while noteworthy variants exist, the emphasis on ancient masculinity is placed heavily on elites.

This association with elite values is important in several aspects. For example, as a marker of elite status, the achievement of masculinity was characterized by high-stakes competition. Ancient masculinity was designed to be a limited commodity, earned by a few, and inaccessible to the rest. Once achieved, it was very difficult to maintain because of the constant striving of others. As Gleason argues, it "was not a state to be definitively and irrefutably achieved, but something always under construction and constantly open to scrutiny."[28] And, the consequences of failure, what Conway calls "the specter of lost manliness . . . was frequently raised before the eyes of the literate male audience."[29]

The visible consequences of loss as well as the tangible rewards for performances of dominance raise the stakes of the competition for achieving masculinity. Those elite males who demonstrate ideal masculinity are truly hegemonic. They claim the task of leadership (ἡγεμονία) in all realms of life: political, military, economic, religious, societal, and cultural. Those who do not demonstrate masculinity risk losing not only their status as a "man," but also their power in all other aspects of life. This hegemonic system, where power is in the hands of a very few, advances their interests at the expense of the many and perpetuates a system where the elite males are the powerful and the powerful are the elite males.

Like other systems of hegemonic masculinity, the association of permanence and strength with ancient ideal masculinity is accompanied by a secondary message of vulnerability and crisis.[30] Gleason refers to this as a "double face," calling masculinity a project "representing itself as natural and inevitable to outsiders, but stressing to insiders the importance of nurture and the vulnerability of the entire project to lapses of taste and self-control."[31] Because ideal masculinity is difficult to achieve, it can be understood to be in short supply, particularly when the masculinity of so many is subjected to frequent critique and challenge. If masculinity is threatened by competition or critique, the need to reassert its dominance becomes prominent.

In the words of Conway, this dynamic produces "a paradox: the rhetoric of instable and threatened masculinity juxtaposed with the reality of stable and continuous masculine power."[32] In the ancient world, this juxtaposition equates to a nearly constant effort to assert dominance and masculine power. Tension between stability and vulnerability brings to mind the work of both Traister and Connell, who stress the ability of hegemonic masculinity to sustain itself. Despite operating in the interests of the very few at the expense of the very many, the power of elite males thrives in the ancient world, making it important to consider what role the ambivalent "double face" plays in this process.

Connell identifies three types of alternative masculinities—subordinate, marginalized, and complicit—and characterizes them in terms of their relationship to hegemonic masculinity.[33] She argues that other forms of masculinity that do not conform to the ideal are still identified with respect to that ideal. "Subordinated" masculinities, for example, are contrasted with ideal masculinity, devalued, and often associated with femininity. They are "foils" set up to fail.[34]

"Marginalized" masculinities, by contrast, may bear some resemblance to ideal masculinity, but are identified with racial, ethnic, or class distinctions that preclude full hegemony. Since these masculinities are subject to "the *authorization* of the hegemonic masculinity of the dominant group" (emphasis original), they are understood to be marginalized.[35] The ambivalence of the imperial world toward the masculinities of its enemies is an example.

Finally, the concept of "complicit" masculinity describes the reality that although most men cannot achieve ideal masculinity, they still benefit from what Connell calls the "patriarchal dividend."[36] These men are not understood to be "slackers" or "bad guys," whose expressions of masculinity are shadows or perversions of the ideal. In some respects, they may even be called "good guys" as they are not overt aggressors and often exhibit support of women or critique of some masculine power. Nevertheless, the system of hegemonic masculinity provides them with advantages and authority that are not available to women in the same way.[37]

As I consider the masculinities described in the Gospel of Matthew, these terms—hegemonic, subordinated, marginalized, and complicit masculinities—may prove to be helpful starting points in describing and understanding what is encountered there. And yet, as imperial critical scholars have pointed out, dealing with hegemonic power is never as simple as it seems.[38] Demetriou's complexified understanding of Connell's categories advocates for a more careful analysis of the ways that alternative masculinities interact with more hegemonic expressions in order to support the prevailing system.[39] Sometimes this can be described as complicit, but sometimes it is not; hegemonic masculinity can co-opt for its own use even those alternative forms that seek to challenge the system.[40]

Bryce Traister offers another way to view the way that masculine power establishes and protects its dominance.[41] According to Traister, discourse on masculinity has frequently employed the concept of "crisis" to claim that masculinity itself is somehow vulnerable or that the phenomenon of masculinity puts "real men," who are separated from the theoretical concept of "masculinity," in a position of threatened vulnerability.[42] Traister finds the crisis narrative to be extremely problematic as it often results in reactionary movements to reassert masculinity's strength and power, as well as removing accountability from human beings for the oppression that hegemonic masculinity can cause.[43]

Building on Traister's work, Conway also raises questions about this "crisis" theory of masculinity and its implications for the New Testament.[44] The idea of masculinity in crisis, although a relatively recent one, fits in well with the ancient understanding of masculinity that simultaneously communicates vulnerability and stability.[45] Scholars like Conway have found it a helpful way to address the paradox apparent in ancient attitudes.

Another implication of the association of masculinity with elite identity is the connection between masculinity and virtue. Prescribing and policing virtuous behavior was a key strategy for defining who qualified for elite status.[46] Catherine Edwards notes that alignment between elite status and virtuous behavior was a key strategy for defining who qualified for elite status, as well as controlling those who had elite status.[47] The intimate tie between elite status and masculinity means the same demonstration of virtue strengthened one's claim to masculinity.

According to Gleason, "to exhibit courage or excellence (*virtus*) was by definition to exhibit the qualities of a man."[48] The close linguistic relationship between the word *vir* (man) and *virtus* emphasizes the connection.[49] The courage and excellence Gleason describes relate to many aspects of a man's life, including and especially military prowess.[50] Through this lens, behaviors that made one "manly" (i.e., military conquest, control over self and others) also made one virtuous.[51] The relationship between the two is not automatic; not all men accomplish or maintain *virtus*. But those who did claimed the association with and demonstration of virtue as part of their achievements, tying virtues and masculinity together.

Ancient Masculinity: Themes of Dominating Control over Self and Others, Divine Service, and Wealth

The resulting picture of masculinity combines elite status, competition, varying roles for non-elites, performative fragility, and connection to virtue into what Wilson calls an "agonistic fixation on affirming one's manliness in the face of the ever-present threat of effeminacy."[52] From this picture of masculinity, three themes emerge that are central to a discussion of masculinity in the Gospel of Matthew: dominating control over self and others, divine service, and wealth. While these themes have distinct expression, it is unsurprising to see that they overlap as they contribute to a larger, interconnected effort to assert masculine status.

First, an essential aspect of establishing masculine status in the ancient world was establishing dominating control over one's self and over others, often centered around bodies and their activities.[53] Self-control meant protecting one's own body from attack or sexual advance, keeping emotions in check, preserving physical mobility and travel, and controlling the narrative about oneself. As Wilson states, "only elite males were able to defend the boundaries of their body from invasive assaults, such as being blinded, beaten, or sexually penetrated.[54] Threats to masculinity came in a variety of forms that threatened a man's personal autonomy and necessitated a response.

Control over one's self was tied to control over others. As Edwards argues, "The elite justified their privileged position by pointing to their superior morals. Their capacity for self-control legitimated the control they exercised over others who were, it was implied, unable to control themselves."[55] The sense of control over others similarly includes efforts to wield social status, physical power, financial influence, and sexual dominance. In order to assert and maintain masculine status, elite men controlled the movements of others, for example demonstrating power over women and slaves with sexual access and economic ownership. They authorized (or not) the movements of others through travel and the public arena, gave large gifts in support of public works to establish the importance of their patronage, and established the laws and rhetorical terms for societal values that reified the connection between masculinity and virtue.[56]

This connection between masculinity and virtue goes hand in hand with an association with divinity. While not all men were gods, Roman emperors were understood to rule with divine sanction and were increasingly declared to be divine after their deaths.[57] The mix of divine and human figures in Roman religious narratives and the presence of heroic, ideal historical figures like Alexander the Great emphasized the connection.[58] The association is not without tension; while the presence of divine sanction solidified success and vice versa, conversely, the absence of virtue or power or the presence of failure was linked to the absence of divine favor.[59] Further, divine sanction both emphasizes and relativizes human power.[60] J. Rufus Fears draws on Seneca to show how Nero was considered "vicegerent of the gods."[61] Such a position acknowledges the ultimate authority of the divine over Nero. From a human perspective, however, the result is increased power and authority over others.[62]

The characteristics associating divinity with power resonate deeply with the second theme of divine service as a component of ancient masculinity. Other aspiring men emulated the power of these figures, and the idea of divine order and blessing persisted.[63] As Carter argues, "being 'equal to (a god or) God' is a matter of honor, of power, of benefaction, of imitating God, of being sent as an agent of the gods."[64] These themes reflect a preoccupation not merely with demonstrating power akin to the divine, but with achieving a certain kind of masculine identity. For his analysis, Carter draws on the work of Price, who quotes a Greek maxim to emphasize the connection: "What is a god? The exercise of power. What is a king? God-like."[65] God-like humans are those who exercise power in the masculine terms of dominance, benefaction, honor, and imitation of the divine.[66]

The third and final theme of ancient masculinity important for this discussion is wealth. Because exercising power required wealth, access to resources was an important part of the establishment of masculine status. An emperor used wealth for benefaction, for status display, and for funding an army. Others followed suit. Gleason emphasizes both the amount of wealth commonly associated with aristocrats in antiquity, as well as the role of benefaction and conspicuous consumption for those who lived into an elite identity.[67] So for those who were already in line to compete for ideal masculinity, wealth was assumed. One could have wealth without status in the ancient world, but it was difficult to have status without wealth.

Mythic or heroic figures such as Alexander the Great or Augustus set the standard for wealth as they do for divinity. Such figures are part of the Roman preoccupation with the past, whether the Greek past or their own, and their mythic quality conveys an almost limitless sense of resources. Conway argues that a figure like Augustus is particularly important because "all the ideals of masculine deportment, and the honor and authority that accompany them, were concentrated in one man."[68] For elites as well as non-elites, a figure like Augustus communicates widely the sense of unlimited power, made possible by and communicated with unlimited wealth, and sanctioned by the gods.

Interestingly, however, there is a sense of tension and ambiguity associated with excess wealth that circles back to virtue. As Edwards notes, "*Virtus*—that quality which marked out the good Roman—consisted of a complex mixture of ancestry, wealth, and personal merit."[69] Gleason articulates a "self-conscious frugality" that competed with the "gross logic of overconsumption: excess is power."[70] Both excess frugality and excess extravagance could be a source of masculine critique.[71] This tension leads to some ambiguity with respect to definitions of masculine behaviors. However, the sense of significant wealth used or disseminated in appropriate ways remains an integral part of the display of masculine status. The constant is the demonstration of power. Whether power is better shown through overconsumption or frugality may be debatable in particular circumstances, but the primacy of power over others through the vehicle of wealth is consistent.[72]

These aspects of elite status—dominating power over self and others, association with virtue and divinity, and connection to wealth marked by limited availability in a competitive environment—all worked together to focus attention on the efforts of the elite to establish masculine identity. The task of competing for ideal masculinity involved a complex combination of behaviors and attributes, as well as their interpretation by others. The effort involved was substantial; it was an all-encompassing project that needed lots of attention.

Ancient Masculinity: Arenas and Contexts for Masculine Behavior

In this next section, I flesh out some arenas that are important sites of negotiation for masculine status, including physiognomy, public debate, and sexuality. The ancient practice of physiognomy, the interpretation of a person's traits and behaviors in terms of some kind of meaningful judgment about character, was a popular site for the vigorous debate over masculine behaviors in the ancient world.[73] Physiognomical discourse both established and enforced coded masculine behaviors. Gleason's work demonstrates the importance of physiognomy for understanding the behavioral interests and assumptions of ancient elites.[74] These interests were not limited to sexual practice, but included and valued what she calls "'languages' of flesh, voice, and gesture."[75] Thus, physiognomical experts studied characteristics such as amount and type of facial and body hair, as well as physical size, but also behaviors connected to those characteristics, including depilation and gait. Everything from grooming to vocal inflection revealed something important about a man's place on the gender spectrum.

With so many different aspects to consider, expertise in physiognomy was both important and difficult. Even with such expertise, physiognomic writing reports both the near-misses of the experts, and the ability of some individuals to conceal their true identity.[76] One's traits and behaviors were understood both to reveal and to conceal. Interpretation of others is key, and a "universal atmosphere of suspicion" was the norm.[77]

Another important arena for the exhibition and evaluation of these behaviors was the public stage.[78] According to Maude Gleason, speech was particularly important for one's masculinity because it was both public and physical. "Public speaking, even more than literary writing, was the hallmark of the socially privileged male."[79] Not only was it practical, in that elite men advocated for their economic and political interests through public speech, but it provided a public context for performing, comparing, and evaluating behaviors that carried symbolic value.[80]

In fact, it was so powerful that it could compensate for other characteristics that would have argued against ideal masculinity. In Gleason's account of the debate between the ancient rhetors Polemo and Favorinus, Favorinus relies on his speaking prowess to defend himself against Polemo's accusations that his sexual behavior as a eunuch compromises his masculinity.[81] Although his deviation from conventional sexual behavior clearly matters to the public, so do his abilities as a public speaker.[82] The indication that sexual behavior is only one aspect of masculinity speaks to the contextual basis for masculinity as well as the process of construction, revision, and negotiation that takes place within that context.

It is important to note the public nature of these contexts, as the judgment of others plays a key role in the competition for masculinity. Polemo and Favorinus are engaged in a public feud that involves both public expectation and perception. Both the erection and the removal of a public statue of Favorinus in Corinth, as well as his need to respond, signal that the debate is conducted in front of a public audience whose decisions have real implications, and whose opinions can be changed.[83] The public domain of these events illustrates some of the ambiguity of the competition involved in the quest to establish masculinity. Not only are actions and traits offered up for evaluation by other people, some of whom matter more than others, these individuals may disagree with one another or change their minds.

This role of public expectation, suspicion, and evaluation, and the resulting ambiguity, is further amplified by the presence of competing or contradictory criteria as well as the presence of paradigmatic male leaders as heroes. The very high standards set by those heroes are designed, in the words of Gleason, "to inspire or excoriate their underachieving descendants."[84] The task of public speaking provides a competitive forum for the demonstration of and debate over masculine behaviors.

What were these behaviors and traits understood to reveal? The story of Favorinus demonstrates how ancient writers frequently associated public behaviors with private ones, specifically sexual habits and preferences. These sexual behaviors provided yet another way to identify and label individuals in terms of their masculinity. It is important to remember that sexual discourse in the ancient world reflects assumptions that differ substantially from modern ones. As previously indicated, gender in the ancient world includes the concept of a spectrum, rather than merely a binary opposition.[85] This gender spectrum plays a crucial role, providing the context for the competitive maneuvering where masculinity is won or lost.

Sexual behavior is one of the ways this movement happens. Ancient writers show a preoccupation with identifying, labeling, and categorizing the sexual behavior with others. Working with ancient sources, both Holt Parker and Craig Williams have studied the ancient terminology and underscore the association between masculinity and the active, penetrative role in sexual behavior.[86] Williams makes the connection quite plain: "Penetration is subjugation and masculinity is dominion."[87] Their work emphasizes that the kind of sexual action, rather than the sex of the partner, determines the categorization.

Parker categorizes ancient sexual behaviors according to what he calls the Teratogenic Grid.[88] It labels both individuals and their behaviors, resulting in a matrix where human beings are categorized both according to their gender and according to their preferred sexual practice. Parker's grid makes plain the difference between an ancient and contemporary construction of sexual behavior. Organization of the grid is based upon sexual activity, whether it is active or passive. A person is categorized not according to the gender of the partner, which is the contemporary preoccupation, but according to his or her own preferred sexual activity.

For the purposes of this book, what is particularly important is Parker's distinction between active and passive behaviors and the connection to masculinity. Although there are six positions open to male sexual activity, the word "*vir*" is given to only three of them, all active and penetrating behaviors. If a male engaged in passive sexual behavior of some kind, a different word is used to categorize the passive male in terms of the penetrated orifice.[89] Certain sexual behaviors contributed to masculine status—others prevented it.

Such a grid is clear enough, even if fitting people into it isn't always easy. Like the physiognomic discussions above, much of the rhetoric around sexual behavior in the ancient world involves rumor and speculation. Accusations are common and physiognomic assessments carry weight. And contradictions further confuse the issue. Craig Williams, for example, notes the ambiguity around prostitution. It is not condoned, but treated as somewhat unavoidable; excess use is judged to be the result of lack of control.[90] Even sex with a man's wife is cause for debate. It was expected, but shouldn't be advertised or enjoyed (too much).[91]

The complexity suggests that something else is at work beyond simply sexual norms and expectations. According to Williams, "what was at stake was less a man's actual behavior and more the *appearance* he gave and the *image* he had; how he was seen and talked about by his peers more than what he actually did in the privacy of his bedroom."[92] At its core, the emphasis on sexual behavior and its interpretation conveys an emphasis on control, which extends to many facets of masculinity.[93]

Sexuality is a particularly important example, and being in control of one's sexual desire and activity is both a demonstration of power on one scale, and a contribution to power on a greater one. The performance of masculinity, however, incorporates many different facets of life, including anger, fear, and hunger.[94] As with sexuality, a certain amount of these emotions or behaviors might be necessary or even good, but excess was frowned upon.[95] The goal was control, because "a man who fails to control his own desires and fears is less than fully masculine."[96]

An integral part of the self-control idealized by the ancient writers involved the ability to protect one's own body. Jonathan Walters underscores this sense of inviolability and connects it directly to the sexual paradigm outlined above.[97] Not only are elite men given the active, penetrative role in sexual activity, but they are immune to such penetration themselves. He argues that these "impenetrable penetrators can most usefully be seen in the context of a wider conceptual pattern that characterized those of high social status as being able to defend the boundaries of their body from invasive assaults of all kinds."[98] Male bodies do the penetrating and asserting. They are not to be penetrated or violated. The ability to keep one's body intact is the hallmark of a man. The inability or choice not to do so threatens his masculine status.

Walters makes an explicit connection between the penetrative sexual behavior named above and other modes of bodily threat, such as beatings.[99] In both cases, an elite male could expect that his body would remain intact and uninjured by others.[100] No such assurance was offered to non-elite males or to women. "To be of high status meant to be able to protect one's body from assault even as a punishment, the mark of those of low status was that their body was available for invasive punishment."[101]

Self-control is also connected to control over others. If one does not have the latter, it's difficult to have the former. As an elite male, this includes being in charge of the women and slaves in his household, including what happens to their bodies, sexually and otherwise.[102] The elite male is in charge of what they do and do not do, and could do to them whatever he pleased. On a larger scale, this extends to the ability to direct groups of people, such as a military regiment/squadron, a group of workers, or clients signaled elite masculine power.

Again, this control is understood to be associated with virtue. The control over self and others is the privilege of those who exhibited virtue. And, conversely, the absence of them signals the absence of virtue and the absence of masculinity. Control over both self and others is considered to be a virtuous expression of one's status as a man, which fits neatly into a larger, equally virtuous, scheme where a connection between *virtus* and *imperium* creates "rule or dominion that magistrates exercised over the Roman people, generals over their armies, the Roman people as a whole over their subjects, and

Roman men over women and slaves."[103] There are other virtues associated with masculinity—wisdom, justice, and courage, for example—but power exhibited by control over self and others is highly dominant.[104]

The preceding description leads to an understanding of masculinity that is marked by ambiguity, flux, and crisis rather than security. Its assertion charges forward in perpetuity; otherwise it is ephemeral at best or completely lost at worst. In the words of Williams, "vigilance was crucial. The house of cards might collapse with the removal of just one card."[105] Its establishment is up to the judgment of others, who may disagree with another, challenge the integrity of the presentation, and/or change their minds along the way.

METHODOLOGY: ADDITIONAL LENSES OF CRITICISM

In this section, I name other methodologies that inform, amplify, or intersect with the masculinity studies methodology I primarily employ: Classics, Imperial Critical Methods, Feminist Biblical Criticism, and theories of character from Narrative Criticism.

Additional Lenses: Classics

Masculinity studies draws heavily on classicists who specialize in ancient masculinity. The work of such scholars has already figured prominently in the previous section, including Maude Gleason, Jonathan Walters, Amy Richlin, Erik Gunderson, Catherine Edwards, and Craig Williams. Utilizing ancient texts, classicists compile observations about behavior, dress, and gendered speech from ancient sources into cogent themes and theories. Their work often focuses on specific areas of interest that, taken as a whole, provide a detailed description (if not a systematic theory) of the phenomenon of masculinity in the ancient world.

Since classicists work with primary source materials, they are attentive to the limits and challenges, as well as the contributions, of their sources. These limitations are based both in what is available and what is not. For instance, Walters characterizes the available resources on masculinity as texts "written by male members of the ruling elite of the Roman world . . . whose primary intended audience was that of other such men, with whom the authors were linked by a common culture that itself rested on wealth and semihereditary social status."[106] In other words, our insight into ancient concepts of masculinity comes from the discourse of highly educated males comparing themselves to one another. Further, Gleason points out that there is a lack of mythic images or symbols in the ancient world that would have functioned as the "media stereotypes" familiar to a modern or postmodern audience.[107] When and if ancient images or statues communicate expectations of masculinity, that communication is implicit.

The available sources concerned with masculinity, then, are elite, subjective, and understood to be a rhetorical tool for public positioning and posturing. There are limits to such material in terms of reliability, trustworthiness, and applicability beyond immediate context. Further, there is a lack of other public cultural symbols that could provide additional perspectives. In light of this difficulty, Gleason advocates for placing the available sources alongside others that may or may not speak explicitly about masculinity but nonetheless contribute to the conversation. These may include statues and images, but also other types of writing. For Gleason, "the overlap between explicit moralizing pronouncements and the assumptions about gender embedded in more technical writings (e.g. medical, rhetorical, physiognomical)" suggest places of resonance where common beliefs may be identified.[108]

Even if such a picture can be drawn, problems remain. If the available sources reflect elite experiences and priorities, then the resulting picture still excludes 98 percent of the population of the Roman Empire from the discussion, including the population in view in this project.[109] What can be said about non-elite conceptions about masculinity? And, on what basis can it be said? First, even if the subtleties were irrelevant to them, the dominance of the elite narrative should not be underestimated. Conway argues that even if the elite obsessions with masculinity "did not represent the lived reality of most men in the empire, it had an effect on them. No matter where one lived in the empire, one would not have to look hard to find an image of masculinity that was intended to evoke admiration and honor and to which one was supposed to aspire."[110]

Understanding the omnipresence of elite attitudes is helpful, but that does not always mean that non-elites agreed with such attitudes. Sometimes elite sources provide cracks for accessing dissenting non-elite perspectives. In her work on public speech, for instance, Gleason notes that men were encouraged to practice their vocal exercises while traveling, even if it was a source of embarrassment in the presence of lower classes.[111] This suggests that while non-elites shared the same context of cultural norms on masculinity as elites did, they did not necessarily view the behaviors in the same way or accepted the dominant values as their own.

The intersection between elite and popular experience also provides a fricative space where possible opinions can be seen. In the case of Favorinus, the city of Corinth first put up a statue in his honor and then removed it.[112] Favorinus reacts to this with a treatise defending himself and attacking their judgment. To be sure, the rhetoric still ignores much of the population, but the public nature of the debate and the physical presence and absence of a statue suggests that conversation might have extended beyond those classes and that public opinion might have played a role. At any rate, lower classes may have witnessed negotiations that involved discourse of masculinity even if they weren't directly involved.

This issue points to a wider area of concern that needs to be addressed. In this methodological context, as in the ones below, scholars face the tricky question of anachronism in the application of contemporary theories to ancient texts. Conclusions that are rushed or too facile will, at best, fail to capture nuance, and at worst, misconstrue or misrepresent the historical reality. However, I consider contemporary theories and ancient texts to be valuable conversation partners. Humility and healthy suspicion are important, as is a willingness to look for places of both resonance and friction. It is important to recognize that the juxtaposition of the two may ultimately produce far more questions than answers, but the emergence of questions produced by the challenging of assumptions and careful analysis of applied theories in historical context can be quite valuable.

In terms of literary perspectives, Teresa Morgan has attempted to identify material that could be seen as representative of popular morality.[113] She posits that when texts are considered on the basis of their type, distribution, and subject matter, there is a convincing "degree of agreement."[114] Further, she challenges the concept of a strict separation between popular and elite culture, suggesting that "the landscape of ethics in the Roman Empire is ultimately one landscape."[115] Her approach represents a methodological attempt to identify material that would have been representative of popular reality, and thus indicative of popular assumptions or ideas about issues like masculinity.

Despite this attempt, there are limitations to her methodology that curb its usefulness for this project. Morgan asserts that her sources are "popular," but her classification of sources as "popular," and their identification with other scholarship on non-elites is not explicit or definitive. Further, Morgan emphasizes the similarities between the elite and non-elite perspectives. Are there no differences between elite and non-elite realities? If so, what are they? Finally, Morgan does not offer a compelling potential sketch of non-elite masculinity, which is the focus of this project.

One scholar who has brought these perspectives together with an eye toward masculinity is Robert Knapp.[116] Knapp's book, *Ordinary Romans*, contains a chapter on "Ordinary Men," whom he defines as "every free person below the elite and above the poor day-laborer or peasant."[117] Knapp argues that while this group is aware of elite priorities, some of which they echo (i.e., sexual morality), they are different in some key ways. Ordinary men, for example, do not share all of the prejudices of the elite, particularly when it comes to labor.[118] In addition, they demonstrate a larger interest in religion and/or magic than do elites, evidenced by both their worries and their practices.[119] Like elites, they are concerned about social status, but he argues that their worries and efforts were more intense because of their vulnerability.

Knapp posits that the desire of ordinary men for control in uncertainty drives their attitudes and efforts, whether toward work, social status, or religious interest.[120] It is here where his analysis intersects with other theories of masculinity in classical studies. Once again, the red thread is control. Like Morgan, the question of sources remains a key concern for Knapp's work, but his analysis engages the question of the difference between non-elite and elite masculinities as well as a possible construction of non-elite masculine values.

Knapp's work is particularly interesting for this project because one of the sources he uses to create a picture of ordinary men is the New Testament. In fact, he refers to the New Testament as "the single richest collection of literature written by what I call invisibles and expressing their outlook."[121] Knapp's interests are broader than mine, as ordinary men constitute only one segment of a population he is trying to capture. But his use of the New Testament brings us back to the question of whether and how it can be a source of non-elite views on masculinity.

The New Testament texts certainly contain non-elite perspectives, some of which make reference to men and their lives. But gender is not the primary focus, and they represent provincial perspectives from a religious and cultural minority. It would be too much to say that the New Testament texts contain a representative, systematic, or comprehensive look at masculinity. However, as noted above, neither do the extant elite texts. Rather, like those texts, the New Testament contains a multiplicity of non-elite viewpoints spanning some geographical and cultural distance. While not comprehensive, the New Testament texts are certainly valuable.

Rather than trying to codify non-elite deviations from dominant masculinity, for example, Conway claims that she is "primarily interested in showing the consistent and pervasive nature of the ideology that any such deviations were up against."[122] Placing this perspective in conversation with Gleason's concept of overlap and Knapp's description of the priorities of "ordinary men" may provide a way forward. Placing the New Testament texts in the context of dominant theories of ancient masculinity challenges the assumptions and posturing of each. The overlap may be small, but the emergence of certain consistent, dominant themes will warrant attention. Even the areas outside the overlay may be helpful, possibly highlighting non-elite particularities. The resulting picture will be incomplete. But it provides one avenue into a conversation that will hopefully only improve with age.

Additional Lenses: Imperial Critical Perspectives

The employment of ancient texts and the work of classical scholars is echoed in imperial critical perspectives, another methodology that is important to this project. Biblical scholars doing imperial critical work bring a highly informed perspective on the Roman Empire, offering fresh interpretations of and provocative possibilities for understanding how the biblical texts might have functioned among early Jesus-believers.[123] Some of this scholarship focuses on mapping the power and structures of the Roman imperial context for the New Testament. Dennis Duling, for example, draws on the work of theorists such as Karl Wittfogel, S. N. Eisenstadt, Gideon Sjoberg, Géza Alföldy, Michael Doyle, Alexander J. Motyl, James Scott, John Kautsky, and Gerhard Lenski to provide and evaluate models of empire.[124] In addition, Warren Carter brings together many different aspects of empire in order to construct a world for the New Testament texts to inhabit.[125]

The social and economic dynamics of the empire and implications for Christian communities have been particularly important for many of these scholars as they provide some access into the world of non-elites. New Testament scholars have explored the implications of the economic realities for early Christian communities elucidated by Robert Knapp and C. R. Whittaker.[126] Justin Meggitt looks at the world of the New Testament within the context of the extreme wealth and privilege of the Emperor, while Steven Friesen's and Bruce Longenecker's poverty scales provide a helpful window into the circumstances of non-elites.[127] Oakman and Hanson have studied the fishing economy that is described in Gospel texts, and Carol Wilson has provided an analysis of food access in the empire.[128]

Also of interest for New Testament scholars has been the political and religious landscape of the Empire, both in Rome and the provinces. In his work on Matthew, Warren Carter has theorized about the implications of the Gospel being experienced in Antioch, an ancient city with a dynamic cultural and religious landscape.[129] Carter also engages scholarship on ancient governors in order to evaluate different portrayals of Pilate in the Gospels, as well as possible interpretations of Pilate's character.[130]

Much good work in imperial critical scholarship has used the contextual framework described above to work with specific New Testament texts and themes, including David Sim's work on the concept of Matthean eschatology, Dorothy Weaver's interpretation Matthean characters, and Warren Carter's new insights into a variety of Matthean texts including the parable of the mustard seed in chapter 13, the coin in the fish's mouth in chapter 17, and the presence of eagles (not vultures) in the eschatology of chapter 24.[131]

In addition to looking for ways that the texts employ language and concepts that belong to imperial rhetoric and practice, imperial critical scholars have struggled with the implications of this interaction, including to what extent the New Testament texts can be understood both to resist and/or accommodate the Empire's dominant narrative. One of the most important contributions of imperial critical scholars is to remind contemporary interpreters that there is no separation—real or imagined—between the religious and the political in the ancient world. Interpretations that have focused on the religious, spiritual, or theological while neglecting the social or political have ignored a fundamental tension. Taking seriously the relationship between the New Testament and the Empire acknowledges that texts like Matthew's Gospel are not merely interested in spiritual or religious matters; they reflect a multifaceted way of being in the world that intersects with political and social life.

The question of potential engagement with empire spans the spectrum of New Testament studies. Richard Horsley, Crossan and Reed, and Neil Elliot have all made contributions to the question of how Pauline texts can be understood to interact with their imperial context.[132] Davina Lopez has worked with similar questions, especially in relation to visual representation, while also foregrounding issues of gender in her analysis.[133] Peter Oakes has provided multiple examples from New Testament texts in response to the question of positionality.[134] And beyond the Matthean work already cited here, Warren Carter has worked extensively with potential engagement with empire in Revelation and the Gospel of John.[135]

The analysis has yielded a rich and complex discussion characterized by tension and ambiguity. Oakes identifies six possible responses to Rome representing a variety of attitudes including awe, resentment, appreciation, contempt, expectation of overthrow, and judgment.[136] Crossan and Reed identify Paul's rhetoric as one that directly challenges Roman domination, while Lopez understands him to be identifying with subjugated nations against Rome. Carter uses the term "rhetoric of distance" to characterize the Gospel of John's encouragement to the Christian communities to resist accommodation and acculturation.[137] Likewise in Revelation, he identifies a strong voice advocating for separation between Jesus-believers and their cultural context, instilling a future hope for divine judgment on a world identified with sin and evil.[138] The encouraged separation is described in terms of one's daily participation in the social world of the empire; Revelation stresses separation and distinction precisely because the writer does not feel there is nearly enough.

Referring to Matthew, Carter articulates the tension that characterizes much of the New Testament texts: "As much as the Gospel resists and exposes the injustice of Rome's rule, as much as it points to God's alternative community and order, as much as it glimpses something of the merciful inclusion of the non-elite in God's love and life-giving reign for all, as much as it offers alternative economic practices, renounces violence, and promotes more egalitarian household structures, it cannot, finally, escape the imperial mindset. The alternative to Rome's rule is framed in imperial terms."[139]

James Scott's insightful work brings helpful language to this phenomenon, describing the variety of ways in which non-elites act and speak within the oppressive context of empire, and the tension and ambiguity that is often associated with those words and actions.[140] Early Christians were marked by relative poverty and powerlessness, and most scholars note the subversive potential for their texts. However, the ambiguity and variety in rhetoric and behavior witnessed in much of the literature points to a much more complex reaction to power that can be loosely termed "negotiation."

The presence of postcolonial studies in the above material is notable. Although imperial critical perspectives are not synonymous with postcolonial approaches, there is sufficient overlap that certain postcolonial concepts are quite helpful in this type of work.[141] Specifically, mimicry, ambivalence, and hybridity have been important concepts as imperial critical scholars have explored the ways that New Testament texts function. As Carter points out, "There is no doubt that opposition and conceptual reframing are important elements in the Gospel's negotiation of, and negation of, Roman power . . . [b]ut they are by no means the whole story. Postcolonial studies of subaltern negotiation of imperial power indicate ambiguity or hybridity, both accommodation and resistance, as a key dimension of daily interaction."[142] Rather than "a monolithic stance of opposition," Carter advocates "attending to a whole span of practices and attitudes signified by the terms—'negotiation,' 'interaction,' and 'engagement'—in which the Gospel engages."[143]

Additional Lenses: Feminist Biblical Criticism

The interest in power dynamics is something that masculinity studies shares with feminist biblical criticism. This approach has roots in and relationships with the larger enterprise of feminist theory, scholarship that provides force and foundation for the arguments of feminist biblical critics.[144] Responding to challenges and opportunities, feminist biblical criticism has evolved in the past few decades into a diverse, expansive conversation within biblical studies.

This current research continues the feminist emphasis on exploring the problematic relationship between gender and power in several different ways. First, it decenters masculinity as the powerful default and opens it to critique. It is often the case that "gender" is equated with "women" or "femininity," while masculinity escapes analysis and consideration. One of the ways that masculinity maintains its power is by upholding its imperceptible omnipotence. Treating masculinity as a concept bound by history and culture joins this project with those that endeavor to expose masculinity as a social construct rather than a normative assumption.

This exposure is a critical facet of feminist discourse. In her book concerning issues of feminism, gender, and sexuality in biblical studies, Deryn Guest includes (among the contributions of masculinity studies) the ability "to remove the invisibility of men as a marked category," and calls this "the most basic, valuable objective" of masculinity studies.[145] From a feminist perspective, attempting to de-center masculinity as the assumed "default setting" for gender interrupts the narrative that femininity is a departure from this default, alternatively understood as inferiority or complementarity. Instead, all concepts of gender are considered to be products of negotiation and subject to change and critique.

Once the category of masculinity is de-centered, then it becomes possible to explore the ways in which it operates to preserve the power structure that reifies it.[146] To that end, this project looks closely and carefully at the ways that the specific association between masculinity and power is assumed in the biblical text. Although this discussion of New Testament texts is situated in scholarly conversation, I recognize that these texts are also foundational and authoritative for many faith communities. Therefore, I engage this research with the knowledge that these texts and their interpretations impact the lived experiences of real human beings and with the feminist commitment to contribute to the wider conversation in a way that advances justice and full inclusion.

This de-centering relies on foundational work by gender scholars on the relationship between gender expression and social values. Particularly important is Judith Butler's claim that gender is something that is socially constructed rather than biologically determined, and that the establishment of gender is achieved by repeated performance of particular behaviors.[147] Drawing on the work of Foucault, Butler argues that "gender ought not to be construed as a stable identity or locus of agency from which various acts follow; rather, gender is an identity tenuously constituted in time, instituted in an exterior space through a stylized repetition of acts."[148] Subsequent scholars have employed this framework in various ways in their work on New Testament and Early Christianity.[149]

The concept of the social construction of gender is not without criticism, even for those who accept its basic premise. In particular, the issue of agency remains problematic in a scheme where Butler questions the idea of an original referent and emphasizes the weight of discursive practice on signification.[150] R. W. Connell seeks to find a way to account for the role of the body in the process of social construction, something she calls "body-reflexive practice."[151] She rejects a return to biological determinism or essentialism as a means for understanding the role of the body in gender practice, but still argues for an acknowledgement of the embodiment of the social construction of gender. "The body," she concludes, "is inescapable in the construction of masculinity, but what is inescapable is not fixed."[152]

This tension between embodiment and the social construction of gender is important in a project like this one that emphasizes control over bodies as an expression of masculinity expressed in Matthew's Gospel. For me, the social construction of gender is a basic assumption that is critically important for an analysis of masculinities. However, I also acknowledge the very complex relationship between that social construction and the bodies it includes.[153]

In terms of this project's approach to masculinity studies, feminist biblical criticism provides both theoretical underpinnings as well as direct engagement with the text. Feminist biblical critics have identified and approached these issues of power in the Gospel of Matthew in a variety of ways.[154] Early work by Janice Capel Anderson, for example, drew attention to the androcentrism that marked the Gospel.[155] Using a different approach, Celia Deutsch has worked with the reinterpretation of symbolic themes, viewing the figure of Jesus through the theme of Wisdom.[156] This early scholarship is textually focused, challenging long-held assumptions about the texts and their interpretations and offering alternatives.

Later feminist work has expanded the methodological possibilities. Elaine Wainwright draws upon both the earlier feminist interpretive framework and the subsequent rhetorical model created by Elisabeth Schüssler Fiorenza for her feminist readings of the Gospel.[157] She combines narrative and reader-response criticism, highlighting the increasingly important role of the interpreter. Using a feminist rhetorical lens, Wainwright identifies more than one reading of a given text, each of which provides options to prior dominant interpretations. These alternative readings often exhibit or create tension with previous scholarship, not only questioning the primacy of certain interpretations, but challenging the notion that there is one definitive understanding of a given text.

Critics of earlier feminist work, such as Musa Dube, have challenged the privileged positionality of many of its interpreters and problematized the notion of a common feminine experience.[158] As a result, consideration of race, class, and colonial imperialism have further refined and shaped feminist biblical criticism. The discourse has shifted to one focused on intersectionality, resulting in a discipline marked by a diversity of voices contributing to a richly complex matrix of feminist perspectives. This has further emphasized the question of how multiple issues can contribute to the construction and manipulation of power. The insights and commitments of this intersectional feminist work inform and shape this project as it approaches questions of masculinity from a feminist perspective.

Finally, the masculinity scholars that I engage and that inform my work are shaped by feminist scholarship in that "objectivity" with respect to the biblical texts is neither possible nor desirable. Rather, they acknowledge the role of the interpreter in the establishment of the meaning of a text, and encourage scholars to prioritize questions of justice in their own interpretive work.[159] While this may not be true of every scholar interested in masculinity, and may take different forms among those who do engage such questions, the articulation of justice issues in the work of scholars such as Moore, Thurman, and Conway indicates some kind of shared commitment that is echoed in this project. This commitment leads, in some cases, to challenging or resisting the biblical text and, in others, to drawing attention to what has previously been minimized or ignored.[160]

Because of these shared assumptions and commitments, I employ masculinity studies as a feminist enterprise. By approaching similar issues and questions from an alternate perspective, masculinity studies contribute something different to an already rich discussion about gender and power. I recognize that some may remain skeptical about the potential for a focus on men and masculinity to be liberative. For example, although Elaine Wainwright acknowledges the need to engage masculinity studies, she urges caution "as the power of the normativity of masculinity in both texts and the consciousness of interpreters remains strong."[161] There is always the risk that putting the focus back on men undermines the work of feminists to challenge and critique what has been a very one-sided tendency to study only men and their experiences.[162] Acknowledging this risk while attending to the feminist insights noted above provides a way forward.[163]

Additional Lenses: Narrative Criticism

Because this project is interested in individual figures within the storyline of a Gospel, it is important to engage the work of narrative critics who specialize in characterization and how those characters function in a text like Matthew's Gospel.[164] While this project is not primarily narrative critical, the insights from narrative criticism provide a helpful set of defined concepts and tools within which to understand and discuss the characters that I explore through the lens of masculinity.

As a methodological perspective, narrative criticism came of age in the 1980's and signaled a move away from the various expressions of historical criticism that had characterized the previous generation of biblical scholarship.[165] Those interested in narrative criticism focused on the literary unity of each Gospel, using conceptual frameworks from literary perspectives outside biblical studies as interpretive lenses. These literary concepts include attention to plot, character, setting, and various constructions of both readers and authors. Although acknowledging the role of both author and reader, the focus shifted away from the meaning "behind" the text in its original context to the meaning inherent "in" the text itself, or the meaning created "in front of" the text through the interactions of the interpreter and text.[166] More recent narrative critical work has refined and expanded the method in a variety of ways by incorporating later insights from poststructuralism and revisiting conclusions about characterization.[167]

Because my goals and parameters vary somewhat from traditional narrative critical work, I have made some conscious choices about the way that I employ narrative concepts. For example, because I am interested specifically in masculinity, retaining historical insights is helpful, engaging ancient ideas not explicitly named in the text but readily available outside the text as dominant cultural constructions. Although I still value the idea of the text as a coherent whole, I am more interested in how Matthew's characters can be understood in relation to the culturally and historically constructed form of masculinity than some narrative critics would be.

My approach to characterization, then, attempts to balance the sense of characters as abstract constructions, on the one hand, and on the other hand, in some sense "real."[168] While I am sympathetic to the postmodern concept of construction as integral to reality, I remain convinced that we *experience* that construction as reality. Therefore, I employ a "mimetic" or "people" conception of characterization, where characters are understood to be entities created and developed as readers or interpreters assemble information about them from the narrative, producing a figure that is "knowable" in some sense by the audience or interpreter.[169]

It is important to acknowledge that there are limits to this "knowing." As Harvey is careful to point out, "This is certainly not speculation of the what-did-Hamlet-study-at-the-university variety. But it *is* a regard for an interest in a character, a human being, as something more than a creation of language or a function in the total context of the play."[170] Balancing the limits and the possibilities, this theory allows an interpreter to make statements about characters and their behaviors while acknowledging the role of both the author and interpreter in the construction of that character.

The process of characters becoming knowable happens as readers compile information present in the narrative, information Seymour Chatman describes as a "paradigm of traits."[171] These traits, however, are not simply random facts revealed about a character; Carter identifies them as "consistent ways of being and doing that distinguish one character from another."[172] So traits are both consistent and identifiable to individual characters, making them a relatively accurate basis for forming expected patterns of speech and behavior.

Information about a character's traits can be conveyed in a narrative either through "showing" or by "telling," and can be achieved in a variety of ways, including a character's language about others or about himself or herself, the narrator's language about the character, the character's actions, or the actions of others toward the character.[173] As a reader experiences a character speaking and acting, that reader incorporates those pieces of information into a given character's paradigm by echoing, expanding, refining, or challenging it.

Not all characters are constructed the same way or with the same results. Chatman uses Forster's concepts of flat and round characters to speak about the different ways this characterization can take place, where round characters can elicit a response more akin to human relationships marked by familiarity and intimacy.[174] Hochman provides a taxonomy of eight different categories, each containing two poles, that provide language for these aspects.[175] Stylization, for example, is the degree to which a character varies from an expected norm, while coherence is the extent to which a character expresses unity in thought and action, rather than dissonance.[176] Literalness attempts to get at a character's ability to be realistically comprehensible in a given historical context, transparency speaks to the degree to which a character is open to a reader, and dynamism refers to the ability of a character to develop or change.[177] These concepts illustrate the wide variety of ways that characters can be constructed and interpreted, and provide common language and concepts for comparison and analysis.

Applying this theory of character to the present study equips me to treat characters in Matthew's Gospel as knowable entities, even if all characters do not exhibit the same kind of depth or dimension. Having language to understand both the opportunities and limitations of this engagement enables me to consider the masculinities of Matthew's characters, who are described and identifiable by traits such as gender.[178] The traits established by the narrative and informed by the historical context offers insight into that character's masculinity, even if such masculinity is not the focus of the narrative and even if the description or development of the character is limited.[179]

Although narrative criticism of the Gospels has often considered character groups, this study focuses on individuals.[180] This means, for example, that I will engage Peter as an individual character, and not as a paradigmatic spokesperson or symbol for the disciples. I recognize that the Gospel describes Peter in both terms.[181] But the extent to which the characterization of Peter has implications for the rest of the disciples is another interesting project; in this one, I will focus on Peter as an individual and how the characterization of his masculinity is potentially knowable.[182]

This book is organized into chapters that focus on characters, tracing the same three themes—divine service, dominating control over self and over others, and wealth—through the Gospel's construction of each figure's masculinity. There are a number of different male characters in Matthew, so criteria are needed to keep the project manageable and facilitate fruitful discussion. Highlighted are four prominent characters that have significant relationships with Jesus: Joseph, John the Baptist, Peter, and Judas. Each of these characters plays an important role in the story of Jesus in Matthew and engages significant questions around masculinity, including the three themes outlined throughout this book (divine service, dominating control over self and over others, and wealth). Although different in many respects, these four also share the complexities and challenges of non-elite masculinity.

In addition to these four characters, drawing on the ancient rhetorical strategy of *synkrisis* (σύγκρισις), I include discussions of King Herod on Joseph in chapter 2 and Herod Antipas on John the Baptist in chapter 3.[183] Graham Stanton argues that this "widespread convention" of *synkrisis*, found in a variety of ancient literature, was used to point out difference or superiority, and he provides several examples of its use in Matthew.[184] Both King Herod and Herod Antipas are integral to the stories of Joseph and John the Baptist, both express a more elite version of masculinity than their counterparts, and both provide a helpful context for various expressions of masculine power.

An obviously important question is how I engage Jesus as a male character. I do not include a separate chapter about Jesus because previous scholarship has already provided compelling arguments about Jesus's masculinity in Matthew, and because a discussion of Jesus would have the potential to be a project all on its own.[185] Further, his prominence limits the potential for comparison that is central to this discussion. And, the emphasis in this project is on the significant way that Jesus functions in the lives of the other characters. He is not simply one character among many. Rather, he plays a pivotal role in establishing the masculinities of the other figures.

The resulting list includes six figures, four focus characters and two discussed in context: Joseph and King Herod, John the Baptist and Herod Antipas, Peter, and Judas. I address each one in chapters two through five and then tie the emerging themes together in a final discussion.

CONCLUSION AND STUDY OUTLINE

A critical focus on masculinity is still relatively new in the field of New Testament studies, but its presence has been growing rapidly in the last several years. Recent scholarship in masculinity and the Gospels has fallen into one of two general groups. First are the scholars who have focused on the masculinities of Jesus. The most comprehensive work is that of Colleen Conway, who has provided a comparative analysis of Jesus' masculinity across the four Gospels.[186] Others have focused on specific portrayals. Jerome Neyrey, for example, has worked on the masculinity of Jesus in Matthew, and Tat-siong Benny Liew has done similarly with Mark.[187] Susanna Asikainen's study on ideal masculinity focuses on Jesus but also includes other male characters in the Synoptics.[188] In a slightly different vein, Eric Thurman has placed the masculinity of Jesus in the Gospel of Mark in conversation with the masculinity of ancient Greek novels.[189]

A second stream of scholarship has traced themes of ancient masculinity through the Gospels, highlighting particular scenes and characters where these themes are mimicked, contested, redefined, or otherwise engaged in some interesting way. For example, Brittany Wilson examines the masculinity of both major and minor male characters in Luke-Acts, arguing that they "refigure" dominant elite masculinity.[190] Janice Capel Anderson and Stephen Moore trace concepts of genealogy, fatherhood, householders, brotherhood, and eunuchs through the Gospel of Matthew; Sébastien Doane discusses the masculinities of the men in Matthew's genealogy of Jesus; and Eric Thurman reads the concept of masculinity in the Gospel of Mark through the lens of mimicry, focusing on both Jesus and his disciples.[191]

Despite some different approaches, the work of these scholars has important similarities and can be understood to occupy the same scholarly conversation. This project is formulated as a continuation and extension of the work named above, utilizing many of the same resources and addressing many of the same issues. It is intended to be another voice contributing to the larger conversation.

However, since masculinity is still a new field in biblical studies, much remains to be explored. For example, there is a lack of scholarly attention to male characters other than Jesus, particularly in Matthew. Bonnie Flessen has worked with concepts of masculinity and Cornelius in Acts, Wilson has worked with several characters in Luke-Acts, and Doane has explored the men in the genealogy in Matthew, but there are many other Gospel figures whose masculinity has not been addressed.[192] Therefore, this project studies a variety of male figures within the Gospel of Matthew. A sustained analysis of the constructed masculinities of male figures in Matthew offers new insights into the multiple ways that masculinity can be understood in the New Testament.

Of course, each of the Matthaean characters I address has already been the subject of significant scholarly work. Biblical scholars have addressed Joseph,[193] King Herod,[194] John the Baptist,[195] Herod Antipas,[196] Peter,[197] and Judas[198] from a variety of approaches, including source, redaction, and literary approaches. However, none of the portrayals of these figures has undergone sustained analysis with respect to Matthean conceptions of masculinity, which is the focus of this project. Since I address these characters through a particular methodological lens that has not been employed before, not all existing scholarship will be directly relevant. However, I use what is appropriate from previous work—particularly material that is important in the understanding of that character or that deals specifically with issues of gender, status, empire, and/or power.

Building on the work of previous scholars, this project arranges some familiar pieces in a new way. This approach stands to make a contribution to the field of New Testament studies, especially in terms of its engagement with questions of gender and power, by addressing the question of non-elite masculinities, providing multiple examples of the characterization of such non-elite men, articulating themes that might constitute alternative or modified masculinities to the Roman ideal, identifying ways that those alternatives interact with their imperial context, and exploring the implications for these alternative, non-elite masculinities for readers of the Gospel.

This contribution is linked to several different areas within the discipline, including masculinity studies, imperial critical approaches, and feminist work. This research is particularly revealing because it provides various examples of how non-elite masculinity may have been understood or constructed. Most ancient sources discuss masculinity exclusively from an elite perspective, creating an ideal that is attainable by very few men. This study, by contrast, focuses on the experience of the many, rather than the few.

For those interested in dynamics of empire, a discussion of masculinity makes several important contributions to the wider conversation. First, imperial critical scholars have provided a persistent, helpful reminder that spiritual, political, and social dimensions are all intertwined in the ancient world. This project provides a specific example of how these concepts interrelate. Second, it provides another specific example of how the rhetoric of the Gospels participates in and engages pervasive Roman imperial ideology. Because masculinity is such an integral part of the way that Romans understood power, I argue that it is an essential part of any discussion that contextualizes the world of the New Testament in terms of imperial realities.

Third, the imperial experience of the non-elite Gospel communities is not merely advantageous to only one group. Imperial critical scholars are not only interested in the ways that the Roman Empire potentially influences texts, but also how such texts interact with and fuel comprehension of Roman imperial ideology. This interaction takes a variety of forms. The presence of imitation or similarity is equally as interesting or important as the presence of challenge or modification. Like the empire, the Gospels are also interested and invested in the idea of masculinity. Because of this shared commitment, this project provides one specific example of this negotiation and points to a larger area of potential interest for those engaged in imperial critical work.

Several Matthean texts figure prominently in the work of feminist biblical interpreters. Dube's work focuses on Matthew 15:21–28, where the Canaanite woman advocates for her daughter and is called a "dog" by Jesus.[199] A number of feminist interpreters, including Janice Capel Anderson, have explored the provocative presence of five women in the predominantly androcentric genealogy of Jesus in Matthew 1.[200] Warren Carter outlines five feminist interpretations of this text, including those of Wainwright, Levine, Anderson, and Schaberg.[201] Elaine Wainwright highlights the contrast between confession and faithful action in the depiction of the women in chapters 27 and 28, while Carolyn Osiek addresses these chapters from the perspective of social history and the culture of women in antiquity.[202] Jennifer Glancy highlights the problematic presence of slavery in Matthew's parables.[203] And, Amy-Jill Levine has provided important critique of feminist anti-Judaism, illustrated by the focus on purity codes in the story of the haemorrhaging woman in Matthew 9:20–22.[204]

Many of the interests and concerns of these scholars are echoed in the work of those engaged with masculinity. In one example, just as feminists have been interested in the story of John the Baptist, Herod Antipas, Herodias, and her daughter in Matthew 15, so those interested in masculinity find much there to consider.[205] Like feminist biblical critics, scholars of masculinity recognize how the social effects and oppressive structures resulting from a relationship between gender and power have been to the detriment of women and femininity. In addition, masculinity critics are interested in the ways that these dynamics have adversely affected men whose gender expressions do not conform to hegemonic expectations, and how oppressive constructions of masculinity perpetuate systems of subjugation.

Ancient masculinity is mysterious and can be elusive; characteristics that argue for masculinity can also be understood to mask others that argue against it. The association of some behaviors with sexuality or masculinity may seem to be arbitrary, particularly to a contemporary eye. And, the application of criteria is not always consistent or predictable, breeding ambivalence. While power and wealth are expected, excesses are not desired; there is even too much of a good masculine thing. However, in the end, the power of masculinity through its connections to power in all aspects of life is unmistakable.

From Connell's perspective, this construction works just as hegemonic masculinity should. It perpetuates itself while oppressing others—both women and men who exhibit alternative forms of masculinity. It is preoccupied with an elite minority, ignoring or subjugating other realities. It works together with social and cultural expectations to reify power structures. It is a fundamental way that the Roman world organized itself and established and maintained its power.

Discussing the characterizations of six male characters—Joseph and King Herod, John the Baptist and Herod Antipas, Peter, and Judas—and noting how they mimic, resist, redefine, and otherwise negotiate the dominant construction of masculinity, I am able to identify assumptions and values of the Empire and place the Gospel in context. This analysis provides answers to my key questions: (1) how masculinity is variously constructed in the Gospel of Matthew and (2) how those constructions relate to the dominant Greco-Roman context.

Based on the resulting analysis, I contend that the constructions of masculinity in Matthew's Gospel involve ambivalence, inscribing certain aspects of the dominant construction of the ancient world while seeking to create distance from others. Matthew's constructions appear to challenge some aspects of dominant characterizations of masculinity, critiquing wealthy elites and emphasizing self-denial and submission to God through discipleship. However, the Gospel's emphasis on discipleship means that other aspects of masculinity, namely divine service and dominating control over self and over others in service to divine purposes, are upheld. In the end, the essential, problematic relationship between masculinity and power is maintained, reinscribing divine sanction of the imperial status quo. I proceed to build this case by considering each Matthean man in turn, beginning with Joseph in Matthew 1–2.

NOTES

1. Mary Daly, *Beyond God the Father: Toward a Philosophy of Women's Liberation* (Boston: Beacon Press, 1990), 19.

2. Maude Gleason, "Elite Male Identity in the Roman Empire," in *Life, Death, and Entertainment in the Roman Empire,* ed. D. S. Potter and D. J. Mattingly (Ann Arbor: University of Michigan Press, 1999), 67–84 and *Making Men: Sophists and Self-Presentation in Ancient Rome* (Princeton: Princeton University Press, 1995); Craig Williams, *Roman Homosexuality: Ideologies of Masculinity in Classical Antiquity* (Oxford and New York: Oxford University Press, 1999).

3. As I discuss shortly, the question of masculinity and women is a complex one that deserves its own treatment. What is in focus for me in this project is the way that men in the Gospel express and negotiate expectations of masculinity.

4. Aspects of the experiences of non-elites have been explored by Dennis Duling, "Empire: Theories, Methods, Models" in *The Gospel of Matthew in its Roman Imperial Context,* ed. John Riches and David C. Sim (New York: T&T Clark International, 2005), 49–74; Steven Friesen, "Poverty in Pauline Studies: Beyond the So-called New Consensus," *JSNT* 26 (2004): 323–61; Gerhard Lenski, *Power and Privilege: A Theory of Social Stratification* (Chapel Hill: University of North Carolina Press, 1984); Bruce Longenecker, *Remember the Poor: Paul, Poverty, and the Greco-Roman World* (Grand Rapids, MI: Eerdmans, 2010); and C. R. Whittaker, "The Poor," in *The Romans,* ed. Andrea Giardina (Chicago: University of Chicago Press, 1993), 272–99.

5. By "divine service," I mean a group of behaviors or characteristics that align a figure with divine intent and thus contribute to power and to masculinity. Alignment

with divine purposes is an important part of imperial authority. Divine sanction for rule and for behavior strengthens a claim both to power and to masculinity. In the Gospel, alignment with the empire of God is deeply valued and expressed in multiple ways. I engage these individual cases in chapter discussions. Embedded in this concept is an inherent tension, whereby acknowledging the ultimate authority of God/the gods relativizes the power of the human being. However, for both Roman and biblical perspectives, divine service is an essential part of establishing credibility, claiming authority over others, and justifying one's behavior.

6. Colleen Conway, *Behold the Man: Jesus and Greco-Roman Masculinity* (Oxford: Oxford University Press, 2008).

7. Susanna Asikainen, *Jesus and Other Men: Ideal Masculinities in the Synoptic Gospels.* (Boston: Brill, 2018).

8. Brittany E. Wilson, *Unmanly Men: Refigurations of Masculinity in Luke-Acts* (New York: Oxford University Press, 2015).

9. Eric Thurman, "Looking for a Few Good Men: Mark and Masculinity," in *New Testament Masculinities* ed Stephen D. Moore and Janice Capel Anderson (Atlanta: Society of Biblical Literature, 2003), 137–61 and "Novel Men: Masculinity and Empire in Mark's Gospel and Xenophon's *An Ephesian Tale*," in *Mapping Gender in Ancient Religious Discourses,* ed. Todd Penner and Caroline Vander Stichele (Atlanta: Society of Biblical Literature, 2007), 185–230. This last piece is notable for its combination of masculinity and empire studies, a combination that it is utilized in this project, as well.

10. Tat-siong Benny Liew, "Re-Mark-able Masculinities: Jesus, the Son of Man, and the (Sad) Sum of Manhood?" in *New Testament Masculinities* ed Stephen D. Moore and Janice Capel Anderson (Atlanta: Society of Biblical Literature, 2003), 93–135.

11. Janice Capel Anderson and Stephen D. Moore, "Matthew and Masculinity," in *New Testament Masculinities* ed Stephen D. Moore and Janice Capel Anderson (Atlanta: Society of Biblical Literature, 2003), 67–91.

12. See R. W. Connell, *Masculinities,* 2nd ed. (Berkeley: University of California Press, 2005) and R. W. Connell and James W. Messerschmidt, "Hegemonic Masculinity: Rethinking the Concept," *Gender and Society* 19, no. 6 (Dec. 2005), 829–59.

13. Connell, *Masculinities,* 77.

14. Demetrakis Z. Demetriou, "Connell's Concept of Hegemonic Masculinity: A Critique," *Theory and Society* 30, no. 3 (June 2001), 337–61.

15. Wilson, *Unmanly Men,* 23

16. Asikainen, *Jesus and Other Men,* 5–12.

17. R. W. Connell, *Gender and Power: Society, the Person, and Sexual Politics* (Stanford: Stanford University Press, 1987), 183.

18. Asikainen retains use of the term "hegemonic" while arguing that more than one type of elite masculinity was competing for hegemonic status. Asikainen, *Jesus and Other Men,* 19–20. Wilson prefers to speak of "elite masculine norms" to refer to the way that hegemonic masculinity took shape in the ancient world. Wilson, *Unmanly Men,* 23.

19. The relationship between masculinity studies and issues of sexuality still faces difficult questions and problematic concerns. Traister calls it an "awkward waltz" that needs time and attention to be worked out. Bryce Traister, "Academic Viagra: The Rise of American Masculinity Studies," *American Quarterly* 52, no. 2 (2000), 276. They are clearly connected in some way, yet the nature of that connection still needs clarifying work.

20. Connell, *Masculinities,* 78.

21. See Judith Butler, *Gender Trouble: Feminism and the Subversion of Identity* (New York: Routledge, 2006) and Michel Foucault, *The History of Sexuality, Volume 1: An Introduction* (New York: Pantheon Books, 1978).

22. Conway, *Behold the Man,* 9.

23. Wilson provides a discussion of ancient masculinity framed similarly within her selected themes. Wilson, *Unmanly Men,* 39–75.

24. Conway emphasizes the contrast between elite men and everyone else. "Understanding what it meant to be a man in the Greco-Roman world meant understanding one's place in a rationally ordered cosmos in which free men were placed at the top and what fell beneath could all be classified as 'unmen,'" Conway, *Behold the Man,* 15.

25. Gleason, "Elite Male Identity," 68–70.

26. Connell and Messerschmidt, "Hegemonic Masculinity; Rethinking the Concept."

27. Gleason, "Elite Male Identity," 70. Gleason here draws on the concept of a "one-sex" model of gender in antiquity advanced by Thomas Laqueur. See Thomas Laqueur, *Making Sex: Body and Gender from the Greeks to the Romans* (Cambridge, MA: Harvard University Press, 1990), 1–62. The implications of this model of gender include the potential loss of masculinity altogether. As Conway observes, "If women were not different in kind, but simply a lesser, incomplete, version of men, what was there to keep men from sliding down the axis into the female realm?" Conway, *Behold the Man,* 18. The answer is that nothing could do so except diligent effort on the part of the man to maintain his standing. Laqueur's model has been critiqued in recent years, notably by Helen King, who challenges Laqueur's assertion of the exclusivity of the one-sex body as well as its longevity, which Laqueur claims extends until the seventeenth century. Helen King, *The One Sex Body on Trial: The Classical and Early Modern Evidence* (Burlington, VT: Ashgate Publishing, 2013), 1–5. Instead, King argues for a more complex understanding of gender in the ancient world, where "one-sex" and "two-sex" models coexist "alongside other ways of understanding the body." King, *One Sex Body on Trial,* 221. In terms of the present discussion concerning ideal masculinity focused on elites, even if the implications of a loss of masculinity are not identical, both the "one-sex" model and the complex fluidity described by King allow for a spectrum of masculinity and an emphasis on elite expressions of it. Both the spectrum and elite emphasis threaten the establishment and retention of masculinity and emphasizes efforts to maintain it.

28. Gleason, *Making Men,* xxii.

29. Conway, *Behold the Man,* 17.

30. Traister, "Academic Viagra."

31. Gleason, "Elite Male Identity," 67.
32. Conway, *Behold the Man*, 11.
33. Connell, *Masculinities*, 78–81.
34. The contemporary "foil" is homosexuality. The forms are different in antiquity, but the same process of subordination takes place and corollary examples are addressed later in this project.
35. Connell, *Masculinities*, 81
36. Connell, *Masculinities*, 79
37. The question of status complexifies this assertion, e.g., individual examples of women of very high status have the potential to express masculine behaviors or authority that men of very low status may not have. See, for example, Mary Taliaferro Boatwright, "Plancia Magna of Perge: Women's Roles and Status in Roman Asia Minor," in *Women's History and Ancient History* ed. Sarah Pomeroy (Chapel Hill: University of North Carolina Press, 1991), 249–72. However, among men and women of the same rank, or even women of slightly higher rank, the system of hegemonic masculinity preserves the power and advantages of masculinity and men benefit from that system.
38. Warren Carter, *John and Empire: Initial Explorations* (New York: T&T Clark, 2008), 13 and *Matthew and Empire: Initial Explorations* (Harrisburg: Trinity Press International), 171.
39. Demetriou, "Connell's Concept."
40. Demetriou, "Connell's Concept," 347–49. He uses Bhabha's concept of "hybridity" to account for this shifting character.
41. Traister, "Academic Viagra."
42. Traister, "Academic Viagra," 288.
43. Interestingly, Traister cautions that the idea of social construction also contributes to this problem. By separating masculinity from human bodies and placing it in the realm of social discourse, both agency and blame shift away from actual human beings, limiting potential for change.
44. Conway, *Behold the Man*, 10–12.
45. Gleason, "Elite Male Identity," 67.
46. For extensive and detailed discussion on this topic, see Catharine Edwards, *The Politics of Immorality in Ancient Rome* (Cambridge: Cambridge University Press, 1993).
47. Edwards, *Politics of Immorality*, 12.
48. Gleason, "Elite Male Identity," 67.
49. For a longer discussion, see Conway, *Behold the Man*, 22–23.
50. Myles McDonnell emphasizes this aspect of *virtus* in his work on its relationship with the Greek terms αρετη and ανδρεια. He argues that the original semantic field for *virtus* included "martial prowess or courage," which corresponds to ανδρεια. Myles McDonnell, *Roman Manliness: Virtus and the Roman Republic* (New York: Cambridge University Press, 2006), 240. Later, under Hellenizing influence, the concept expands to include moral aspects associated with αρετη. Nevertheless, "physical prowess or courage, especially as displayed in war, remained the

central element of manliness throughout the Republican period and into the Empire." McDonnell, *Roman Manliness,* 236.

51. Conway quotes Matthew Kuefler, who is worth noting here: "Virtue was so intimately linked to maleness in the Roman universe that it is impossible to separate Roman definitions of masculinity from more general notions of ideal human behavior." Matthew Kuefler, *The Manly Eunuch: Masculinity, Gender Ambiguity, and Christian Ideology in Late Antiquity* (Chicago: University of Chicago Press, 2001), 19.

52. Wilson, *Unmanly Men,* 43.

53. Wilson calls this "corporeal masculinity." Wilson, *Unmanly Men,* 49

54. Wilson, *Unmanly Men,* 51.

55. Edwards, *Politics of Immorality,* 25.

56. The relationship between virtue and power is not without ambivalence, but tension usually worked to the benefit of the elite. As Edwards notes, "A good Roman citizen did not commit adultery—but at the same time adultery could be associated with power and with masculinity. Adulterers were viewed with ambivalence. Augustus passed a law against adultery but derived advantage from committing it himself." Edwards, *Politics of Immorality,* 48–49.

57. For a discussion of the development of Roman ideology about divine sanction for emperors, see J. Rufus Fears, "The Cult of Jupiter and Roman Imperial Ideology" in *Principat 17/1; Heidentum: Roemische Goetterkulte, Orientalische Kulte in Der Roemischen Welt* (Berlin: Walter de Gruyter, 1981), 3–141.

58. Gleason, "Elite Male Identity," 70.

59. For example, Fears relates the symbolic rejection of the line of Augustus at Nero's demise, including the death of laurel trees used to produce triumph laurels for the emperors and a lightning strike resulting in the loss of heads and scepter from temple statues. J. Rufus Fears, "Cult of Jupiter and Roman Imperial Ideology," 74.

60. For more on this tension and its implications for New Testament scholarship, see Mary Rose D'Angelo, "Theology in Mark and Q: *Abba* and Father in Context," *The Harvard Theological Review* 85, no. 2 (Apr 1992), 149–74 and "*Abba* and Father: Imperial Theology and the Jesus Traditions," *Journal of Biblical Literature* 111, no. 4 (Winter 1992), 611–30. I draw on this scholarship more fully in my discussion on Joseph in chapter 2.

61. See J. Rufus Fears, "Nero as the Vicegerent of the Gods in Seneca's de Clementia," *Hermes* 103, no. 4 (1975), 486–96.

62. I revisit this tension over divine service in the characterization of Joseph, John the Baptist, and Peter.

63. In this study, I am focused on the connections between human male emperors and divine behavior identified as masculine, and how that relationship contextualizes the masculinity of non-elite humans in the Gospel of Matthew. However, the question of females in the Roman Pantheon, their expression of gendered behaviors, and the potential connection with human men and women in the Gospel is an interesting question for another project.

64. Carter, *John and Empire,* 370.

65. τί θεος; τὸ κρατον. τί βασιλεύς; ἰσόθευς. S. R. F. Price, "Gods and Emperors: The Greek Language of the Roman Imperial Cult," *The Journal of Hellenistic Studies* 104 (1984), 95.

66. The range of behaviors and characteristics I call "divine service" includes both those that imitate divine behavior, noted here, as well as those that carry out divine purposes. The way that divine service functions in the context of human limitations echoes the tension present in the characterization of emperors, which I explore in more detail in subsequent chapters.

67. Gleason, "Elite Male Identity," 82–83.

68. Conway, *Behold the Man,* 39.

69. Edwards, *Unmanly Men,* 185.

70. Gleason, "Elite Male Identity," 83. The "self-conscious frugality" is connected to expressions of self-control noted above.

71. For more on this tension, see Emma Dench, "Austerity, Excess, and Failure in Hellenistic and Early Imperial Italy" in *Parchments of Gender: Deciphering the Body in Antiquity* (New York: Oxford University Press, 1998).

72. There are parallels between the way that wealth functions and how other aspects of masculine performance function, namely sexuality, which I discuss below. While excess or misplaced sexual desire might infringe upon a claim of masculine power, the "right" amount directed in "appropriate" ways was an essential part of establishing masculinity. The same is true for wealth.

73. Gleason, *Making Men,* 55–81. The aforementioned Polemo was an expert physiognomist.

74. Gleason, "Elite Male Identity," and *Making Men.*

75. Gleason, "Elite Male Identity," 84.

76. Both Gleason and Conway mention the story of a man who nearly got away with deception except for the efforts of the intrepid physiognomist. Gleason, *Making Men,* 76–78; Conway, *Behold the Man,* 19–20.

77. Gleason, "Elite Male Identity," 78

78. It is important to note that this does not refer to entertainment, which was often viewed negatively, but with public debate. See Craig Williams, *Roman Homosexuality,* 153–55.

79. Gleason, "Elite Male Identity," 67.

80. Gleason, "Elite Male Identity," 67. See also Erik Gunderson, *Staging Masculinity: The Rhetoric of Performance in the Roman World* (Ann Arbor: University of Michigan Press, 2000) and Amy Richlin, "Gender and Rhetoric: Producing Manhood in the Schools," in *Sex and Difference in Ancient Greece and Rome,* ed. M. Golden and P. Toohey (Edinburgh: Edinburgh University Press, 2003), 202–20.

81. Gleason, *Making Men,* 3–20.

82. Gleason characterizes their reaction as a "fascinated ambivalence about effeminate rhetorical style" Gleason, "Elite Male Identity," 81.

83. Gleason, *Making Men,* 8–9.

84. Gleason, "Elite Male Identity," 70.

85. Gleason, "Elite Male Identity," 70.

86. Holt N. Parker, "The Teratogenic Grid," in *Roman Sexualities,* ed. Judith P. Hallett and Marilyn B. Skinner (Princeton: Princeton University Press, 1997) and Craig Williams, *Roman Homosexuality,* 18–19.

87. Williams, *Roman Homosexuality,* 18.

88. Parker, "The Teratogenic Grid," 49. Craig Williams also includes a detailed chapter on the same subject of classification and sexual behavior. Williams, *Roman Homosexuality,* 177–245.

89. Parker, "The Teratogenic Grid," 51. The specific terms are *fellator* "male penetrated with respect to the mouth," *cinaedus/pathicus* "male penetrated with respect to the anus," or *cunnilinctor* "male penetrated with respect to the vagina."

90. Williams, *Roman Homosexuality,* 43.

91. Williams, *Roman Homosexuality,* 50–59.

92. Williams, *Roman Homosexuality,* 18.

93. Williams, *Roman Homosexuality*, 145–69.

94. Conway, *Behold the Man,* 23–30.

95. As Gleason notes, this extended even to exercise. While there was some respect for the military service in terms of its physical expectations, it was seen as irregular and out of one's control. Far better would be the elite male ability to exercise in moderation when desired. Military service might produce a body that is the correct shape, but "health requires autonomy." Gleason, "Elite Male Identity," 73.

96. Williams, *Roman Homosexuality,* 151.

97. Jonathan Walters, "Invading the Roman Body: Manliness and Impenetrability in Roman Thought," in *Roman Sexualities,* ed. Judith Hallett and Marilyn Skinner (Princeton: Princeton University Press, 1997).

98. Walters, "Invading the Roman Body," 30.

99. Williams cautions against equating all forms of bodily violation as the same, arguing that the experiences can be quite different. Williams, *Roman Homosexuality,* 260. His point is well-taken, but the relationship among them on some level is persuasive as it contributes to the establishment of the larger matrix of power.

100. One interesting exception that Walters offers to this rule is that of the soldier. His body is subject to his military superior. Walters posits that this violation is reconcilable with masculinity because 1) it is not sexual and 2) the wounds received are seen as honorable. However, the exception is interesting and will be incorporated into subsequent discussions about the violation of bodies in Matthew's Gospel.

101. Walters, "Invading the Roman Body," 38.

102. Walters notes that "slaves could be beaten, tortured, killed, and the fact that a slave, male or female, was at the disposal of his or her master was so commonplace as to be scarcely noted in Roman sources." Walters, "Invading the Roman Body," 39.

103. Williams, *Roman Homosexuality,* 146.

104. Conway, *Behold the Man,* 23–26.

105. Williams, *Roman Homosexuality,* 156.

106. Walters, "Invading the Roman Body," 29.

107. Gleason, "Elite Male Identity," 68.

108. Gleason, "Elite Male Identity," 70.

109. This is a best-case scenario. True elites comprised only one half of one percent of the population. Even if one includes the retainer class as those aware of and aspiring to elite status, the population excluded from the conversation is still an overwhelming majority. Lenski posits that the cooperation of as little as 6 or 7 percent of the population was needed to subdue and rule the rest in Agrarian Empires. Lenski, *Power and Privilege,* 246. According to Friesen's poverty scale, the first three levels of society (what he calls PS levels 1–3: imperial elites, provincial elites, and municipal elites) comprised 1.23 percent of the population, with the percentage being somewhat higher (2.8 percent) in urban centers. Friesen, "Poverty in Pauline Studies," 340–47.

110. Conway, *Behold the Man,* 16.

111. Gleason, "Elite Male Identity," 74–75.

112. Gleason, *Making Men.*

113. Teresa Morgan, *Popular Morality in the Early Roman Empire* (New York: Cambridge University Press, 2007).

114. Morgan, *Popular Morality,* 160.

115. Morgan, *Popular Morality,* 299.

116. Robert Knapp, *Invisible Romans* (Cambridge, MA: Harvard University Press, 2011).

117. Knapp, *Invisible Romans,* 5.

118. Like elites, however, they did carry a prejudice against the poor. Knapp, *Invisible Romans,* 7–8.

119. Knapp, *Invisible Romans,* 13–24.

120. Knapp, *Invisible Romans,* 13.

121. Knapp, *Invisible Romans,* 321.

122. Conway, *Behold the Man,* 16.

123. Carter, *Matthew and Empire;* Wendy Cotter, "Greco-Roman Apotheosis Traditions and the Resurrection Appearances in Matthew;" in *The Gospel of Matthew in Current Study,* ed. David Aune (Grand Rapids, MI: Eerdmans, 2001), 127–53; Amanda Miller, *Rumors of Resistance: Status Reversal and Hidden Transcripts in the Gospel of Luke* (Minneapolis: Fortress Press, 2014); Robert Mowery, "God, Lord and Father: the Theology of the Gospel of Matthew;" *Biblical Research* 33 (1988), 24–36; John Riches and David Sim, eds., *The Gospel of Matthew in its Roman Imperial Context* (London: T&T Clark, 2005); Ian E. Rock, *Paul's Letter to the Romans and Roman Imperialism: An Ideological Analysis of the Exordium (Romans 1:1–17)* (Eugene, OR: Pickwick, 2012); and Carol Wilson, *For I Was Hungry and You Gave Me Food: Pragmatics of Food Access in the Gospel of Matthew* (Eugene, OR: Pickwick, 2014).

124. Duling, "Theories, Models, and Concepts;" Karl Wittfogel, *Oriental Despotism: A Comparative Study of Total Power* (New Haven, CT: Yale University Press, 1957); S. N. Eisenstadt, *The Political Systems of Empires: The Rise and Fall of the Historical Bureaucratic Societies* (Glencoe: Free Press, 1963); Gideon Sjoberg, *The Preindustrial City: Past and Present* (New York: Free Press, 1960); Géza Alföldy, *The Social History of Rome* trans. David Braund and Frank Pollock (Baltimore, MD: The Johns Hopkins University Press, 1985); Michael Doyle, *Empires* (Ithaca, NY: Cornell

University Press, 1987); Alexander J. Motyl, *Imperial Ends: The Decay, Collapse, and Revival of Empires* (New York: Columbia University Press, 2001); John Kautsky, *The Politics of Aristocratic Empires* (Chapel Hill: University of North Carolina Press, 1982); Lenski, *Power and Privilege;* and James C. Scott, *Domination and the Arts of Resistance: Hidden Transcripts* (New Haven, CT: Yale University Press, 1990), *Moral Economy of the Peasant: Rebellion and Subsistence in Southeast Asia* (New Haven, CT: Yale University Press, 1985), and *Weapons of the Weak: Everyday Forms of Peasant Resistance* (New Haven, CT: Yale University Press, 1999).

125. Warren Carter, *The Roman Empire and the New Testament: An Essential Guide* (Nashville: Abingdon Press, 2006).

126. Knapp, *Invisible Romans* and Whittaker, "The Poor."

127. Justin Meggitt, "Taking the Emperor's Clothes Seriously: The New Testament and the Roman Emperor;" in *The Quest for Wisdom: Essays in Honor of Philip Budd,* ed. Christine Joynes (Cambridge: Orchard Academic, 2002), 143–69; Friesen, "Poverty in Pauline Studies;" Longenecker, *Remember the Poor,* 36–59. Longenecker recognizes a larger level 4 than Friesen does (17 percent instead of 7 percent) and somewhat smaller level 6 (30 percent, not 40 percent). But the contrast between the circumstances of elite and non-elite remains stark in both.

128. K. C. Hanson and Douglas E. Oakman, *Palestine in the Time of Jesus: Social Structures and Social Conflicts,* 2nd edition (Minneapolis, MN: Fortress Press, 2008), 107–9 and Carol Wilson, *For I Was Hungry.*

129. Carter, *Matthew and Empire.*

130. Warren Carter, *Pontius Pilate: Portraits of a Roman Governor* (Collegeville: Liturgical Press, 2003).

131. David C. Sim, "Rome in Matthew's Eschatology;" in *The Gospel of Matthew in its Roman Imperial Context* ed. John Riches and David C. Sim (New York: T&T Clark, 2005), 91–106; Dorothy Jean Weaver, "'Thus You Will Know Them By Their Fruits;' The Roman Characters of the Gospel of Matthew," in *The Gospel of Matthew in its Roman Imperial Context* (New York: T&T Clark, 2005), 107–27; and Warren Carter, "Matthew's Gospel, Rome's Empire, and the Parable of the Mustard Seed (Matthew 13:31-32)," in *Hermeneutik der Gleichnisse Jesus,* ed. R. Zimmermann, *WUNT 271* (Tubingen: Mohr Siebeck, 2008), 181–201; "Paying the Tax to Rome as Subversive Praxis: Matthew 17:24–27," *JSNT* 76 (1999), 3–31; and "Are There Imperial Texts in the Class? Intertextual Eagles and Matthean Eschatology as 'Lights Out' Time for Imperial Rome (Matthew 24-27-31)," *Journal of Biblical Literature* 122 (2003), 467–87.

132. Richard A. Horsley, "The Apostle Paul and Empire;" in *In the Shadow of Empire: Reclaiming the Bible as a History of Faithful Resistance,* ed. Richard A. Horsley (Louisville: Westminster John Knox Press, 2008), 97–116; John Dominic Crossan and Jonathan L. Reed, *In Search of Paul: How Jesus's Apostle Opposed Rome's Empire with God's Kingdom* (New York: Harper Collins, 2004); and Neil Elliot, *The Arrogance of Nations: Reading Romans in the Shadow of Empire* (Minneapolis: Fortress Press, 2010).

133. Davina Lopez, *Apostle to the Conquered: Reimagining Paul's Mission* (Minneapolis: Fortress Press, 2008).

134. Peter Oakes, "A State of Tension: Rome in the New Testament," in *The Gospel of Matthew in its Roman Imperial Context*, ed. John Riches and David Sim (London: T&T Clark, 2005), 75–90.

135. Warren Carter, *What Does Revelation Reveal? Unlocking the Mystery* (Nashville: Abingdon Press, 2011); *John and Empire*; and *Matthew and Empire*.

136. Oakes, "A State of Tension," 90.

137. Carter, *John and Empire*, 335.

138. Carter, *What Does Revelation Reveal*, 27–49.

139. Carter, *Matthew and Empire*, 171.

140. Scott, *Domination and the Arts of Resistance*.

141. Homi Bhabha, *The Location of Culture* (New York: Routledge, 1994); Fernando Segovia, "Postcolonial Criticism and the Gospel of Matthew;" in *Methods for Matthew*, ed. Mark Allan Powell (Cambridge: Cambridge University Press, 2009), 194–237; Gayatri Spivak, *A Critique of Postcolonial Reason: Toward a History of the Vanishing Present* (Cambridge, MA: Harvard University Press, 1999); R. S. Sugirtharajah, *Exploring Postcolonial Biblical Criticism: History, Method, Practice* (Chichester, West Sussex: Wiley-Blackwell, 2011).

142. Carter, *John and Empire*, 13.

143. Carter, *John and Empire*, 13.

144. Representative works include: Simone de Beauvoir, *The Second Sex*, trans. Constance Borde and Sheila Malovany-Chevallier (New York: Alfred A. Knopf, 2010); Susan Bordo, *Unbearable Weight: Feminism, Western Culture, and the Body* (Berkeley: University of California Press, 1993); Butler, *Gender Trouble;* Mary Daly, *Gyn/Ecology: The Metaethics of Radical Feminism* (Boston: Beacon Press, 1990); Anne Fausto-Sterling, *Sexing the Body: Gender Politics and the Construction of Sexuality* (New York: Basic Books, 2000); Betty Friedan, *The Feminine Mystique* (New York: Norton, 1963); Foucault, *The History of Sexuality: Vol. 1*; bell hooks, *Talking Back: Thinking Black, Thinking Feminist,* (Boston: South End Press, 1989); Luce Irigaray, *The Irigaray Reader,* ed. Margaret Whitford (Cambridge: Basil Blackwell, 1991); Elizabeth Cady Stanton, *The Woman's Bible* (Amherst: Prometheus Books, 1999); Mary Wollstonecraft, *A Vindication of the Rights of Woman* (London: Farnborough, Gregg, 1970).

145. Deryn Guest, *Beyond Feminist Biblical Studies* (Sheffield: Sheffield Phoenix Press, 2012), 125.

146. This sense of opening masculinity to feminist critique is seen in the trajectory of feminist scholar Lilly Nortje. Jeremy Punt, "Lilly Nortje-Meyer's (En)Gendered New Testament Hermeneutics," *Neotestamentica* 53, no. 2 (2019), 231–48. Her decidedly feminist work also extends to inquiries into masculinity in Jude and Ephesians.

147. Butler, *Gender Trouble*.

148. Butler, *Gender Trouble*, 191.

149. In addition to the many examples already utilized in this project, see also Todd Penner and Caroline Vander Stichele, *Contextualizing Gender in Early Christian Discourse: Thinking Beyond Thecla* (New York: T&T Clark, 2009), 228–29.

150. Butler, *Gender Trouble*, 197.

151. Connell attempts to account for both the presence of the material body as an agent as well as discursive practice that utilizes that body: "Through body-reflexive practices, bodies are addressed by social process and drawn into history, without ceasing to be bodies. They do not turn into symbols, signs, or positions in discourse. Their materiality (including material capacities to engender, to give birth, to give milk, to menstruate, to open, to penetrate, to ejaculate) is not erased, it continues to matter. The *social* process of gender includes childbirth and child care, youth and ageing, the pleasures of sport and sex, labour, injury, death from AIDS." Connell, *Masculinities,* 65.

152. Connell, *Masculinities,* 56. The current discourse about and among those who are transgender is illustrative. For some, bodies themselves have been deconstructed from biological sex, and yet biological alignment with gender expression and understanding remains a goal for many.

153. Wilson provides a helpful discussion on this topic, landing in a similar place she terms a "pragmatic-constructionist" approach. Wilson, *Unmanly Men,* 22.

154. For a detailed discussion of recent feminist work in Matthew including material cited here, see Elaine Wainwright, "Feminist Criticism and the Gospel of Matthew," in *Methods for Matthew,* ed. Mark Allan Powell (New York: Cambridge University Press, 2009), 83–117.

155. Janice Capel Anderson, "Matthew: Gender and Reading," *Semeia* 28 (1983), 3–27.

156. Celia Deutsch, "Jesus as Wisdom: A Feminist Reading of Matthew's Wisdom Christology," in *A Feminist Companion to Matthew,* ed. Amy-Jill Levine (Sheffield: Sheffield Academic Press, 2001), 88–113 and *Lady Wisdom, Jesus, and the Sages: Metaphor and Social Context In Matthew's Gospel* (Valley Forge, PA: Trinity Press, International, 1996).

157. Elaine Wainwright, *Towards a Feminist Critical Reading of the Gospel According to Matthew, BZNW* 60 (Berlin: deGruyter, 1991) and *Shall We Look for Another? A Feminist Rereading of the Matthean Jesus* (Maryknoll: Orbis, 1998); Elisabeth Schüssler Fiorenza, *Rhetoric and Ethic: The Politics of Biblical Studies* (Minneapolis: Fortress Press, 1999).

158. Musa Dube, *Postcolonial Feminist Interpretation of the Bible* (St. Louis, Chalice Press, 2000).

159. Specifically, I am including the work of Conway, Moore, and Thurman, each of whom benefits from the pioneering work of feminist critics led by Elisabeth Schüssler Fiorenza. See Schüssler Fiorenza, *But She Said: Feminist Practices of Biblical Interpretation* (Boston: Beacon Press, 1992).

160. Judith Fetterley's concept of a "resisting reader" is helpfully demonstrated in the work of Adele Reinhartz on the Gospel of John. See Reinhartz, *Befriending the Beloved Disciple: A Jewish Reading of the Gospel of John* (New York: Continuum, 2001).

161. Wainwright, "Feminist Criticism and the Gospel of Matthew," 95.

162. Indeed, there are current movements hoping to do just that. Various representations of a "Men's Movement" have been prevalent in American popular culture in the wake of feminist action and conversation. Such groups vary in their tactics

and rhetoric, from the Promise Keepers of the 1990's to the much more strident "Men's Rights Movement" found in Reddit threads, TikTok videos, and in groups like A Voice for Men (http://www.avoiceformen.com). Feminists are understandably concerned about the effects that voices like these have on popular culture and even academia, and about the potential for academic work to support or validate them.

163. Wilson comes to a similar conclusion weighing the same concerns. Wilson, *Unmanly Men,* 2–4.

164. Examples of such work include David Rhoads, Joanna Dewey, and Donald Michie, *Mark as Story: An Introduction to the Narrative of a Gospel,* 2nd ed (Minneapolis: Fortress Press, 1999); Stehen D. Moore, *Literary Criticism and the Gospels: The Theoretical Challenge* (New Haven: Yale University Press, 1989); and Mark Allan Powell, "Literary Approaches and the Gospel of Matthew," in *Methods for Matthew,* ed. Mark Allan Powell (Cambridge: Cambridge University Press, 2009), 44–82. For other narrative critical work, see Janice Capel Anderson, *Matthew's Narrative Web: Over, and Over, and Over Again* (Sheffield: Sheffield Academic Press, 1994); Cornelis Bennema, *A Theory of Character in New Testament Narrative* (Minneapolis: Fortress Press, 2014); David Bauer, *The Structure of Matthew's Gospel: A Study in Literary Design* (Sheffield: Sheffield Academic Press, 1988); Robert Charles Brandon, *Satanic Conflict and the Plot of Matthew* (New York: Peter Land, 2006); Jeannine K. Brown, *The Disciples in Narrative Perspective: The Portrayal and function of the Matthean Disciples* (Atlanta: Society of Biblical Literature, 2002); William H. Shepherd, *The Narrative Function of the Holy Spirit as a Character in Luke-Acts* (Atlanta: Scholars Press, 1994); Warren Carter, "Kernels and Narrative Blocks: The Structure of Matthew's Gospel," *Catholic Biblical Quarterly* 54 (1992): 463–81 and *Matthew: Storyteller, Interpreter, Evangelist* (Peabody, MA: Hendrickson, 2004); Richard A. Edwards, *Matthew's Story of Jesus* (Philadelphia: Fortress Press, 1985) and *Matthew's Narrative Portrait of the Disciples: How the Text-Connoted Reader is Informed* (Harrisburg: Trinity Press International, 1997); and Jack Dean Kingsbury, *Matthew as Story* (Philadelphia: Fortress Press, 1986).

165. The relationship between historical critical and narrative critical scholarship has continued to evolve. For some scholars, narrative criticism has been a tool to address established issues from a fresh perspective, such as the issue of structure in Matthean studies. Others emphasize the distinction between the two, and narrative criticism's ability to introduce new questions not in focus in historical critical scholarship. These two may not be mutually exclusive, but rather indicate a negotiation of place and relationship over time within biblical studies and among other methodological approaches. But they further illustrate the variety within the approach and the need for clarity in terms of one's employment of the methodology.

166. Narrative critics differ in the extent to which they emphasize one or the other of these *loci* of meaning. But some interaction of the two is commonly present in narrative approaches, and both are emphasized over the prior focus on historical, original, meaning. Many early narrative critics speak of bracketing historical questions or privileging literary questions over historical ones. But scholars disagree about the extent to which this is necessary or possible. In an attempt to organize these different approaches, Powell suggests three categories: audience-oriented, text-oriented, and

reader-oriented narrative criticism. See Mark Allan Powell, "Narrative Criticism: The Emergence of a Prominent Reading Strategy," in *Mark as Story: Retrospect and Prospect,* ed. Kelly R. Iverson and Christopher Skinner (Atlanta: Society of Biblical Literature, 2011), 19–43. Although Powell's categories may merit some critique or adaptation, their usage underscores the variety of ways to address the relationship between narrative criticism and questions of historical context. For such a critique, see Warren Carter, "Narrative Readings Contextualized Readers, and Matthew's Gospel," in *The Oxford Handbook to Biblical Narrative,* ed. Donna Nolan Fewell (New York: Oxford University Press, 2016), 307–18 and Moore, *Literary Criticism and the Gospels.*

167. For examples of this more recent work, see Scott Elliott, *Reconfiguring Mark's Jesus: Narrative Criticism after Poststructuralism* (Sheffield: Sheffield Academic Press, 2011) and Elizabeth Struthers Malbon, *In the Company of Jesus: Characters in Mark's Gospel* (Louisville, Westminster John Knox, 2000). For excellent summaries of the trajectory of narrative critical work in the Gospels, see the introductory chapter of *Characters and Characterization in the Gospel of John,* ed. Christopher Skinner, (London: Bloomsbury T&T Clark, 2013); *Character Studies and the Gospel of Mark,* ed. Christopher Skinner and Matthew R. Hauge (London: Bloomsbury T&T Clark, 2014) and *Character Studies in the Fourth Gospel,* ed. Steven A. Hunt, D. Francois Tolmie, and Ruben Zimmermann (Tübingen: Mohr Siebeck, 2013).

168. Different scholars utilize different terms for these concepts. Marvin Mudrick coined the terms "mimetic" and "purist." Marvin Mudrick, *On Culture and Literature* (New York: Horizon, 1970), 150–51. Shlomith Rimmon-Kenan uses the simpler distinction "people" and "words" to describe the same phenomenon. Shlomith Rimmon-Kenan, *Narrative Fiction: Contemporary Poetics,* 2nd ed, (London: Methuen, 1983), 31–34.

169. See W. J. Harvey, *Character and the Novel* (Ithaca, NY: Cornell University Press, 1965), 201–204; Baruch Hochman, *Character in Literature* (Ithaca, NY: Cornell University Press, 1985), 28–58; and Seymour Chatman, *Story and Discourse: Narrative Structure in Fiction and Film* (New York: Oxford University Press, 1978), 107–38.

170. Harvey, *Character and the Novel,* 204.

171. Chatman, *Story and Discourse,* 127–31.

172. Carter, *Matthew: Storyteller, Interpreter, Evangelist,* 167. This concise description is drawn from the longer discussion in Chatman, *Story and Discourse,* 121–26.

173. Wayne C. Booth, *The Rhetoric of Fiction* (Chicago: University of Chicago Press, 1961), 3–16. For more on this distinction in the context of how Matthew creates characters, see Anderson, *Matthew's Narrative Web,* 78–83 and Carter, *Matthew; Storyteller, Interpreter, Evangelist,* 92–95.

174. Chatman, *Story and Discourse,* 131–34. For discussion on the presence of round and flat characters in the Gospel of John, see the introduction of Skinner, *Characters and Characterization in the Gospel of John.*

175. Hochman, *Character in Literature,* 89.

176. Hochman, *Character in Literature,* 89–102.

177. Hochman, *Character in Literature,* 116–37.

178. For more examples of those "thinking with" ancient characters in the context of gender, see Stephanie Cobb, *Dying to be Men: Gender and Language in Early Christian Martyr Texts* (New York: Columbia University Press, 2008); Judith Perkins, *The Suffering Self: Pain and Narrative Representation in the Early Christian Era* (London: Routledge, 1995) and *Roman Imperial Identities in the Early Christian Era* (London: Routledge, 1995); and Helen Morales, *Vision and Narrative in Achilles Tatius' Leucippe and Clitophon* (Cambridge: Cambridge University Press, 2004). Although these works all deal with later literature than the New Testament, their approaches of working with gender representation in characters of ancient literature are similar and relevant to this project.

179. For another example of NT scholars reading characters explicitly alongside a theme present in the Gospel, see Skinner, *Characters and Characterization in the Gospel of John* and Skinner and Hauge, *Character Studies in the Gospel of Mark.* The variety present in these volumes indicate a preference for diversity, rather than one dominant or "consensus" strategy, in approaches to characterization.

180. Brown, *The Disciples in Narrative Perspective,* and Edwards, *Matthew's Narrative Portrait of the Disciples.*

181. In 16:15–16, for example, Peter replies when Jesus asks a question of the group of disciples. Jesus's reaction to him in verse 17 suggests that his response both speaks for them and sets him apart from the others. For an example of a fuller discussion, see Janice Capel Anderson, *Matthew's Narrative Web,* 90–97.

182. I am focusing specifically on theories of character in narrative criticism. Other important elements, such as plot, are the subject of intense debate in Matthean scholarship, but of less importance to this project. For me, the question of definitive plot of the Gospel is secondary. Rather I am interested in the ways that plot further illuminates the characters' traits, particularly their masculinities, and how that masculinity functions in the sequence of events presented in the narrative. The complex relationship between plot and characters is a substantial topic of discussion in narrative criticism. While some inquiry into the influence of one over the other may be fruitful, I prefer to work more with the tension inherent with the two operating together. In any case, I agree with Chatman that working to separate them is troublesome and not meaningful. Chatman, *Story and Discourse,* 113.

183. See Graham N. Stanton, *A Gospel for a new People* (Louisville, KY: Westminster John Knox, 1993), 77–84.

184. Stanton, *A Gospel for a New People,* 79. Although Stanton does not mention Joseph and Herod the Great among his examples; they are a further example of the kind of comparison he highlights.

185. Conway, *Behold the Man,* 107–26; Jerome Neyrey, "Jesus, Gender, and the Gospel of Matthew," in *New Testament Masculinities,* ed. Stephen Moore and Janice Capel Anderson (Atlanta: Society of Biblical Literature, 2003), 43–66.

186. Conway, *Behold the Man.*

187. See Neyrey, "Jesus, Gender, and the Gospel of Matthew," and Tat-siong Benny Liew, "Re-Mark-able Masculinities."

188. Asikainen, *Jesus and Other Men.*

189. Thurman, "Looking for a Few Good Men, and "Novel Men."
190. Wilson, *Unmanly Men.*
191. Anderson and Moore, "Matthew and Masculinity;" Sébastien Doane, "Masculinities of the Husbands in the Genealogy of Jesus (Matt. 1:2–16)," *Biblical Interpretation* 27 (2019), 91–106; and Thurman, "Looking for a Few Good Men."
192. Bonnie J. Flessen, *An Exemplary Man: Cornelius and Characterization in Acts 10* (Eugene, OR: Pickwick, 2011).
193. Derek S. Dodson, *Reading Dreams: An Audience-Critical Approach to the Dreams in the Gospel of Matthew* (London: T&T Clark, 2009); Joseph Fitzmyer, *Saint Joseph in Matthew's Gospel* (Philadelphia: Saint Joseph's Press, 1997); and Matthew J. Marohl, *Joseph's Dilemma: "Honour Killing" in the Birth Narrative of Matthew* (Cambridge, UK: James Clark, 2010).
194. Warren Carter, *Matthew and the Margins: A Sociopolitical and Religious Reading* (Maryknoll: Orbis, 2000), 73–89; Richard A. Horsley, *The Liberation of Christmas: The Infancy Narratives in Social Context* (New York: Crossroad, 1989); Ulrich Luz, *Matthew in History: Interpretation, Influence, Effects* (Minneapolis: Fortress Press, 1994); Adam Kolman Marshak, *The Many Faces of Herod the Great* (Grand Rapids, MI: Eerdmans, 2015); Dorothy Jean Weaver, "Power and Powerlessness: Matthew's Use of Irony in the Portrayal of Political Leaders," in *Society of Biblical Literature 1992 Seminar Papers,* ed. E. H. Lovering, Jr. (Atlanta: Scholars Press, 1992), 637–63.
195. Carter, *Matthew and the Margins,* 90–105, 250–55, 301–5; Catherine Murphy, *John the Baptist: Prophet of Purity For a New Age* (Collegeville: Liturgical Press, 2003); and Gary Yamasaki, *John the Baptist in Life and Death: Audience-Oriented Criticism of Matthew's Narrative* (Sheffield: Sheffield Academic Press, 1998).
196. Carter, *Matthew and the Margins,* 301–305; Kathleen Corley, *Private Women, Public Meals: Social Conflict in the Synoptic Tradition* (Peabody, MA: Hendrickson, 1993); Gerd Theissen, *The Gospels in Context: Social and Political History in the Synoptic Tradition* (Minneapolis: Fortress Press, 1991); and Weaver, "Power and Powerlessness," 454–66.
197. Raymond Brown, Karl Donfried, and John Reumann, eds., *Peter in the New Testament: A Collaborative Assessment by Protestant and Roman Catholic Scholars* (Eugene, OR: Wipf and Stock, 2002); Carter, *Matthew and the Margins,* 121–22, 308–12, 332–37, 341–43, 519–20; Jack Dean Kingsbury, "The Figure of Peter in Matthew's Gospel as a Theological Problem;" *JBL* 98, no. 1 (1979), 67–83; Ulrich Luz, *Matthew in History,* 57–74.
198. Raymond Brown, *The Death of the Messiah: From Gethsemane to the Grave: A Commentary on the Passion Narratives in the Four Gospels,* 2 vols. (New York: Doubleday, 1994); Carter, *Matthew and the Margins,* 503–506, 512, 522–23; W. D. Davies and D. C. Allison, *A Critical and Exegetical Commentary on the Gospel According to St. Matthew,* vol. 3 (Edinburgh: T&T Clark, 2004), 568–71; Ulrich Luz, *Matthew 21–28: A Commentary,* trans. James E. Crouch, ed. Helmut Koester, Hermeneia (Minneapolis: Fortress Press, 2005), 478–90.
199. Dube, *Postcolonial Feminist Interpretation,* 127–202.

200. Janice Capel Anderson, "Mark and Matthew in Feminist Perspective: Reading Matthew's Genealogy," in *Mark and Matthew II,* ed. Eve-Marie Becker and Anders Runesson (Tübingen: Mohr Siebeck, 2013).

201. Carter, *Matthew and the Margins,* 58–61.

202. Wainwright, "Feminist Criticism and the Gospel of Matthew," 100–17, and Carolyn Osiek, "The Women at the Tomb: What Are They Doing There?" in *Feminist Companion to Matthew,* ed. Amy-Jill Levine (Sheffield: Sheffield Academic Press, 2001), 205–20.

203. Jennifer Glancy, "Slaves and Slavery in the Matthean Parables," *JBL* 119 (2000), 67–90.

204. Amy-Jill Levine, "Discharging Responsibility: Matthean Jesus, Biblical Law, and haemorrhaging Woman," in *Feminist Companion to Matthew,* ed. Amy-Jill Levine and M. Blickenstaff (Sheffield: Sheffield Academic Press, 2001), 379–97.

205. Some examples of previous work include Ross Kraemer, "Implicating Herodias and Her Daughter in the Death of John the Baptizer: A (Christian) Theological Strategy?" *JBL* 125, no. 2 (2006), 321–49; Caroline Vander Stichele, "Herodias Goes Headhunting," in *From the Margins II: Women of the New Testament and Their Afterlives,* ed. Christine Joynes and Christopher Rowland (Sheffield: Sheffield Phoenix Press, 2009), 164–75 and Weaver, "Power and Powerlessness." For a companion piece on Mark, see Janice Capel Anderson, "Feminist Criticism: The Dancing Daughter," in *Mark & Method: New Approaches in Biblical Studies,* 2nd ed., ed. Janice Capel Anderson and Stephen D. Moore (Minneapolis: Fortress Press, 2008), 103–34.

Chapter 2

Joseph and King Herod

In this chapter, I discuss the figure of Joseph in Matthew's Gospel through the three categories of masculinity identified in chapter 1: wealth, dominating control over self and others, and divine service. I argue that Joseph's masculinity is constructed not primarily in terms of wealth or control, but primarily in terms of divine service. His masculinity does exhibit ambivalence, particularly with respect to control over his own and others' bodies. However, despite some expected limitations, Joseph's divine service conveys conventional ancient masculine status as one who expresses obedient righteousness through control over himself and others.

As outlined in chapter 1, I also include reflections on the masculinity of King Herod in the course of this chapter. In his work, Graham Stanton argues that *synkrisis* (σύγκρισις), an ancient rhetorical strategy of comparison used to point out difference or superiority, was found in a variety of ancient literature, including the Gospel of Matthew.[1] Since (1) the stories of Joseph and King Herod are intertwined, and (2) Joseph's masculinity is built, in part, on a contrast with Herod, this prevalent ancient strategy of comparison is helpful and appropriate for this discussion.

Joseph is not a major character in the New Testament narratives. The bulk of his story is found in the Gospel of Matthew, primarily in chapters 1–2 with one other brief reference to an un-named Joseph in 13:55 when the crowds identify Jesus as "the carpenter's son" (ὁ τοῦ τέκτονος υἱός).[2] Even in Matthew, where his role is arguably quite important for the trajectory of the narrative and the safety of God's plan in Jesus, the development of his character itself is severely limited. In addition to being what Davies and Allison call "practically a faceless figure," he is also voiceless.[3] What the reader knows about Joseph comes from narrative description of his thoughts and actions, as well as selected observations of his relationships and background.

From this information, Davies and Allison describe the Joseph in Matthew's Gospel in broad, but significant, brushstrokes: "Davidid, upright, a man of visions, and obedient to the Lord."[4] This chapter will address the complexities and implications of these qualities, exploring what roles they play in constructing Joseph's masculinity. In addition, I add to this list the important characteristic of dominating control, a fundamental aspect of ancient masculinity. The resulting picture both builds on and expands Davies and Allison's image and understanding of Joseph.

Herod's story is also found in chapters 1–2, but his character is quite different. He is "Rome's representative and puppet," and acts accordingly.[5] He speaks and acts with power, is given a royal title, and is identified as an enemy of God's work in the birth of Jesus. He does not have divine dreams; the divine dreams of others instruct them how to avoid Herod's brutality and thwart his plans to destroy God's agent, Jesus. His exercise of power through dominating control is highly conventional, but circumvented in interesting ways. Herod is the default masculine power whose actions are thwarted by those faithful to God.

WEALTH

Although it is of interest in other parts of the Gospel, wealth is neither a major focus in chapters 1–2 of Matthew's Gospel nor a defining aspect of Joseph's character. In this section, I will consider the implications of this observation, arguing that the lack of emphasis on wealth allows Joseph's character, including his masculinity, to be defined by other aspects. This shift in focus not only has implications for Joseph's character but also creates an opening for a potential redefinition of wealth as it is commonly associated with ancient masculinity. The Joseph story demonstrates that this Gospel doesn't value wealth in the way that the dominant imperial culture does. The distinction comes in the intimate cultural association of wealth with virtue. While wealth is still an important measure of value, in this Gospel one can be righteous or obedient to God without it. In fact, the story of Joseph is one in which the Gospel seems to suggest that righteousness and divine obedience may be easier to achieve in the absence of wealth.

In Matthew 1–2, both abundance and lack of wealth are present in the economic status of the characters, as well as in the gifts of the magi, but there is no direct discourse about wealth or its significance. Taken together, these indirect references form a composite picture of wealth that has considerable ambiguity, particularly when viewed through the lens of ancient masculinity. Joseph embodies this ambiguity. Chapter 1 places both Jesus and Joseph in a lineage that includes many powerful men.[6] In verse one alone, in addition to being called "Messiah" or "Christ" (Χριστοῦ), Jesus is also called "son of David" (υἱοῦ Δαυὶδ) and "son of Abraham" (υἱοῦ Ἀβραάμ). The verses that follow trace his lineage through many other men of status—including royalty such as Solomon, Jehoshaphat, Uzziah, and Hezekiah—ending up with Joseph and Mary. The list also includes Boaz, who, although not royal, is described in the book of Ruth as a man with economic resources and status in the community.[7]

In the ancient world, higher status often, though not always, involved some wealth, so the mention of Joseph in the company of these other men of status and wealth introduces the concept of wealth with respect to Joseph, whether by association, contrast, or both.[8] The presence of kings in this lineage is important, as they are ultimate symbols of earthly power and impressive wealth, if not always righteousness or fairness.[9] At the same time, the list also includes figures who are not well-known outside of this chapter (1:13–15) and those who are presumably poor, such as the more recent ancestors of Joseph. Whatever the economic resources of these figures, inclusion in the genealogy does not assume status or wealth, and it certainly does not translate into financial power or access to wealth either for Joseph or for Jesus. However, the association of wealth and status with some in this group still conveys something important about both of them.

Scholars have long pointed out how important the lineage is to establishing Jesus's meaningful heritage in the history of Israel.[10] As Luz states, "Jesus is descended from the progenitor Abraham through Israel's royal dynasty. He is not only an authentic Jew; he is a descendant of David."[11] This lineage attaches Jesus to the core figures in Jewish history, solidifying his identity (1:20). By placing Jesus in this context, Matthew "elucidates Jesus' Davidic sonship," legitimating his identity and status.[12] At the risk of being pedantic, if it's true for Jesus, then it's true for Joseph, too. If the status Joseph passes on through adoption establishes and reinforces a certain status for Jesus, then it does the same for Joseph.

For Greeks and Romans, the turn to the past is an important part of constituting elite status.[13] Attaching oneself to ancient, esteemed, authorities reflects glory and power on the present. In other words, as Carter asserts, in the dominant culture of the ancient world "antiquity is authority."[14] In this respect, then, Joseph has a claim to authority and identity through his association with Jewish antiquity.

For Romans, however, this elite status would have usually been accompanied by wealth, solidifying the claim to masculine power.[15] For Joseph, this is not the case. 13:55 identifies Joseph as a builder (ὁ τέκτων), which gives him a trade and means of income, but nothing approaching elite status. Friesen places artisans, which would include those who were builders like Joseph, anywhere from PS4-PS6 on his poverty scale.[16] However, he argues that the percentage of artisans in the more economically stable category of PS4 is quite small, perhaps 7 percent. It is more likely that Joseph and his family hovered between PS5 and PS6, right around subsistence level, sometimes slightly above, and often slightly below. So, from an ancient imperial perspective, there is an inherent tension in the royal lineage of Joseph and of his adopted son, Jesus. There is a claim to powerful ancient heritage, but no wealth to accompany it.

An ambivalent attitude toward wealth is further visible in Joseph's decisions and actions. While Joseph is not wealthy, particularly from a Roman perspective, he is also not destitute. The family is not described in terms of its resources, but neither are they described in terms of what they lack. The narrative assumes that he is able to get his family to Egypt and back and lack of wealth is not discussed as a barrier. (2:13–16, 19–23) While the narrative lacks detail about what such a journey would entail, Lionel Casson's work describes the options open to a first-century traveler like Joseph.[17] Travelers had access to the extensive network of famed Roman roads, which they could access by foot, by cart, or by hired carriage.[18] Along the way, a loose system of official inns (*mansiones/stationes*) and smaller, unofficial, hostels (*mutationes*) provided periodic stops for food and rest.[19] Travelers could also arrange to stay with friends or relatives. Lacking access to either of these, people would need to bring bedding for sleeping in the open air, as well as kitchenware and food for cooking.[20]

While some travelers could no doubt afford hired carriages or carts, Catherine Hezser argues that "the large majority of people would have walked," some with a pack animal and others without. Walking would have been cheaper, but also extended the length of a trip and possibly altered travelers' courses through less-direct routes that would be safer or afford better options for accommodations.[21] For example, she suggests that Jews could have utilized synagogues either for lodging or for connections, or sought out hostels owned or kept by Jews.[22] This would have increased the options for support along the way but limited routes to places where such connections were available.

All of this suggests that a flight to Egypt was certainly possible for Joseph, Mary and the child, but would have required some resources. Even if they literally took the cheapest route possible (walking, carrying all their own supplies rather than using a pack animal, utilizing synagogues when possible and sleeping in the open air the remainder of the time), they still would have needed access to enough money and supplies to last their trip, which would have taken longer on foot than by cart.

In his work on homelessness in the Gospel of Matthew, Robert Myles emphasizes the systemic forces at work in the flight to Egypt.[23] He resists a romantic notion of homelessness, pointing to their status as "displaced outsiders" and calling into question ideas of agency.[24] I agree with Myles' critique that the external, political dynamics surrounding the flight to Egypt have not received sufficient attention and that too often the agency of biblical figures has been overestimated and/or reflected through the experiences of contemporary Western interpreters.[25]

I resist, however, his assessment that this means Joseph shows little to no agency in the flight to Egypt.[26] While agency in the ancient imperial context will be defined differently than in other contexts, that does not mean it doesn't exist either in the text or in lived historical experience.[27] The dynamics of travel described above speak to the broad range of necessary actions and decisions required to complete such a journey. And while the text does emphasize Joseph's righteousness and obedience, it also assumes much in the way of Joseph's action and competence in carrying out the dreams' instructions. Once again, ambiguity and ambivalence, obedience and agency, mark Joseph's portrayal.

Tension with respect to status and wealth is also present in the depiction of King Herod. Matthew 2:1–6 contextualizes the birth narrative within Herod's reign. As "Rome's vassal king," Herod wields great power over the world into which Jesus is born.[28] The text is focused on Herod's physical power, but he also had economic power. Herod's reign was marked by multiple large-scale building projects, including temples, monuments, cities, and palaces, as well as lavish expenditures on gifts for the emperor and contributions to the Olympic games, all funded by tax income.[29]

The elision of Herod's wealth from the narrative perhaps misses an opportunity to emphasize another aspect of his power, but it also leaves no room for the narrative to attach positive significance to him in the form of patronage.[30] Herod is the villain of the story who resists God's purposes. 2:16–18 emphasizes his anger and brutality, recounting his desperate order to murder the children around Bethlehem in an effort to eliminate a threat to his power. While the narrative does not mention wealth, the economic disparity between Herod and other characters can be assumed, and Herod's wealth is coupled with brutality.[31] The overall effect is a disruption of any automatic association between wealth and virtue and a suggestion of the opposite, that brutality and grandiose demonstrations of economic power are linked.[32] While the Gospel associates Joseph with the absence of wealth and presence of virtue, Herod is associated with the opposite.

Comparison with Joseph yields additional cracks in Herod's status. Unlike Joseph, Herod has no genealogy; in fact, as an Idumean, his identity as a foreigner threatens his power.[33] And his wealthy status does not give him unlimited power; the story is about how Herod is outsmarted and outmaneuvered, despite the vast resources at his disposal. Joseph lacks wealth, but his inclusion in the genealogy gives him status. Herod clearly has wealth, and the royal title, but his status is marked by instability. I will further explore Herod's character and related themes in the subsequent sections on dominating control and divine service. For now, it is sufficient to note an interruption between wealth and virtue and a critique of Herod's conventional wealthy status.[34]

This interruption among wealth, status, and virtue is also evident in the depiction of other characters. For example, the news of a new baby king is brought to Herod by the wise men. Carter notes that as priestly-court figures from Persia, the magi "had access to the centers of power," and yet were "a destabilizing influence" that could threaten that power through their predictions.[35] Further, the authority of their predictions was a source of disagreement, despite their claims to legitimacy.[36] Also, any claim to status or power in a Roman imperial context would be mitigated by their identity as outsiders from the East, what Edward Said identifies as "Orientalism."[37] Finally, the wise men exhibit some ambivalence in their decisions and actions. They initially expose, rather foolishly, the identity and location of the infant, obeying the instructions of the fearful and dangerous Herod, but later return home without reporting back to him, obeying the instructions of the angel and defying Herod. This portrayal contributes to a problematic association among wealth, status, and virtue.

Ambivalence with respect to financial resources is also present in presentation of the gifts by the magi, the one significant reference to wealth in the context of Joseph's story (2:7–12). On the one hand, these gifts denote earthly value and wealth, but the meaning of the gifts or an assessment of their value is not explicitly extrapolated or continued in the story (e.g., Are they used to finance the trip to Egypt? Arrange for assistance at home while they are gone? Pay taxes?). Luz emphasizes their monetary value, calling frankincense and myrrh "very expensive (imported) luxury items."[38] When combined with gold, he argues that their meaning is that "the magi bring the child the most costly gifts possible."[39]

Others disagree, arguing that while the gifts undoubtedly have some monetary value, that value is not the reason for their use in the story. Carter, for example, declines to automatically associate them with "excessive wealth," pointing to the reference in 10:9 that associates gold with people of lower status. Instead, he focuses on the gifts as part of a larger biblical pattern in which Gentiles bring whatever they have to celebrate and contribute to "God's universal purposes."[40] Davies and Allison agree, referring to this as "the firstfruits of the eschatological pilgrimage of the nations and their submission to the one true God."[41] As those who may relate to or serve powerful rulers, the male magi who bear the gifts may be associated with power or status in their own context. But, from the point of view of the narrative, what matters is their acknowledgement of God's purpose in the child Jesus. The gifts symbolize this recognition.

In addition to the gifts' monetary value, the context for their bestowal is also curious. The original news of Jesus' birth is received and interpreted on a large stage in Jerusalem, as "all Jerusalem" (πᾶσα Ἱεροσόλυμα) was frightened with King Herod (2:3). Yet, the birth of the child and delivery of the gifts meant to honor him take place in Bethlehem (2:1); here, no crowds are mentioned. From a Roman perspective, the giving of gifts or lavish displays of wealth were meant to happen in public places and to enhance the status of the giver.[42] This one happens in private and appears to communicate a sense of value about the child Jesus. This demonstration of value does not resonate with dominant notions of wealth.

A disruption between wealth and virtue is present in a different way in the depiction of Joseph and Mary. After their forced flight to Egypt, the builder and his family settle in Nazareth (2:23), at a distance from the center of attention and of power in Jerusalem. The parents who protect the infant Jesus are neither wealthy nor powerful. In fact, a discussion of wealth is notably absent in the drama of what Marohl calls "Joseph's dilemma."[43] (1:18–25) Wealth is not an important motivator for Joseph's actions; he is motivated by righteousness and obedience to God (1:19).

Further, Joseph's lack of wealth does not appear to inhibit his efforts at righteous obedience. Despite their limited means, Joseph and Mary exhibit righteousness and virtue in their adherence to God's direction and care for Jesus. The significance of Joseph's lack of wealth with respect to righteousness may be understood to be consistent with ambivalence toward wealth reflected in the broader biblical context. For example, Matthew 1:19 identifies Joseph as "a righteous man" (δίκαιος). In Deuteronomistic perspective, righteous adherence to the law brings material blessing; see Deuteronomy 28:1–14. However, in the book of Job, an automatic association between the two is challenged when Job loses all his material possessions despite his righteousness.

As I have shown, there is considerable ambivalence in the depiction of wealth in the story of Joseph. What does this mean for Joseph's masculinity? From an ancient perspective, an ideal male would have both wealth and status. Joseph is not defined in these terms. Whether he is understood to lack wealth, or if he is simply not defined by it, Joseph's claim to masculinity is not made or bolstered by his financial status. Despite this, he still plays a pivotal role in the Gospel, one that can be described in other terms that convey ancient masculinity. For example, even though Joseph is not associated with wealth, this does not appear to undermine his righteousness, his status as a descendant of David, or his ability to protect his wife and child.

It is possible that the role of wealth in Joseph's story is simply overshadowed by these other, more positive, characteristics attributed to him in the Gospel. As I will argue later in this chapter, Joseph's righteousness and relationship with God are very strong. In the Gospel's view, these characteristics are prioritized, and so might mitigate any potential negative association with

Joseph's social status. While Matthew is not averse to talking about wealth in other areas, it does not seem to be a defining characteristic of Joseph's character or the dynamics of this particular story.[44] So perhaps the ambivalence of the Gospel's attitude toward wealth in the depiction of Joseph allows him to be defined by other characteristics.

Even so, I want to suggest that something else may be going on, as well. The elite male in this story, the one who would ordinarily qualify for ideal masculinity, is Herod.[45] However, Herod is established in this Gospel as an enemy of God's purpose. He is the dangerous royal pretender who threatens the will of God. Herod's connection to danger and opposition undercuts any association of virtue with his character, including potentially associated wealth. It also contrasts starkly with Joseph's obedience and righteousness. If this set of relationships is indicative of the larger perspective of the Gospel, then Joseph's dissociation from wealth can be seen as either neutral or perhaps even positive, enhancing his status in the Gospel's view. The fact that he is able to exhibit core masculine values of righteousness and devout obedience to the divine, even without the wealth that would have been assumed by an ancient thinker, suggests a shift in focus.

This shift away from wealth as a major factor in the narrative might indicate a subtle rejection or at least downgrading of the importance of wealth in the construction of Matthean masculinity. Rather than being overshadowed by his other good qualities, Joseph's disassociation with wealth in some ways *facilitates* those other qualities of righteousness and divine obedience, contributing to his masculinity rather than mitigating it. This potentially redefines the way that masculinity is associated with wealth. They can go hand in hand, Joseph's reliance on God and not on wealth, his connection to God and not to mammon. The antithesis, the choice between these two, is emphasized in 6:24 as an important part of discipleship. Viewed in this context, the same tension has implications for the definition of masculine status.

While it may be too much to say that the Gospel's depiction of Joseph openly challenges or opposes imperial values of wealth, it is clear that the Gospel doesn't necessarily value wealth in the same way as the dominant imperial culture. Wealth is still used somewhat as a measure of value, indicated by the association with royal lineage and the gifts of the wise men, but wealth is not a prerequisite for being righteous or obedient. Rather, in this story, material wealth is associated most closely with the enemy of God assumed to have it, rather than with the righteous ones. Contrary to the dominant imperial assumptions, Joseph is able to be both righteous and obedient even without overt association with significant financial resources.

DOMINATING CONTROL OVER SELF AND OVER OTHERS

We turn now to the question of control over self and over others, which is a fundamental part of ancient masculinity and a contested site where masculine status can either be achieved or lost. I use the general term "control" because it includes the wide variety of behaviors associated with masculinity. But, as I discuss in chapter 1, it is good to note that the type of control connoted in ancient constructions of masculinity is characterized by exerting dominating power over self and others in an active, even aggressive, manner that is intended to raise the status of the subject and limit the actions and reactions of the object of control.[46]

Control over others covers a wide variety of things, from physical location to bodily violation, including the power over life and death. Control over self is related to a balance of certain emotions, like anger, where some is allowed, but too much is problematic. It is also indicative of a man's ability to protect himself from unwanted interactions. In addition to the obvious benefit of increased power, dominating control over self and others is associated with virtue, which can be lost if that control is diminished.[47]

While full domination over self and others expected of elites is not realistic for Joseph, non-elite imitation of elite behavior in imperial or colonial contexts is common and unsurprising. The question is how Joseph executes this imitative behavior and what sort of masculine status it achieves. In this Gospel, Joseph's power over himself and others is both emphasized and limited; this tension is an essential part of the dramatic narrative in Matthew.

In the dominant construction of masculinity, a virtuous man exhibits control over himself, his desires, and his emotions.[48] Joseph's character is primarily described as righteous (1:19), which in this context might be understood as reasoned adherence to the law and to divine guidance. Based on this distinction, one would expect Joseph to demonstrate his masculinity through control over his various appetites. This bears out both in Joseph's words and actions, which are not marked by excess, but measured and thoughtful responses. Although he contemplates divorcing Mary in 1:19, which is a weighty and dramatic act, he is not described as angry or sexually aggressive. When the angel arrives, he is told to listen and obey (1:20–21), which he does (1:24–25). In v. 24, he submits to divine authority, responding just as the angel commands. Joseph is characterized as one who does not lose control over his emotions.

The angel's reference to fear in 1:20 does introduce the possibility of fear being associated with Joseph. This is notable because fear had a negative connotation with respect to masculinity in the ancient world.[49] Ancient emphasis on power and especially military prowess associated masculinity with courage. Williams notes that "military discipline, pertinacity, endurance, and bravery in the face of death are all coded as masculine, and their absence as effeminate."[50] Fear showed a lack of courage as well as a lack of control over one's emotions, and could be both accusation and proof of compromised masculinity.

For example, Matthew 2:3 identifies Herod's primary emotional reaction to the news of the wise men as fear (ἐταράχθη). In this case, I contend Herod's fear is exactly the kind of emotion that threatens masculinity. Davies and Allison note that the verb ταράσσω "goes beyond 'startled;' it is closer to 'disturbed,' 'unsettled.'"[51] The news of a baby who is called "king" deeply disturbs the sitting king because it threatens his masculine power. Further, this fear produces violent actions and anger as Herod first tries to murder the new king, and, when that fails, to have all the children in Bethlehem killed. Herod's legendary paranoia often produced this dangerous combination; in just one example, Josephus relates the story of Herod making arrangements for his wife, Mariamne, to be killed if she is unfaithful during his absence.[52] The intensity of Herod's fear and anger is underscored by the reference in 2:3 to "all Jerusalem" being frightened with him. I read this collective fear to be related to Herod's reputation for brutal violence when threatened.[53] If Herod's masculine power is challenged, excessive violent action borne of fear commonly results, putting everyone in danger.

Herod's outsized fear, paranoia, and anger mark him as someone who is out of control, who responds in excessive ways because he does not exhibit self-mastery. This diminishes his masculine status. It is important, then, to consider whether the association of fear with Joseph is also a threat to his masculinity. However, the situation with Joseph is quite different. First, Joseph is responding to the angel of the Lord, but Herod to the news delivered by the wise men. Second, the text does not explicitly say that Joseph is afraid; it says that the angel tells him not to fear.

Third, even if he is afraid, the fear might be seen as appropriate to the situation. The presence of this phrase in other biblical dream sequences suggests that its usage here may not be anything related specifically to Joseph's character, but rather what Davies and Allison call a "standard element" of angelophanies.[54] Fear prompted by an angelic visitor is a typical and expected human response, and quite different from the exhibition of fear in the face of battle or other threat. Unlike Herod, then, the mention of fear in Joseph's story cannot be assumed to be a character-building trait, but can be understood rhetorically as formulaic and conventional. This suggests that it would be unwise to read too much into Joseph's exercise of control based on this reference, particularly because there is no sustained mention of fear with respect to Joseph's character. If he was ever afraid, it does not limit him. He shows consistent submission leading to action, responding to the angel by getting up and obeying each time (1:24, 2:14, 21–22).

In addition to emotions, control over self can be expressed in one's ability to control one's own movements and safety. The ideal male has the agency and authority to move about freely and keep himself safe. Herod demonstrates aspects of this kind of control. He holds a position that affords him authority and agency; when that position is threatened, he takes steps to secure it. In his encounter with the wise men, Carter says that Herod "takes the initiative, as he will do often throughout the scene."[55] Although Herod's authority is questioned, his body is not in immediate danger. He speaks and his words are heard and have consequences. In the story, he is not represented as subject to anyone.

At the same time, there are ways that Herod's control over himself is limited. Although the narrative does not depict this, as a client king of Rome, Herod is surely subject to pressure "from above," limiting his choices.[56] In addition, his position is clearly threatened "from below," as news of a newborn king greatly disturbs him. Also, significantly, this narrative records Herod's death, mentioning it three times (2:15, 19, 20). If Herod's desire is to oppose God, his death proves that he is still subject to God. Although the text gives no indication of the manner of death, the fact that it is mentioned three times emphasizes Herod's ultimate loss of power and security.

While some tension may be present in Herod's character with respect to control over movements and body, more substantial tension is prevalent in Joseph's character. He is able to exercise some control with respect to his own movements. In the wake of Herod's threats, he is able to get to Egypt and back again. He is neither restrained nor detained, but apparently is able to move freely.[57] On the way back, he senses that danger remains once he hears Archelaus is now ruling (2:22). This sense is confirmed with a dream, and the destination is changed to Galilee. The text does not indicate whether the dream specified the location, or whether that was Joseph's choice. But regardless, Joseph's attentiveness to the situation and ability to shift gears demonstrates some determinative agency as well as considerable courage. As Davies and Allison remark, "Mary, like her son Jesus, is a completely passive character throughout Matthew 1–2. It is Joseph who does what needs to be done."[58]

Another example of Joseph's relative control over himself is the lack of attention paid to his body. Montserrat argues that one indicator of lower status in Roman discourse on gender is the description of one's body.[59] He finds numerous descriptions of bodies in the Oxyrynchus papyri in Egypt but asserts that they are primarily descriptions of (1) slaves and (2) men who have been victims of violence. The compromised status of these individuals gives them a passive quality that is to be observed and recorded. By contrast, he says, "the bodies of free people are described quite differently in the same circumstances; or rather, they are not described at all."⁶⁰

This observation is interesting in light of the presentation of Joseph in Matthew. There is no description of Joseph's body at all. While it might be too much here to argue that this means something specific for Joseph's status, I do think the lack of description, along with the indirect references to agency and mobility outlined above, indicates that Joseph is seen more as a subject than an object. His body is not the issue; Mary's is. His control over himself is not violated by a narrative description that puts him in a passive position.

At the same time, it must be emphasized that there are very significant things about his body and his life that Joseph does not control. As discussed in chapter 1, the performance of rhetoric is a critical element in the establishment of masculinity.⁶¹ While other men in the Gospel talk, including both Herod and the angel, Joseph does not. He is not given the ability to speak for himself to establish his own power and perspective. Further, the fact that he is forced to move around is the result of the whim of Herod and the will of God. He goes to Egypt because the angel warns him about Herod, and only returns when it is safe (2:20). Even this safe return is mitigated by the presence of Archelaus; the family relocates rather than returning to their home.⁶² Further, as discussed in the previous section, according to Friesen's scheme, Joseph is not a man of wealth or status. Instead, he is a provincial builder (ὁ τέκτονος), subject to ruling authority figures such as Herod and Archelaus, the client kings of the Roman Empire. If a soldier or elite person wanted to do something with Joseph, that person could with little consequence.

Not only is Joseph subject to Herod, but he is also subject to God. This is apparent in Joseph's lack of ability to control his participation in the difficult situation he faces. While he shows considerable control over his own emotions and choices *in response*, Joseph's involvement is not the result of his own actions, but by an act of God. Joseph is forced into a reactive position, rather than a proactive one, making consequential choices that impact his own life that do not result from his own volition.

This lack of control is emphasized in the story itself, as the reader initially knows more about Joseph's dilemma than he does.⁶³ In verse 18, Mary is described as being "with child by the Holy Spirit" (ἐν γαστρὶ ἔχουσα ἐκ πνεύματος ἁγίου), but this is directed at the reader, not at Joseph. It is not until verse 20 that the angel spells this out for him, after he has already resolved in verse 19 to respond by divorcing her. Joseph's response to his delayed inclusion into the truth of Mary's pregnancy both allows the reader to learn something about Joseph and reinforces the idea that Joseph does not have command of the situation.

God's control or domination over Joseph's body has another implication, as well. Montserrat emphasizes the phallocentric nature of ancient masculinity in architecture, household objects, and art.[64] The presence and use of the phallus conveyed masculine power both symbolically and literally, through the dominant role in sex and the fathering of children. God's role in Mary's pregnancy means that Joseph is excluded from this aspect of masculinity; he is unmanned by the irrelevance of his body to Mary's pregnancy.[65]

I will revisit the issue of whether God's control over Joseph diminishes his masculinity in the next section on his divine service, but here it is important to note that Joseph's choices and movements are not only limited by earthly powers but are also understood to be guided or directed by God. So, while Joseph may be able to move about with some agency on a small scale, on a larger scale he does not qualify as one in dominant control of himself.

This same story of Joseph's response to Mary's pregnancy also provides a framework for considering his potential domination over others, a second sphere of this aspect of Joseph's masculinity. Once again, ambivalence predominates. On the one hand, we see evidence of Joseph's lack of dominating control over others. While he does demonstrate agency, he is consistently in the reactive position. Mary's pregnancy, holy or not, has occurred without Joseph's participation, assent, or knowledge.[66] He responds to this pregnancy with a plan that is eventually rejected by God, and he dutifully abandons his own plan in favor of the instructions of the angel. He is unable to challenge openly those who threaten his family, either Herod or the more immediate soldiers, and is forced to take evasive action. The fact that the reader knows before Joseph does that there is something unusual and divine about Mary's pregnancy puts the reader in a position of power, reinforcing the idea that Joseph does not demonstrate control over his environment.

Despite these limits, Joseph clearly benefits from what Connell calls the patriarchal dividend.[67] We can see the effects of this dividend in Joseph's domination over Mary, namely, he exercises the power of life and death over her. The idea of divorcing her unilaterally is *not* challenged by the angel in vv. 20–25. Neither does the angel tell Joseph that his authority over her is wrong. Rather, the angel says that God wishes Joseph to use that power differently. Joseph has the right and ability to do so; the power is his. Divorce remains an approved response. But in this case, God desires another outcome.

As I discuss below, it is important to remember that the command is given by the angel of the Lord, so his response to that command may be limited. But it is clear that the narrative considers Joseph capable of impacting reality in particular ways that would be contrary to God's purpose. So God intervenes with an angel to guide and influence those ways according to God's plan and preference. In other words, Joseph's agency matters.

Joseph's domination over Mary extends beyond this dramatic choice to all facets of life. He is understood to have control over her and the infant, deciding and facilitating their protection (2:14–15, 21–23). The dream sequences come to him, not to Mary (1:20, 2:13, 19, 22), and he is given the authority and ability to decide and direct their movements. This dominant control is not just a privilege, but his assumed responsibility as a man over his household. Exerting this kind of control is intrinsic both to his masculine identity and to his identity as a righteous person. The fact that his control over the others is subject to divine control further legitimates Joseph's control.

Joseph's actions with Mary can be understood as imitative of the ideal of masculine dominance. Control over others is a crucial aspect of establishing masculine status, and this can be carried out on small or large scales. A comparison here with Herod is helpful. King Herod possesses the same kind of control that Joseph does, but on a larger scale and with fewer restrictions. Herod commands the military forces who secure his place as ruler, and who travel at his command to kill the infants in Bethlehem. The threat of Herod's actions impacts others, from Joseph and Mary's flight to Egypt to the fear of those in Jerusalem. Herod decides whether others live or die, whether they are free or not.

It is the expectation of Herod's domination over others that gives tension to the story as his assertion of control meets resistance. Herod's power must be considered to be real; if he had been able to find Jesus, then he would have been able to kill Jesus. The murder of the other male infants emphasizes the deadly potential of Herod's control over others, telling "of Herod's dangerous anger and thus how great the danger was that the child escaped."[68] Even after Herod's death, his line lives on in Archelaus, whose presence changes Joseph's final destination to Galilee. The movements of the wise men, Joseph, and Mary all resist Herod's domination of them and avoid Herod's physical dominance over Jesus. While Herod's domination over others is not complete, it is real and dangerous.

It is important to note here that it is God who ultimately limits Herod's power. As Carter says, Herod's "attempts to thwart God's purposes are thwarted through a dream."[69] In this respect, God is operating with the kind of domination and control that is indicative of a hegemonic male.[70] Masculine domination, then, is a key element in this part of the Gospel. It is the loss of control that drives Herod, and the narrative, forward. It is the combination of resistance to and expression of control that gives tension to Joseph's story. And it is the assertion of dominant control over others by God that ultimately saves Jesus.

Beyond his interactions with Mary, other behaviors also contribute to the overall picture of Joseph's negotiation of control over others. For example, Joseph's evasive movements can also be understood to convey a blunting or deflecting of Herod's power. While this is more of a responsive action than "control" in the dominant sense, it is a successful countering of Herod's efforts. Scholars of empire often speak of resistance to empire not as direct action, but as indirect and opaque, but nonetheless effective.[71] While Joseph does not openly challenge Herod's authority or control his actions, he is able to keep Herod from doing what he wants. Given this social location, this is as close to effective control as someone like Joseph could have over Herod.

One other important way that Joseph has control over others is his role in giving Jesus an identity. Regardless of how one understands Jesus's conception, it is clear that Joseph is not the biological father. In 1:16, Joseph is identified as the husband of Mary (τὸν ἄνδρα Μαρίας), but the feminine singular relative pronoun (ἐξ ἧς ἐγεννήθη Ἰησοῦς) refers not to him, but to Mary. This break in the pattern of the genealogy emphasizes Mary's role in Jesus's conception and birth, not Joseph's. Despite the absence of biological association, Joseph follows the angel's bidding to claim the child by giving him a name. This is how he is included in the Davidic line that Matthew traces, what Luz calls "the grafting of the virgin's son onto the stock of David."[72]

This adoption does two things. First, as Schaberg reminds us, "Of all the possible fates in store for the child of a woman in the situation Matthew depicts, adoption into the family and protection of her husband was the kindest and most humane. But because of the emotional obstacles and prejudices that would have been involved in such a decision, we can conjecture that it may have been the rarest and most unexpected."[73] According to Sirach and Wisdom of Solomon, these consequences could have included public humiliation, inquisition, and ostracization.[74] Joseph's choice creates a space for Jesus to be born and live in relative security. His choice to adopt Jesus puts Joseph in line not only with the emphasis on righteousness and obedience in chapter 2, but also with the Gospel's larger theme of mercy (9:13, 12:7).

Second, not only does Joseph's decision legitimate the child's existence, he also provides him with an identity. This is what happens in Matthew's genealogy, when Joseph is connected to Mary and to Jesus. Like Joseph, Jesus becomes part of the line of David. This adopted identity is fully legitimate, not halfway or watered down. "Davidic sonship is a legal sonship which does not demand biological descent. All that is required is that his mother's husband, a Davidid, acknowledge Jesus as his own. This Joseph does when he chooses to remain with Mary and give Jesus his name."[75]

Scholars make much of this adoption in terms of Jesus's identity, and they focus on Joseph's role. "By his actions, Joseph the Davidid proves that he has made Jesus his own."[76] He is seen as the way Jesus enters the house and line of David. Without Joseph, Jesus doesn't have much of an identity.[77] But with Joseph, Jesus is "Abraham's Son and royal messiah, and thus the bearer of all Israel's messianic hopes in accordance with God's plan."[78] This lineage and future are important for Matthew; they set the tone of the rest of the book. Once again, Joseph's obedient, righteous responses effect significant change for those around him.[79]

In this section, I have explored the complex dynamics of dominating control over self and others, an integral part of ancient masculinity, in the characterization of Joseph. This analysis suggests that there is no singular statement about Joseph's ability to control human beings. Ambivalence abounds. On the one hand, Joseph is in control of his own body in the sense that he is righteous and he exercises domination over Mary both in his decision over Jesus as well as his responsibility for Mary's protection. And yet, his own body and choices are subject to God, Herod, and political authorities associated both local and imperial rule, as well as to the laws that govern a righteous man's life. He is able to exercise control in significant ways, but that control faces serious limitations.

So how does this ambiguity function within the larger context of masculinity? While he demonstrates admirable control over his own emotions, Joseph's socioeconomic status does not afford him the kind of domination over others that matches the assumptions of the ancient imperial elite. In terms of his relationship with Mary, he exercises relative authority over her marital status and movements, but their situation also points to his lack of control of her sexuality. Even if his choice to adopt a child who was not "his" can be explained, the perception of betrayal by Mary is problematic from the perspective of masculine control over others. Even his domination over himself is limited. In terms of emotions, he is commendable, but the indignity of having to run around because bigger powers are playing dangerous games underscores Joseph's lack of importance and even invisibility to elites.

However, the question remains whether Matthew's characterization of Joseph is intended to convey that failure, or whether the ambivalence can be understood differently. Within the context of the narrative, it does not appear that Joseph is understood to be a failure as a man. If anything, he is the opposite. He is not a large character, but his actions are terribly important with respect to the progression of the narrative. Without Joseph's adoption of Jesus, there is no Davidic identity. Without Joseph's protection, Herod the tetrarch, the client of Rome, destroys God's plan before it even gets going.

I contend that the ambiguous portrayal of Joseph's control over others and himself ultimately contributes to a positive composite picture of him because it emphasizes his identity as a faithful, righteous, obedient man, all of which are important within the Gospel's framework. He is subject to divine purposes, which is a positive trait, and one I explore more fully in the next section. He able to carry out the mission entrusted to him by God, and he does it despite the odds and the forces at work. The limited resources and control over others that Joseph exhibits do not disqualify him from a positive portrayal. Rather than focusing on these limitations, Joseph is portrayed with considerable dignity.

If this is the case, then it is important to consider how this conceptualization relates to the one promoted in the ancient world. Does it reflect a difference in priorities in the early Christian community from those of the empire? Or, is it indicative of Connell's marginalized mindset, where the man is seen as necessarily inferior, but as good as can be hoped given his status? If it is the latter, then Joseph is a good example of a non-elite male whose masculinity is portrayed in a positive light, but also realistically. There are limitations placed upon him and he does the best he can with them. There is no real challenge to the dominant cultural construction, but an imitative desire to fulfill the expectations as completely as possible given the circumstances.

If it is the former, then a more fundamental critique may be at play, where the community represented in Matthew's writing is attempting to redefine masculinity along different lines. If Joseph is, in some ways, an ideal, then that ideal differs dramatically from the dominant elite ideal male. In fact, Joseph's portrayal may challenge the very concept of an "ideal male" who has ultimate control over himself and others, offering another option of someone who is admirably masculine in some ways while quite unsuccessful in others. This leaves room for the possibility that the association between masculinity and power that is inherent to ancient masculinity is porous and that there is potential space for redefinition and reshaping.

The change is not altogether revolutionary. Exhibition of control, even if it is mitigated, is still seen as essential to masculinity in this paradigm. Non-elite imitation of elite values is not surprising and even expected. Some interpreters have understood this control as positive. For Brown, Joseph is "a Jew who is 'upright,' i.e., scrupulously faithful to the Law, and he protects Jesus from the hostile authorities of his own people and brings him safely to Galilee of the Gentiles."[80] Here, Joseph's control and Joseph's "uprightness" are connected. However, for Schaberg, Joseph "becomes the protector of the mother and child, incorporating them into 'the male sphere,' the ordinary scheme of things."[81] Here, Joseph's control has an edge, connoting domination. Yes, he protects the child and his mother. But what does his protection guarantee?

Feminist interpreters have argued that it places Mary's life squarely and "safely" in the male sphere. As Janice Capel Anderson states, "although it is not their main purpose, the Gospels of Matthew and Luke embody male conceptions of female gender."[82] Because of this androcentric embodiment, the preoccupation of a story about women and children is with incorporating them into appropriate male institutions. If, as Schaberg says, "This story is primarily about and for males,"[83] then Joseph's "protection" of Mary may not be understood as righteous by those who challenge androcentric structures and assumptions.

However, as many have pointed out, the woman and child in this story simply do not fit neatly into the boxes designated by male society. It takes an act of God to save the child's life and incorporation into the male system takes the obedience of Joseph. Even afterward, there is something different about this child and his mother that is beyond the control of Joseph, or even of those with considerably more masculinity.

Like the ambivalence surrounding Joseph's control over self and others, this instability can be taken two ways. On the one hand, the instability can be downplayed in favor of the story that Mary and the child are "rescued" from their liminal status and re-inserted into the male social hierarchy. On the other hand, instability is also a marker of possibility, and this story has plenty of cracks, including anomalous genealogical women,[84] numbers of generations that don't add up,[85] the use of passive voice for paternity,[86] and Joseph's final rescue role that defies cultural expectations.[87] In light of this instability, Janice Capel Anderson characterizes both this story and the birth narrative in Luke as texts that "simultaneously project and undermine male ideology and its associated patriarchal institutions."[88] Joseph's masculinity is a focal point where this tension is exhibited quite clearly.

DIVINE SERVICE

So far in this chapter, I have described the ambivalence and mitigating factors associated with Joseph's wealth and his control over himself and others. One intriguing aspect of these discussions has been the limitation of Joseph's control over himself and others because of his obedience to God. God's control over Joseph means Joseph has less control over himself and others. At the same time, Joseph's credibility is enhanced by his connection to the divine purpose and his own righteousness. Divine service is an integral part of Joseph's characterization as well as the understanding of masculinity in the ancient world.[89] In the final section of this chapter, I explore the relationship between Joseph and the divine and how his divine service contributes to the construction of Joseph's masculinity.

As previously stated, Joseph's adoption of Jesus places Jesus in the Davidic line. Since Joseph is of the Davidic line, so is Jesus (1:20). This is a key factor in associating Joseph with the divine. In addition to his behavior, which is discussed below, Joseph is connected to God through his Davidic status. Building on the sonship references in the royal Davidic language in Israelite tradition, Brown argues for a "very tight connection between Davidic and divine sonship."[90] In 2 Samuel 7, for example, Nathan delivers the message to David that the Lord will raise up a descendant for him; in verse 14, a father/son relationship is established between that descendant and the Lord.[91] Brown understands Matthew's depiction of Joseph's adoption of Jesus to be "a most literal fulfillment" of this promise to David.[92] While this particular argument is intended to focus on Jesus's Davidic and divine identity, it is easy to overlook the implications for Joseph, who secures the tight connection.

The association among Joseph, Jesus, and God is also important in terms of Joseph's righteousness. In 1:19, Joseph is initially and primarily introduced as a man who is righteous (δίκαιος ὤν, "being righteous").[93] Because of its prominence, and perhaps the lack of other descriptors, many interpreters have emphasized Joseph's righteousness, not just in comparison with other characteristics (i.e., Joseph is more righteous than he is wise), but in comparison with *other people* (i.e., Joseph is more righteous than others are). Luz, for example, calls him "an exemplary righteous man."[94] Brown notes that δίκαιος is used 19 times in Matthew, so the idea of "a just man" is very important.[95]

The emphasis on Joseph's righteousness may have further dimension, as well. Annelies Moeser has argued that one function of Joseph's righteousness is to "mitigate the stigma of low birth," and that "Matthew's depiction of Joseph exhibiting self-control and *pietas* are literary creations warding off threats to Jesus' masculinity."[96] Drawing on Erving Goffman's theory of stigma, which addresses how differences that are perceived as inferior affect social status, Moeser argues that the emphasis on Joseph's righteousness falls under Goffman's category of "normification," which contains attempts at restoring social identity by emphasizing similarities and eliding differences with the dominant or elite group.[97] Thus, Joseph's righteousness functions as an important claim to masculinity that downplays or mitigates other factors that detract from his masculine status.[98] I agree with Moeser that the emphasis on righteousness is significant, but further argue that it is important not just for mitigating Jesus's low birth, but for establishing Joseph's masculinity.

The exact nature of Joseph's righteousness, however, is open for discussion. Joseph's righteousness is often associated with his adherence to the Law. Typical is Brown, who characterizes Joseph as "a man who acted in accord with God's will as expressed in the law."[99] But which of Joseph's actions are "in accord with God's will?" His decision to divorce Mary? His decision not to divorce Mary? Both? While Joseph is consistently understood to be righteous, interpreters make contradictory claims about what behavior best reflects this characteristic.

As a sense of righteousness is important for determining divine service, for the purposes of this discussion it is helpful to review some of the possibilities.[100] First, Joseph's righteousness could be indicated by his decision to divorce Mary.[101] Here the priority is orientation to God and God's law. While there is no specific commandment to divorce, Deuteronomy 24:1 assumes divorce as an option for Jewish men. Jesus modifies this assumption in

Matthew 5:32 and 19:9 by prohibiting divorce in all cases except adultery. In that case, divorce remains lawful.

More than lawful, however, it can be understood to be appropriate or even necessary. M.N.A. Bockmuehl has argued that the Judaism reflected in Matthew's community would have understood adultery as a breach in the marriage contract which "precludes a resumption of that marriage."[102] In this understanding, divorce is the appropriate response because it makes legal and formal what has already happened; the marriage has ended.

Concerning Matthew's prohibition of divorce in Matthew 5:32, Luz highlights a reverse association with the same assumption. Here, divorce *is* adultery, except in cases where adultery is the *cause* of divorce, because the consequence of the action has already occurred.[103] "Since adultery already destroys the marriage, for Judaism, divorce is mandatory when adultery happens."[104] To illustrate this point made in 5:32 and in 19:9, Dale Allison actually uses the example of Joseph, citing the internal cogency of the narrative.[105] Without the exception noted in both 5:32 and 19:9, Joseph's decision would have been considered unlawful. Because of the exception in cases of adultery (μὴ ἐπὶ πορνείᾳ), Joseph's actions can be considered righteous even within the context of Jesus's teaching in Matthew.[106]

According to this understanding, divorcing Mary adheres to the law and keeps Joseph right with God. Because Joseph believes Mary's infidelity has introduced impurity into the marriage, divorce is the righteous option that obeys God's law. By making the choice understood to be right, removing the impurity of Mary's adultery from his life, he is righteous. Joseph is righteous, *therefore* he plans to divorce Mary.[107]

Or, slightly differently, Joseph's righteousness could be indicated by his decision to divorce Mary rather than choosing another punishment that would be worse.[108] This is no insignificant choice; Matthew J. Marohl strongly makes the case that other options could have included an honor killing, either by Joseph or Mary's family.[109] Challenging previous biblical scholarship that has assumed that the stoning punishment mentioned in Deuteronomy 22:13–27 was no longer practiced, Marohl argues that stoning would have been a very real option for Joseph.[110] He finds evidence for this in several places: the continued prevalence of honor killings that have an articulated basis in tradition, the dynamics of honor/shame culture, and references to honor killings in ancient literature, including the woman caught in adultery in John 8:1–11.[111]

In this case, the righteousness exhibited by Joseph's decision is identified, at least in part, by mercy.[112] Rather than subjecting Mary to public trial and/or punishment that may have been life-threatening, Joseph chooses divorce.[113] This sets up an interesting potential relationship between righteousness and mercy. Although they are not synonymous, in this scenario mercy marks an act as righteous. Joseph is righteous, *therefore* he divorces Mary *instead of* inflicting another punishment.[114]

A third option for understanding Joseph's righteousness is to consider Joseph's choice as one primarily of avoiding public shame. The fact that the text mentions his desire to avoid exposing her to public disgrace (μὴ θέλων αὐτὴν δειγματίσαι) could be considered indicative of Joseph's desire to minimize Mary's shame and public pain. In this case, the idea of divorce isn't what is righteous, either as opposed to stoning or in obedience to the law, but what spares Mary from public shame. Joseph is righteous, *therefore* he chooses private divorce rather than public disgrace.[115]

This last possibility introduces another question: Whose honor/shame is at stake? Many interpreters focus on Mary's potential shame, which can be supported by the reference to public disgrace in v. 19. Then there is Joseph's honor; Deuteronomy 22 emphasizes that the killing of the adulterous individual will remove evil. In the case of an adulterous wife, this leaves the innocence of the husband intact. In addition, Marohl also suggests that the shame of Mary's family may play a role, citing both ancient and contemporary rhetoric around honor killings as an attempt to preserve the honor of the woman's family of origin.[116] If so, their shame could translate into an honor killing. Both possibilities suggest that preserving Mary's honor is not the same as preserving Joseph's honor or that of Mary's family. This leaves the "righteous" choice less clear, and illustrates the complex dynamics of honor and shame and the potential difficulty of narrowing choices to a single motivation.

The final option for Joseph, the one that the angel says God desires, does several important things. It prevents whatever negative consequences would befall Mary and the baby. It gives the baby a name and a lineage. It fulfills God's wishes. And it befits a man who is described as "righteous." According to Schaberg, "Matthew intends the angelic solution to the dilemma of Joseph to be a righteous and a legal one. It does not contradict, but properly interprets and applies the Law, removing Joseph's scruple."[117] Joseph no longer has a dilemma, because Mary's pregnancy is revealed to be holy. Here, the final option is all things: it is both righteous, preserving Joseph's status with respect to God and public opinion, and merciful, preserving the health and safety of Mary and the child. No tension remains; both Mary and Joseph emerge from the situation intact.

That being said, this final option does leave some questions unanswered. From within the world of the narrative, it is possible to imagine that even with this legitimacy, there might be some social consequences for Joseph from those who might have known *some* of the story, or even *all* of it. It is difficult to imagine a scenario in which Joseph can provide a satisfying public explanation for their situation, leaving Joseph's honor somewhat in question. If this is the case, it is worth considering whether his choice to put the needs of someone else before his own needs for vindication and public honor is part of what makes Joseph righteous in God's eyes, if not in public view.

What is interesting in these different options is that Joseph's righteousness can be accomplished in several ways that have very different effects on those around him. Luz sums up two possible interpretations this way: "Joseph's 'righteousness' consists either in that he follows the appropriate halakah and divorces his betrothed, or in that he doesn't want to shame Mary the suspected adulteress by subjecting her to a trial for adultery-thus in his kindness and gentleness."[118] While Joseph's righteousness may be intact in both scenarios, the consequences are very different for Mary, and perhaps even for Joseph. Although it is possible to associate both with divine purpose, righteousness coupled with "kindness and gentleness" manifests itself in this story quite differently than righteousness that, although obedient, has casualties. It is God's solution, the one Joseph did not initially choose, that preserves both.

One issue related to righteousness that is both yet to be considered and critical to a conversation about masculinity is the concept of obedience. Albright and Mann quote Josephus's words on δίκαιος as follows: "one *obedient* to the command of God, an upright man, a man of character" (emphasis mine).[119] More than kindness, mercy, or respect for God, Brown sees obedience as the key manifestation of righteousness in Joseph's dilemma.[120] Luz says that the "main scope" of this story in Matthew is Jesus's identity and purpose. But he asserts that an "ethical secondary scope is the figure of the righteous Joseph *and his obedience*" (emphasis mine).[121]

Clearly, obedience is important for righteousness. The drama of Joseph's story leaves the precise relationship between these two fuzzy. Is Joseph righteous and therefore obedient, making all his actions potentially righteous? Or is Joseph obedient and therefore righteous? This may seem like semantics, but the question finds some significance in the turning point of Joseph's encounter with the angel. Is Joseph righteous because he does the thing that is righteous? Or is he righteous because he leaves behind what is righteous and does what God wants him to do instead? Luz's reading of the story seems to suggest that while Joseph's adherence to the law is respected, it is his obedience that sets him apart.

The importance of obedience is particularly evident when one expands the conversation to include Joseph's other dreams in Matthew. Joseph's dreams are arguably the most obvious way that he is connected to God, and they create the opportunity for his righteous, obedient, divine service. The combination of connection to God, obedience, and righteousness illustrated by the dreams sets Joseph apart and makes an important contribution to his masculine status.

The connection between Joseph and God manifested by Joseph's obedience to his dreams is emphasized both by the narrative and by interpreters. Luz, for example, notes the dreams foreground "the idea of divine guidance and Joseph's obedience."[122] In ancient understanding, dreams are considered to be "a medium of revelation," as well as a strong and trustworthy way of measuring divine association or access.[123] The content, number, and clarity of Joseph's dreams are all very important. The dream in 1:20–22 is the most direct and vivid; Joseph is addressed by name in 1:20, and the angel shows intimate knowledge of both Joseph's situation and his mental deliberations. Although briefer, the repetition of the dream pattern three additional times emphasizes this connection, particularly in God's investment in Joseph's location and movements guaranteeing the safety of the family.

Together, they indicate that he is connected to God, so his words and actions carry out the will of God and his priorities align with those of the divine. In this respect, Joseph is no ordinary man. He is rather extraordinary. He is not rich, does not demonstrate the expected level of control over others, and yet is a connected and obedient divine servant. Matthew depicts him as having, essentially, a direct line to God.[124] This sets him apart within the context of a Gospel that values familiarity with and advancement of the purposes of God. While Joseph's masculinity may be compromised in some respects, he convincingly demonstrates the crucial element of divine service.

Matthew makes reference to four dreams with respect to Joseph, and three are narrated. The first, 1:20–25, communicates the divine desire that Joseph claim Mary and the baby, and that he name the child Jesus. The second, 2:13–15, contains the warning from the angel of Herod's wrath and the command to flee to Egypt. After Herod's death, the third dream (2:19–21) instructs Joseph to take the family to Israel. These three have a dramatic, immediate, quality, as well as several common elements, namely the identification of the angel, the spoken message, and the immediate response by Joseph. These three will be explored below.

The fourth and final dream (2:22) confirms Joseph's unease about Archelaus, and changes the family's destination to Galilee. This dream is not narrated. More than the other three Joseph dreams, it resembles the dream given to the wise men in 1:12. These two dreams are spoken of in the past tense, issue a warning about the ruler (Herod for the wise men and Archelaus for Joseph) and prompt a detour.[125]

Scholars have noted the similar elements, in the first three dream sequences, of what Luz calls the "dream motif and related vocabulary:" the identification of the angel, the spoken message, and the immediate response by Joseph.[126] Dodson, doing careful work in patterns and categories, places these dreams in context with other Greco-Roman literature, and concludes that "there is nothing peculiarly biblical or Jewish about the form of these dreams, as if Matthew was imitating the dream reports of the Jewish scriptures or a particular dream in Jewish tradition."[127] By contrast, Viljoen emphasizes relationships with both Jewish and Greco-Roman understandings of dreams.[128] Likewise, Davies and Allison call dreams "important for both Jewish and Greco-Roman worlds," but do note how the pattern of these dreams fits with Greco-Roman examples.[129]

Connections to both Jewish and Greco-Roman literature emphasize that the concept of dreams had currency outside of the Jewish tradition. Rather than being insider language that would require intertextual knowledge of other Jewish texts, these dreams would have been recognized and understood by the dominant culture surrounding the early Jesus communities. The larger themes of inspiration, connection to the divine, and special status of the recipient would have been communicable to an outside audience.

What do these dreams mean in the context of the narrative? First, as stated above, they emphasize Joseph's obedience and its relationship to Joseph's virtue. For example, the second two dreams include the same phrase, "Then he got up, took the child and his mother" (ὁ δὲ ἐγερθεὶς παρέλαβεν τὸ παιδίον καὶ τὴν μητέρα αὐτοῦ; 2:14, 21). According to Dodson, the obedience itself is not surprising. He argues that this is "a typical feature of the dream report, and would be expected by an ancient audience."[130] Likewise, Davies and Allison claim that "biblical tradition has a habit of observing that visionaries arise or stand up after an encounter," citing, among others, Exodus 2:1–12, Daniel 8:27, and Luke 1:39.[131]

But while the immediacy of Joseph's response might be expected, Dodson notes that its repetition in parallel stories might be more significant.[132] The fact that Joseph is said to obey the dreams' instructions four different times (1:24, 2:14, 21, 22), twice with the same wording (2:14, 21), and once that infers that he does so immediately ("by night," νυκτὸς in 2:14), may contribute to a composite picture that emphasizes obedience in a different way that other accounts might.

In addition, the dreams make sure that God's will is done. "Matthew is interested in elucidating the grafting of the virgin's son onto the stock of David."[133] Although I have previously highlighted Joseph's role here, it is good to acknowledge that he would not have done this on his own. It took an act of God making God's will known to him through the angel in a dream for this to be accomplished. Schaberg underscores the importance of communicating these divine intentions, including "the nature of the child to be born, and its fate and safety, which are dependent on Joseph's obedience."[134]

For the purposes of this project, the repetition of the theme of obedience is important because it reinforces Joseph's divine service expressed in righteousness. This righteousness, in turn, plays a very important role in the construction of Joseph's character. Of all three of the characteristics of masculinity addressed in this chapter, this one has the least ambiguity or ambivalence. Joseph is definitely righteous. He demonstrates this by his control over his own emotions, his direct communication with the divine through dreams, and his repeated, immediate, obedience to God's will revealed in those dreams.

Joseph's obedience and righteousness are further emphasized through a contrast with King Herod. Herod is the villain of the story, an enemy of God. His fear, rage, and desperation to preserve his own status threaten God's purposes. The opposition to God cannot be overstated. According to Carter, he "represents 'the kings of the earth' who resist God and God's anointed but are thwarted by God (Mt 17:24–27; Ps 2:1–6)."[135] When God intervenes in the narrative, it is to direct others to avoid Herod and sabotage his plans. Herod does not have the approval or sanction of the divine for his actions. It is no surprise, then, that the narrative records his death three times (2:15, 19, 20). God has defeated him.

Herod's opposition to God, and his defeat, have significant ramifications for his masculinity because of the critical role divine service plays in demonstrating elite masculine status. Access to or association with the divine established incredible status for the most elite males: Emperors. During his lifetime, Augustus cultivated an image of himself as a pious leader, in tune with the will of the gods.[136] Not only did he restore temples and refill priesthoods that had fallen away during the years of war, Augustus emphasized his own piety and accepted the title *pontifex maximus*.[137] On the Ara Pacis, what Galinsky calls the "most representative work of Augustan Art," Augustus is depicted with his head covered, leading both priests and the imperial family in a pious sacrificial procession that also participates in the ancient story of Rome.[138] The message is clear: Augustus honors the gods and the gods honor Augustus.

The connection between Augustus, divinity, and masculinity is only strengthened and made more explicit after his death.[139] Brian Bosworth argues for an interpretation of the *Res Gestae* that includes a justification for apotheosis.[140] "On one level," he argues, "it is a record of achievement, at another justification of divine status."[141] According to Bosworth, the argument for apotheosis takes place along traditional Hellenistic lines, namely, conquest and benefaction. In other words, Augustus's military domination and administration of the state, both masculine expressions of power, make the case for his divinity.

Similarly, Wendy Cotter emphasizes the role of apotheosis in granting masculine power both to the deified and to the power associated with him. "The political significance of a hero's *apotheosis* is obvious. His counsels are the will of the gods. If the Romans are masters of the civilized world, it is due to their greater virtue and valor, i.e., their superiority over others."[142] The established association of masculinity with both virtue and valor within the context of apotheosis underscore the strong ties between masculinity, divinity, and Augustus.

Augustus's association with divinity continues after his death, including his connection to the divine Caesar and the development of the imperial cult. This status then becomes the aspiration of subsequent Roman emperors. Vespasian provides an example closer to the historical context of Matthew. The biographer Suetonius records a number of signs pointing to Vespasian's divine blessing and election: a stray dog brings him a human hand during a meal, an ox bows to him, and a statue of the deified Julius turns toward the East.[143] In addition, Vespasian himself is associated with divine power, healing a blind man with his spittle and a lame man by stepping on his leg.[144] Vespasian, too, exhibits the tight connection between imperial power, divinity, and masculinity.

But even if divinity became an increasingly prevalent assumption of imperial status, it also could be questioned as a way of undermining imperial authority. In the satirical *Apocolocyntosis (divi) Claudii* ("Gourdification of [the divine] Claudius"), Seneca imagines the process of deification for the departed Claudius in terms of a heavenly debate over his credentials.[145] It is Augustus himself, at home in the company of the gods, who presents the multiple charges of murder that are the basis for precluding him from joining the gods.[146] Seneca contrasts Claudius with his mighty predecessor, Augustus, but also with his successor, Nero, claiming that the new emperor has the character and ability to bring about the will of the gods in ways where Claudius failed.

Significantly, this separation from the gods is accompanied by a number of other accusations that resonate with compromised masculinity. Claudius is ridiculed by Seneca in terms of physical disability, diminished intelligence, foreign heritage, and lack of control over his own bodily functions.[147] Further, he is criticized for his harsh control of his subjects, who now party at his death.[148] His masculinity, then, is undermined in several intersecting ways, which find a focal point in his rejection by the gods. This story underscores the potential for masculinity to be lost or diminished, even among the most powerful of men. Seneca sees a hierarchy among the emperors where Claudius's claim to deification is not equal to the demonstrated claim of Augustus or the potential claim of Nero. So, while divine service may be an expectation of emperors, it is not a guarantee. Even emperors are subject to competition and comparison in terms of their ability to qualify for divine status and accompanying masculine power.

Joseph's claim to divine service does not include deification.[149] However, like the Roman emperors, he is portrayed as someone who pays attention to and seeks the will of the divine in his actions. And God's will is made known to him directly through dreams and expressed in his actions. Joseph is much less powerful than earthly emperors in terms of his control over others and his wealth. But with respect to divine service, Joseph makes a claim to masculinity that the earthly ruler in this story, Herod, does not have. Herod is established as an enemy of God. Joseph's dreams "are the divine means by which the child Jesus is protected from the threat of Herod."[150] Joseph, by his obedience, is the one who makes this happen.

As I mentioned previously, it is important to consider whether this submission to God might be interpreted as mitigating Joseph's authority. Joseph's encounter with God highlights how he is not in charge of his own actions and how God's desire changes Joseph's plans. The question is heightened if one focuses on the masculinity traditionally identified with God. Eilberg-Schwartz highlights this tension in the biblical tradition, arguing that a male God diminishes or confuses the masculinity of human males who relate to that God.[151] Mary Rose D'Angelo makes a related point, arguing that Jesus's use of father language for God emphasizes power, not intimacy.[152]

If masculinity is a competition for status, the human males will always lose by comparison with God. And, if part of the definition of masculinity is to exert bodily control over others who are women or feminized men, then a male God who exercises hegemonic masculinity does the same to human males in divine service. This is illustrated in Joseph's story in his exclusion from the event of Jesus's conception, as well as in God's direction over Joseph's choices and movements. Rather than boosting Joseph's masculinity, then, the narrative potentially diminishes it in favor of what D'Angelo calls the "absolutely patriarchal claim of God."[153]

At the same time, for an ancient audience, submission to or partnership with the gods did not necessarily undermine the authority of earthly leaders. In the case of emperors such as Augustus, it strengthened and sanctioned it by association. So, in terms of ancient masculinity, whatever agency Joseph might lose could be outweighed by the authority he would gain by knowing and doing the will of the divine. In other words, close proximity to God does mean that Joseph cedes some authority to God. But this doesn't necessarily diminish his masculinity if that translates into relative authority in the realm of humanity.

Acknowledging these complex dynamics, I assert that a male God relating to human males in a hegemonic system, in the words of Eilberg-Schwartz, "renders the meaning of masculinity unstable."[154] Instead of automatically undermining the perceived masculinity of any one individual, it points to the tension inherent in the system itself. This tension produces another potential place for critique and change. In Matthew's Gospel, a strong case for Joseph's masculinity is found in his divine service. The realities and complexities of this relationship, however, reveal the instability of the larger system that perpetuates this understanding of masculinity.

CONCLUSION

From the perspective of Roman imperial ideology about masculinity, Joseph is not an ideal candidate. He is feminized by his lack of wealth and lack of control over his and others' bodies. His promised wife is pregnant, and he is not the father. King Herod, who does have access to money and power, is threatening their lives. Despite these compromising factors, however, I argue that the Gospel makes a good case for Joseph's masculinity, and does so using criteria familiar to the dominant ancient cultural perspective.

Joseph demonstrates that he is a righteous and obedient divine servant, which is very important for ancient constructions of masculinity, and he exerts as much power over himself and others as is realistic for his social location. With God's help, he is able to avoid the danger posed by Herod. While he does not demonstrate the wealth assumed for ancient males, his relationship to powerful and wealthy ancestors is emphasized by the Gospel, while the status of Herod and the overall relationship between wealth and virtue are questioned. Although he is not an ideal candidate, Joseph's characterization does exhibit important aspects of conventional values consistent with ancient masculinity.

I interpret the ambivalence associated with Joseph's masculinity not as an attempt to compromise Joseph's masculinity, but rather as an expected part of a non-elite existence. From the point of view of the narrative, there is no status inconsistency for Joseph. The only inconsistency would be from the point of view of the ancient elite. Dissonance and ambivalence would be the assumed norm for the Gospel, as it represents the perspective of non-elites negotiating the expectations of the culture that surrounds them. The question for readers of Matthew is whether the Gospel understands Joseph's masculinity to resonate with this dominant cultural ideology, or whether some implicit or explicit alternative is being presented.

In this chapter, I have shown that the Gospel does not seek to undermine Joseph's masculinity, even as it recognizes the factors that would mitigate his masculine status to the outside world. In some ways this relatively positive portrayal differs from the dominant cultural understanding of masculinity by emphasizing different values. Particularly in terms of wealth, the Gospel could even be said to demonstrate ambivalence or implicit challenge to the values of the empire.

In other respects, however, Joseph's masculinity resonates with the dominant narrative, even if it is imperfect in its execution. Although he can never control others to the extent that is expected of elites, he demonstrates imitative behavior in his complete control over Mary's life and future. His efforts to thwart unrighteous Herod are successful; he preserves the life of the child that is central to God's plan. Direct visitation from the angel of the Lord is met with his repeated obedience. His righteous decision to divorce Mary quietly is outdone only by his next even more righteous decision to obey God and marry her.

Many of these moves can be seen as preferable to dominant ancient values. Joseph's power over Mary preserves her life, rather than leaving her vulnerable to an honor killing. He is willing to endure long, difficult journeys over significant distances to secure their safety. But the underlying association of masculinity with power so important to ancient masculinity, while circumscribed by the limited options of non-elite males, is retained.

Matthew's construction of Joseph's masculinity clearly exhibits some departure from elite criteria, but also reinscribes ancient values. While Joseph's masculine behavior is limited by factors of control and wealth, he can be described as "elitely-imitative" in his connection to the divine. In terms of the larger emphasis of the Gospel, Joseph's obedience to God's will carries significant weight. This is a priority for the Gospel, and Joseph's successful demonstration of righteousness and obedience establishes him as a good man and example for others.[155] As I have shown, there are potential cracks in the overall façade of ancient masculinity that are visible in Joseph's characterization. But, from the perspective of the Gospel, Joseph is a non-elite man who does what God wants him to do, and that is a good thing.

NOTES

1. See Graham N. Stanton, *A Gospel for a new People: Studies in Matthew* (Louisville: Westminster John Knox, 1993), 77–84. Although Stanton does not mention Joseph and Herod the Great among his examples, they are a further example of the kind of comparison he highlights.

2. Louw and Nida stress that this term includes those who work in wood, stone, and metal, making "carpenter" a bit restrictive and "builder" perhaps more appropriate. I use the latter term in this chapter. J. P. Louw and Eugene Albert Nida, eds, *Greek-English Lexicon of the New Testament: Based on Semantic Domains* (New York: United Bible Societies, 1989), 45.9. References are also made to Joseph of Nazareth, the father of Jesus, in Luke 1:27; 2:4, 16; 3:23; and John 1:45, but he is not the focus of those narratives. This figure is, of course, distinct from Joseph of Arimathea, referenced in Mark 15:43, Matthew 27:57, Luke 23:50–53, and John 19:38–42.

3. W. D. Davies and D. C. Allison, *The Gospel According to Saint Matthew,* vol. 1 (Edinburgh: T&T Clark, 1988–1997), 183.

4. Davies and Allison, *The Gospel According to Saint Matthew,* 1:183.

5. Warren Carter, *Matthew and the Margins: A Sociopolitical and Religious Reading* (Maryknoll: Orbis, 2000), 74.

6. Sébastien Doane argues that Joseph's masculinity is compromised in this chapter. Sébastien Doane, "Masculinities of the Husbands in the Genealogy of Jesus (Matt. 1:2–16)," *Biblical Interpretation* 27 (2019), 91–106. While I agree that Mary's prominence in the genealogy emasculates Joseph with respect to bodily control (and echo this assertion in the next section), I am convinced that the situation shows more nuance and complexity, particularly around the current issue of status.

7. Boaz is described in Ruth 2 as "a prominent rich man" who owns the fields in which Ruth goes to glean as well as servants. In chapter 4, he is a public authority figure in the negotiation of the redemption of Ruth and Naomi.

8. The assumed connection between wealth and status is reflective of Rome's identity as an "aristocratic empire." See Warren Carter, *Matthew and Empire: Initial Explorations* (Harrisburg: Trinity Press, International, 2001), 9–16. It is important to note, however, that while wealth accompanied status, status did not always accompany wealth. Freed slaves such as Trimalchio in Petronius' *Satyricon* could amass significant wealth without gaining elite status. See Petronius, *Satyricon,* 45–183. Trimalchio focuses on his material wealth in a speech on 177–81.

9. This moral ambiguity with respect to royalty in Jesus's lineage includes several figures but is epitomized by David, a morally ambiguous figure who is exhibits great wealth and power, but also comes from humble beginnings and experiences vulnerability and loss. See 1 Samuel 16–31, 2 Samuel 1, 18.

10. See Carter, *Matthew and the Margins,* 55–57, 61–62, 65–66; Davies and Allison, *The Gospel According to Saint Matthew,* 1:156–63, 167–68, 174, 187–88; Ulrich Luz, *Matthew 1–7: A Commentary,* trans. James E. Crouch, ed. Helmut Koester, Hermeneia (Minneapolis: Fortress Press, 2007), 82–83, 85–88; Richard J. Erickson, "Joseph and the Birth of Isaac in Matthew 1," *Bulletin for Biblical Research* 10, no. 1 (2000): 35–51.

11. Luz, *Matthew,* 1:81.

12. Luz, *Matthew,* 1:82.

13. For a full discussion of this phenomenon, see Warren Carter, *John and Empire: Initial Explorations* (New York: T&T Clark, 2008), 93–101.

14. Carter, *John and Empire,* 97.

15. While wealth alone was not enough to secure status (women and freedmen could amass significant fortune without gaining a place in the upper orders), acceptance into the highest orders of society did usually require wealth (e.g., 1 million sesterces for senatorial rank and 400,000 for equestrian rank). See Valerie Hope, "Status and Identity in the Roman World," in *Experiencing Rome: Culture, Identity, and Power in the Roman Empire*, ed. Janet Huskinson (London: Routledge, 2000), 95–123.

16. Steven J. Friesen, "Poverty in Pauline Studies: Beyond the so-Called New Consensus," *Journal for the Study of the New Testament* 26, no. 3 (Mar 2004), 341–47.

17. Lionel Casson, *Travel in the Ancient World* (Toronto: Hakkert, 1974).

18. Casson, *Travel,* 178.

19. Casson, *Travel,* 184.

20. Casson, *Travel,* 176.

21. Catherine Hezser, *Jewish Travel in Antiquity* (Tübingen: Mohr Siebeck, 2011), 100.

22. Hezser, *Jewish Travel,* 89–96.

23. Robert J. Myles, *The Homeless Jesus in the Gospel of Matthew* (Sheffield: Sheffield Phoenix Press, 2014), 52–81.

24. Myles, *Homeless Jesus,* 64.

25. Myles, *Homeless Jesus,* 9, 52–55, 194.

26. Myles, *Homeless Jesus,* 64.

27. Working with these themes of agency and activity in response to and in the context of systems of power is an essential part of imperial critical approaches outlined in chapter 1.

28. Carter, *Matthew and the Margins,* 73.

29. For discussion on these lavish displays of wealth, see Richard A. Horsley, *The Liberation of Christmas: The Infancy Narratives in Social Context* (New York: Crossroad, 1989), 40–52; Amy-Jill Levine, "Herod the Great," *Anchor Bible Dictionary,* ed. David Noel Freedman (New York: Doubleday, 1992), 3:161–69; Byron R. McCane, "Simply Irresistible: Augustus, Herod, and the Empire," *Journal of Biblical Literature* 127, no. 4 (2008): 725–35; Adam Kolman Marshak, *The Many Faces of Herod the Great* (Grand Rapids, MI: Eerdmans, 2015), 191–217, 250–64, 312–34; Ehud Netzer, "Herod's Building Program," *Anchor Bible Dictionary,* ed. David Noel Freedman New York: Doubleday, 1992), 3:169–72; Peter Richardson, *Herod: King of the Jews and Friend of the Romans* (Columbia, SC: University of South Carolina Press, 1996): 174–215.

30. In fact, both Herod's building projects and his euergetism are considered by Marshak to be intentional efforts at bolstering his image and self-presentation. Marshak notes Herod's efforts at tax relief, as well as one particular instance where Herod arranged for a a delivery of grain during a drought in 25/24 BCE. Marshak, *Many Faces of Herod,* 247–49. On the whole, Marshak considers these efforts to be successful, due to Herod's long tenure. But the Gospel of Matthew notes no benefaction or virtuous behavior on Herod's part.

31. According to Marshak, "By all accounts, Herod's Judea was extremely wealthy; he, personally, as the largest landowner in the realm, was also extraordinarily rich." Marshak, *Many Faces of Herod,* 232.

32. This is consistent with Josephus's depiction of Herod in *Jewish Antiquities.* In one example, Herod provides monetarily for the funeral of Aristobulus, who had been murdered at Herod's order. According to Josephus, Herod "made all the more display of lavishness in the burial rites, providing a very fine tomb and a great quantity of perfumes and burying with him a great amount of fine apparel." Josephus, *Jewish Antiquities,* 15.61.

33. Carter points this out during the visit of the magi; "As an Idumean without a royal genealogy . . . Herod is especially touchy despite Roman support." Carter, *Matthew and the Margins,* 76.

34. This disruption is present elsewhere in the Gospel, as well, notably in the depiction of John the Baptist in 11:7–19 and 14:1–12. I will explore these issues further in chapter 4.

35. Carter, *Matthew and the Margins,* 74.
36. Carter, *Matthew and the Margins,* 74–75.
37. Edward Said, *Culture and Imperialism* (New York: Vintage Books, 1979). For an example of this, see Davina C. Lopez, *Apostle to the Conquered: Reimagining Paul's Mission* (Minneapolis: Fortress Press, 2010), 26–55. Lopez provides an analysis of Roman imperial representations of conquered peoples, which were personified both as female and male figures. The masculinity of these figures was compromised in various ways, including being diminutive in size, being bound behind the back, or exhibiting feminine characteristics that echoed their barbarian identity. In particular, Lopez focuses on the Parthian figure on the cuirassed state of Augustus from Prima Porta. In her description, the Parthian "has unruly, uncut hair and a big beard. He wears a loose-fitting, short tunic with trousers that the Romans associated with exotic eastern barbarian peoples who had not achieved their level of masculinity. . . . The Parthian's stance, dress, and passivity betray *effeminacy*." Lopez, *Apostle to the Conquered,* 40. The assumption was that foreign peoples were inferior to Romans in every way, and this inferiority was no more obvious when proven on the masculine territory of military combat.
38. Luz, *Matthew,* 1:114.
39. Luz, *Matthew,* 1:115.
40. Carter, *Matthew and the Margins,* 81–82. Examples of this pattern of gifts include Psalm 72:10, 15 and Isaiah 60:5–11.
41. Davies and Allison, *The Gospel According to Saint Matthew,* 1:249.
42. From a Roman perspective, the giving of such gifts was meant to give honor just as much to the giver as to the recipient. The ability to give lavish gifts said something important about the status of the giver. Here, the connotation is more about the honor ascribed to the infant Jesus. See Warren Carter, *The Roman Empire and the New Testament: An Essential Guide* (Nashville: Abingdon Press, 2006), 8–10; Maud Gleason, "Elite Male Identity in the Roman Empire," *Life, Death, and Entertainment in the Roman Empire,* ed. D. S. Potter and D. J. Mattingly (Ann Arbor: University of Michigan Press, 1999), 83–84.
43. Matthew J. Marohl, *Joseph's Dilemma: "Honour Killing" in the Birth Narrative of Matthew* (Cambridge: James Clark, 2010), 21–37.
44. In addition to the texts concerning John the Baptist, examples of Matthean texts dealing with the many complex aspects of wealth and its relationship with the kingdom of God include 4:8–10, 6:1–4, 6:16–18, 6:24, 10:5–10; 17:24–27; 18:23–35; 19:16–30; 20:1–16; 22:1–14; 22:15–22; 25:14–30; 26:14–16; 27:3–10, 57–61; and 28:11–15.
45. In chapter 3, I will address the tension and ambiguity associated with Herod's portrayal. For now, it is enough to say that he *ought* to be the one who demonstrates ideal masculinity.
46. In subsequent discussions, I will use both "domination" and "control" to describe this kind of behavior, the former often used to denote instances of more significant expressions of power.
47. As noted in chapter 1, *virtus* connoted, among other things, courage. So the demonstration of courage through control over others heightened claims to

masculinity. I will explore this connection more fully below. See Myles McDonnell, "Roman Men and Greek Virtues," *Andreia: Studies in Manliness and Courage in Classical Antiquity*, ed. Ralph Mark Rosen and I. Sluiter (Niger: Brill, 2003), 240.

48. Colleen M. Conway, *Behold the Man: Jesus and Greco-Roman Masculinity* (Oxford: Oxford University Press, 2008), 23–24; Craig Williams, *Roman Homosexuality: Ideologies of Masculinity in Classical Antiquity*, 2nd edition (Oxford: Oxford University Press, 2010), 151–56. Conway notes that, by the first century CE, "self-control emerges among the most important keys to ideal masculinity." Conway, *Behold the Man*, 24

49. Williams, *Roman Homosexuality*, 152. See also Conway, *Behold the Man*, 29–30; L. Stephanie Cobb, *Dying to be Men: Gender and Language in Early Christian Martyr Texts* (New York: Columbia University Press, 2008), 89; and Myles McDonnell, *Roman Manliness: Virtus and the Roman Republic* (New York: Cambridge University Press, 2006), 141.

50. Williams, *Roman Homosexuality*, 152.

51. Davies and Allison, *The Gospel According to Saint Matthew*, 1:238.

52. Josephus, *Jewish Antiquities* 15.65–67.

53. Here I disagree with Luz, who thinks that the news of a royal baby should have been good news to the people because Herod was so unpopular. Therefore, he understands their negative reaction to Jesus to be a precursor to the rejection of Jesus by Jerusalem later in the narrative. Luz, *Matthew*, 1:113. I don't think this interpretation takes Herod's reputation for violence seriously enough and the possibility that many would be caught up in his anger. In another example from Josephus, when Herod demands an oath of loyalty of the Pharisees, they refuse. In response, Herod executes the leaders and violently punishes others. Josephus, *Jewish Antiquities*, 17.41–45. The prevalence of this kind of violence allows for the possibility that those in Jerusalem were afraid *of* Herod rather than *with* him.

54. Davies and Allison, *The Gospel According to Saint Matthew*, 1:208. See also Raymond Brown, *The Birth of the Messiah: A Commentary on the Infancy Narratives in the Gospels of Matthew and Luke* (New York: Doubleday, 1993), 155–59. This formula can also be found in Luke's birth narrative (1:13, 30; 2:10), as well as other biblical texts, including Daniel 10:12, 19; Acts 27:24; and Revelation 1:17.

55. Carter, *Matthew and the Margins*, 77.

56. For a good discussion of Herod as a client king in the Augustan world, see Marshak, *Many Faces of Herod*, 139–73.

57. As will be noted shortly, it's true that Joseph moves at God's command, but God does not orchestrate the actual movements or guarantee safe passage. The angel departs, and the execution of the move depends on Joseph.

58. Davies and Allison, *The Gospel According to Saint Matthew*, 1:208.

59. Dominic Montserrat, "Reading Gender in the Roman World," in *Experiencing Rome: Culture, Identity and Power in the Roman Empire*, ed. Janet Huskinson (London: Routledge, 2000), 178–80.

60. Montserrat, "Reading Gender," 179.

61. Maud Gleason, *Making Men: Sophists and Self-Presentation in Ancient Rome* (Princeton: Princeton University Press, 1995); Montserrat, "Reading Gender," 175–77.

62. The sense of movement is perhaps more exaggerated in Luke where Joseph and Mary are from Nazareth, so the birth of the baby takes place in Bethlehem, far from home. However, as Luz notes, the assumption in Matthew is that Joseph and Mary are from Bethlehem. So their "return" from Egypt is actually a relocation. They leave behind their life and settle somewhere else. Luz, *Matthew,* 1:75.

63. Some scholars have questioned whether we can assume that Joseph is ignorant of this fact, or whether his decision to divorce her can be understood within the context of knowing and desiring to keep his distance from a holy pregnancy. However, most argue that Joseph's ignorance fits better the trajectory of the narrative, highlighting both the danger in the situation and the reason for God's intervention. See Brown, *Birth of the Messiah,* 125–28; Luz, *Matthew,* 1:94; and Carter, *Matthew and the Margins,* 67.

64. Montserrat, "Reading Gender," 168–74.

65. Because of this dynamic, Doane refers to Joseph as "expressing a subordinate masculinity when compared to God's." Doane, "Masculinities of the Husbands in the Genealogy of Jesus," 103. While I explore additional nuance relative to Joseph's masculinity, I think Doane's assessment of Joseph's compromised masculine power relative to Mary's pregnancy and God's power is correct. Both Howard Eilberg-Schwartz and Mary Rose D'Angelo are helpful for understanding the scope of this dynamic. I will return to this discussion in the next section on Joseph's relationship with the divine. See Howard Eilberg-Schwartz, *God's Phallus: And Other Problems for Men and Monotheism* (Boston: Beacon Press, 1994); Mary Rose D'Angelo, "*Abba* and 'Father': Imperial Theology and the Jesus Traditions," *Journal of Biblical Literature* 111, no. 4 (Winter 1992), 611–30; and "Theology in Mark and Q: *Abba* and 'Father' in Context," *Harvard Theological Review* 85, no. 2 (Apr 1992), 149–74.

66. Many scholars have attempted to explain the legal status (sexual relationship, living arrangements, role of family of origin) of Mary and Joseph during this betrothal period, including differences between practices in Galilee and Judea. For the purposes of this project, Schaberg's comment is enough: "Whether or not Joseph was legally allowed to have sexual relations with Mary during this period, according to Matthew, he had not." Jane Schaberg, *The Illegitimacy of Jesus: A Feminist Theological Interpretation of the Infancy Narratives* (San Francisco: Harper & Row, 1987), 44. What matters for this current project is that the pregnancy occurred "before they came together," (πρὶν ἢ συνελθεῖν αὐτοὺς) so they had *not* had sexual relations. Mary's pregnancy was not Joseph's. See Carter, *Matthew and the Margins,* 67.

67. R.W. Connell, *Masculinities,* 2nd ed (Berkeley: University of California Press, 2005), 79.

68. Luz, *Matthew,* 1:121.

69. Carter, *Matthew and the Margins,* 82.

70. I will revisit this issue in the next section with respect to Joseph and obedience to the divine.

71. James Scott calls this rhetoric and action the "hidden transcript," and it includes not only "behind-the-scenes griping and grumbling" but "is enacted in a host of down-to-earth, low-profile strategems designed to minimize appropriation. In the case of slaves, for example, these strategems have typically included theft, pilfering, feigned ignorance, shirking or careless labor, footdragging, secret trade and production for sale, sabotage of crops, livestock, and machinery, arson, flight, and so on. In the case of peasants, poaching, squatting, illegal gleaning, delivery of inferior rents in kind, clearing clandestine fields, and defaults on feudal dues have been common strategems." James C. Scott, *Domination and the Arts of Resistance: Hidden Transcripts* (New Haven: Yale University Press, 1990), 188.

72. Luz, *Matthew*, 1:95.

73. Schaberg, *Illegitimacy*, 58. While adoption may have been not an uncommon strategy in the ancient world for solidifying political alliances and establishing lines of succession for elites, those examples largely involve elites maneuvering for gain. The details of this particular situation involving possible infidelity, lower social class, and potential shame would argue that there is little to gain from adoption in this situation for Joseph.

74. See Sirach 23:22–26, and Wisdom of Solomon 3:16–19 and 4:3–6. Both sources utilize metaphorical agronomical/viticultural imagery, but it is not difficult to imagine real-world experienced consequences. For example, Sirach 23:25 says that the children born to a woman who has engaged in adultery "will not take root" (οὐ διαδώσουσιν τὰ τέκνα αὐτῆς εἰς ῥίζαν). Wisdom of Solomon 3:16–18 is more graphic: "But the children of adulterers will not come to maturity, and the offspring of an unlawful union will perish. Even if they live long they will be held of no account, and finally their old age will be without honor. If they die young, they will have no hope and no consolation on the day of judgment." (τέκνα δὲ μοιχῶν ἀτέλεστα ἔσται, καὶ ἐκ παρανόμου κοίτης σπέρμα ἀφανισθήσεται. ἐάν τε γὰρ μακρόβιοι γένωνται, εἰς οὐθὲν λογισθήσονται, καὶ ἄτιμον ἐπ' ἐσχάτων τὸ γῆρας αὐτῶν. ἐάν τε ὀξέως τελευτήσωσιν, οὐχ ἕξουσιν ἐλπίδα, οὐδὲ ἐν ἡμέρᾳ διαγνώσεως παραμύθιον.)

75. Davies and Allison, *The Gospel According to Saint Matthew*, 1:220.

76. Davies and Allison, *The Gospel According to Saint Matthew*, 1:208.

77. In her paper, "Joseph's Masculinity in the Synoptic Gospels," Annelies Moeser makes this case about Luke's incorporation of Jesus into Joseph's genealogy. I would argue that the same thing is working in Matthew, perhaps even more so because of Joseph's enhanced role in the birth narrative. Annelies Moeser, "Joseph's Masculinity in the Synoptic Gospels," paper presented at the Annual Meeting of the Society of Biblical Literature, Baltimore, MD, November 24, 2013, 7–9.

78. Luz, *Matthew*, 1:85.

79. Since this project is focused on characters within a narrative, I share the assumption of the narrative that it is God who is the creative force behind Mary's pregnancy. Of course, scholars interested in other perspectives have argued for an understanding of Jesus's origins that involve a human father. See Andrew J. Lincoln, "Contested Paternity and Contested Readings: Jesus' Conception in Matthew 1:18–25," *Journal for the Study of the New Testament* 34, no. 3 (2012), 211–31; and Schaberg, *Illegitimacy of Jesus*. In terms of Joseph's role, the inclusion of the possibility of a human

father does not diminish his actions but underscores his obedience to the divine in his willingness to raise another man's child, especially in the circumstances described by Matthew where Joseph's arrangement with Mary would have been violated.

80. Brown, *Birth of the Messiah*, 231–32.

81. Schaberg, *Illegitimacy*, 74.

82. Janice Capel Anderson, "Mary's Difference: Gender and Patriarchy in the Birth Narratives," *The Journal of Religion* 67, no. 2 (Apr 1987), 184.

83. Schaberg, *Illegitimacy*, 74.

84. References to women in the genealogy are found in Matthew 1:3, 5, 6b, and 16. For various interpretations of the four women (Tamar, Ruth, the wife of Uriah, and Mary), see Carter, *Matthew and the Margins*, 58–61; Davies and Allison, *The Gospel According to Saint Matthew*, 1:170–72; and Luz, *Matthew*, 1:83–85.

85. The number of generations catalogued in Matthew 1:1–17 does not match the scheme outlined in v. 17. For discussion, see Carter, *Matthew and the Margins*, 65; Davies and Allison, *The Gospel According to Saint Matthew*, 1:161–65; Luz, *Matthew*, 1:85–86; and Schaberg, *Illegitimacy*, 36–38.

86. On the shift in the pattern of paternity in Matthew 1:16, see Carter, *Matthew and the Margins*, 64–65; Davies and Allison, *The Gospel According to Saint Matthew*, 1:184–85; and Luz, *Matthew*, 1:85

87. For discussions of possible cultural expectations in Matthew 1:18–25, see Carter, *Matthew and the Margins*, 68–69; Davies and Allison, *The Gospel According to Saint Matthew*, 1:197–219; and Luz, *Matthew*, 1:93–97.

88. Anderson, "Mary's Difference: Gender and Patriarchy," 186.

89. See my discussion in chapter 1 for more about the association between divinity and masculinity.

90. Brown, *Birth of the Messiah*, 137.

91. Other examples of a Davidic/divine sonship connection include Ps. 89:27–8 (MT; Ps. 88:27–8 in the LXX); Ps. 2:6–7; and Ps. 110:1 (MT; 109:1 in the LXX).

92. Brown, *Birth of the Messiah*, 137.

93. I read this as an adverbial participle conveying cause. "Because Joseph was righteous." Other possibilities—concessive, purpose, or result—do not make sense in the flow of the narrative. The exact nature of this righteousness, and its implication for Mary, will be explored below. But I contend that the text here *presumes* Joseph's righteousness.

94. Luz, *Matthew*, 1:97.

95. Brown, *Birth of the Messiah*, 125.

96. Moeser, "Joseph's Masculinity," 1.

97. Erving Goffman, *Stigma: Notes on the Management of Spoiled Identity* (New York: Simon & Schuster, Inc., 1963), 3, 5. Moeser defines stigma as the "undesirable and discrediting difference between a person's virtual or expected social identity and their actual social identity." Moeser, "Joseph's Masculinity," 5–6.

98. The implications of this kind of move in terms of accepting the criteria of the dominant narrative will be explored later. Presently, I note simply that righteousness itself, a connection to the divine, makes an argument for Joseph's status.

99. Brown, *Birth of the Messiah*, 125–28.

100. For more detailed discussions beyond this summary, see Brown, *Birth of the Messiah*, 125–28; Schaberg, *Illegitimacy*, 42–62; Luz, *Matthew*, 1:94–95; Davies and Allison, *The Gospel According to Saint Matthew*, 1:202–4; Marohl, *Joseph's Dilemma*, 21–37.

101. Dale C. Allison, Jr., "Divorce Celibacy, and Joseph (Matthew 1:18–25 and 19:1–12)," *Journal for the Study of the New Testament* 49 (Jan 1993), 3–10; Markus N. A. Bockmuehl, "Matthew 5:32, 19:9 in the Light of Pre-Rabbinic Halakah," *New Testament Studies* 35, no. 2 (Apr 1989): 291–95.

102. Bockmuehl, "Matthew 5:32, 19:9," 294.

103. Luz, *Matthew*, 1:251.

104. Luz, *Matthew*, 1:255.

105. Allison, "Divorce, Celibacy, and Joseph," 3–5.

106. There are different possibilities for the translation of this phrase, but a common and reliable interpretation is simply "adultery," meaning sexual infidelity on the part of the woman. See Allison, "Divorce, Celibacy, and Joseph," 5; Bockmuehl, "Matthew 5:32; 19:9," 292; Carter, *Matthew and the Margins*, 148; and Luz, *Matthew*, 1:253–55.

107. Of course, this interpretation is quite problematic when considering the likely consequences for Mary. If Joseph's decision to divorce Mary is understood as righteous, then what is to be concluded about the possible physical, social, and legal consequences for Mary?

108. Carter, *Matthew and the Margins*, 68; Brown, *Birth of the Messiah*, 128.

109. Marohl, *Joseph's Dilemma*, 38–61.

110. Here, Marohl departs from most biblical scholars. For example, Luz asserts that stoning referenced in Deuteronomy "was no longer practiced" in the first century. Luz, *Matthew*, 1:94. Marohl questions the assumptions underlying such assertions. Marohl, *Joseph's Dilemma*, 21–37.

111. Marohl's examples of such references include Susanna 19–22; Jubilees 20, 30; Judges 19; Greco-Roman writers including Cato the Elder, Livy, and Suetonius; Ancient Jewish literature including Josephus, Philo, and the Mishnah; metaphorical usage in Hosea 2 and Ezekiel 16; the *Protoevangelium of James*; and the writings of St. John Chrysostom.

112. Schaberg says Joseph chose "what amounted to a merciful alternative offered by the Law." Schaberg, *Illegitimacy*, 60. Alternatively, Carter troubles the association between righteousness and mercy, saying that while they are not completely distinct, the meaning of righteousness has more to do with acting in accordance with the expectations of God. Carter, *Matthew and the Margins*, 68.

113. Schaberg concludes that the death penalty for an adultress, if not enforced, was at least "discussed and threatened." Schaberg, *Illegitimacy*, 53. So even if an honor killing cannot be assumed, the threat of severe punishment and desire to avoid it are realistic.

114. It is important to note that Marohl asserts that this particular choice by Joseph would not necessarily prevent an honor killing, which would likely have been the responsibility of her family of origin after she was returned to them. In their current liminal state, unilateral control over Mary does not rest with Joseph, her family of

origin also has a role to play. So, while it might be desirable to infer a sense of mercy or safety in this choice, it is not a guarantee. Or, exoneration and righteousness may exist for Joseph, washing his hands of Mary's death and transferring the guilt to her family, but if she were killed anyway then it makes little difference to her. Marohl, *Joseph's Dilemma*, 34–37.

115. This option begs the question of what happens to Joseph's shame when he ultimately decides neither to divorce Mary *nor* to have her stoned. He is aware of Mary's innocence, but the accusation of adultery is still a public reality. Does God's private direction to him also remove public shame?

116. Marohl, *Joseph's Dilemma*, 36–37.

117. Schaberg, *Illegitimacy*, 61. Part of Schaberg's point here is to contradict other scholarship which has pitted Joseph's strict adherence to Jewish law against the (supposedly) more grace-filled approach of "Christian" righteousness. Instead, Schaberg sees a consistency in God's expectations for Joseph. Once the possibility of Mary's guilt has been removed, Joseph can go back to fulfilling his expectations as a husband, taking on the additional expectations God places upon him to be Jesus's father.

118. Luz, *Matthew*, 1:95.

119. W. F. Albright and C. S. Mann, *Matthew*, Anchor Bible 26 (Garden City, NY: Doubleday, 1971), 8.

120. Brown, *Birth of the Messiah*, 125.

121. Luz, *Matthew*, 1:97.

122. Luz, *Matthew*, 1:117.

123. Luz, *Matthew*, 1:95.

124. Moeser makes the point that the final dream does not tell Joseph where to take the family, but that Joseph somehow knows where to go. His choice is said to fulfill Scripture, so it must have been right. As she says, "Joseph is so perfectly of one mind with God's plans that he goes to Nazareth. " Moeser, "Joseph's Masculinity," 11.

125. It is, perhaps, interesting that the final three dreams all pertain to travel. Only the first is about something else, the adoption of Jesus. And, yet, the three final dreams share with the first an emphasis on keeping the child safe. In this case, the theme of travel may serve the larger divine purpose of Jesus's survival. One of the primary tools for achieving this purpose in chapter 2 involves visiting Joseph in a dream.

126. Luz, *Matthew*, 1:90.

127. Derek S. Dodson, *Reading Dreams: An Audience-Critical Approach to the Dreams in the Gospel of Matthew* (New York: T&T Clark, 2009), 147.

128. Francois P. Viljoen, "The Significance of Dreams and the Star in Matthew's Infancy Narrative," *HTS Theological Studies* 64, no. 2 (Jun 2008): 845–60.

129. Davies and Allison, *The Gospel According to Saint Matthew*, 1:207.

130. Dodson, *Reading Dreams*, 145.

131. Davies and Allison, *The Gospel According to Saint Matthew*, 1:218.

132. Dodson, *Reading Dreams*, 145.

133. Luz, *Matthew*, 1:95.

134. Schaberg, *Illegitimacy*, 59.

135. Carter, *Matthew and the Margins*, 74. Davies and Allison speak in terms of a direct confrontation: "Herod, although he could boast no royal genealogy, was a king,

and our evangelist is interested in contrasting his rule and kingdom with the rule and kingdom of Jesus the Davidic messiah." Davies and Allison, *The Gospel According to Saint Matthew,* 1:227.

136. See Werner Eck, *The Age of Augustus,* 2nd ed., trans. Deborah Lucas Schneider (Malden MA: Blackwell, 2007), 46–75; Karl Galinsky, *Augustan Culture: An Interpretive Introduction* (Princeton, NJ: Princeton University Press, 1996), 288–331; Paul Zanker, *The Power of Images in the Age of Augustus*, trans. Alan Shapiro (Ann Arbor: University of Michigan Press, 1990), 101–66; and Lorna Hardwick, "Concepts of Peace," in *Experiencing Rome: Culture, Identity and Power in the Roman Empire,* ed. Janet Huskinson (London: Routledge, 2000), 337–50. For coins bearing images identifying Octavian (later Augustus) as the son of divine Caesar, see Valerie Hope, "The City of Rome: Capital and Symbol," in *Experiencing Rome: Culture Identity and Power in the Roman Empire,* 73. Themes of divinity and piety in Augustus's leadership are prominent in contemporary Roman literature. See especially Virgil, *Aeneid,* 63: 262–97, 64: 2–367; and *Res Gestae Divi Augusti,* 344–405.

137. See Galinsky, *Augustan Culture,* 288–331. In the *Res Gestae,* Augustus claims to have restored 82 temples. *Res Gestae,* 376–79.

138. Galinsky, *Augustan Culture,* 141–55; Zanker, *Power of Images,* 118–25.

139. For more on the process that led to the deification of Augustus, see Galinsky, *Augustan Culture,* 312–22.

140. Brian Bosworth, "Augustus, the Res Gestae, and Hellenistic Theories of Apotheosis" *Journal of Roman Studies* 89 (1999): 1–18.

141. Bosworth, "Augustus, the Res Gestae and Hellenistic Theories of Apotheosis," 13.

142. Wendy J. Cotter, "Greco-Roman Apotheosis Traditions and the Resurrection Appearances in Matthew," in *The Gospel of Matthew in Current Study,* ed. David E. Aune (Grand Rapids, MI: Eerdmans, 2001): 134.

143. Suetonius, *Lives of the Caesars,* 38:275–79.

144. Suetonius, *Lives of the Caesars,* 38:283–85.

145. Seneca, *Apocolocyntosis (divi) Claudii,* 436–83.

146. Seneca, *Apocolocyntosis,* 463–69.

147. In addition, Claudius's hegemonic power is completely removed. His sentence in the underworld is to rattle dice forever in a box with holes, a Sisyphean task marked by futile repetition. Seneca, *Apocolocyntosis,* 480–81.

148. Seneca, *Apocolocyntosis,* 469–75.

149. Actually, it is quite the opposite. He plays no role in the story after chapter 2, except for the brief reference in 13:55.

150. Dodson, *Reading Dreams,* 166.

151. Eilberg-Schwartz, *God's Phallus,* 2.

152. See Mary Rose D'Angelo, "'*Abba*' and 'Father': Imperial Theology and the Jesus Traditions." D'Angelo is arguing against those who claim that Jesus's use of "Abba" as a name for God connotes familiarity, intimacy, and egalitarian impulses in the early Christian communities, emphasizing similar imperial hegemonic aspects of patriarchal masculinity highlighted in this book. While she acknowledges that the desire for rejection of patriarchy may exist *within* the community, utilizing language

that is marked so heavily by the Roman Empire reinforces androcentrism and patriarchy with respect to God. See also Mary Rose D'Angelo, "Theology in Mark and Q: *Abba* and 'Father' in Context."

153. D'Angelo, "'*Abba*' and 'Father': Imperial Theology and the Jesus Tradition," 629.

154. Eilberg-Schwartz, *God's Phallus,* 2.

155. For overall themes of discipleship and identity-formation in terms of God's will, see Carter, *Matthew and the Margins,* 7–11.

Chapter 3

John the Baptist and Herod Antipas

For this chapter, I employ the three criteria of ancient masculinity central to this study to examine John the Baptist. I first consider divine service, then dominating control over self and over others, and finally wealth, changing the order of the criteria to reflect their importance in my analysis of John's characterization. I argue that the Gospel makes a strong case for John's masculinity across all three categories, despite the fact that John demonstrates deficiencies with respect to the dominant masculine ideal of the Roman empire. The case for John's masculinity comprises a combination of mimicry, redefinition, rejection, and successful performance.

In the course of this chapter, I also include reflections on the masculinity of Herod Antipas. As in chapter 2, I highlight the prevalent ancient rhetorical strategy of *synkrisis* (σύγκρισις), which denotes a comparison that is used to point to difference or superiority.[1] Graham Stanton's work has demonstrated the use of σύγκρισις in Matthew, and in chapter 2 I employed it in the discussion of Joseph and King Herod. Here, John the Baptist and Herod Antipas are another good example of its use in the Gospel, since their intersecting stories highlight their differences in terms of wealth, dominating control over self and over others, and divine service. To a lesser extent, I engage some comparison between John and Jesus, reflecting the Gospel's pairing of the two in terms of divine service and resulting status.

What surfaces from this discussion is the Gospel's preference for an alternative form of masculinity that combines an emphasis on divine service, a rejection of wealth, and a complex negotiation and reinterpretation of control over self and over others. This construction finds unique expression in John the Baptist but resonates with larger priorities in the Gospel. John compensates for a lack of elite status with an altered claim to masculinity, which is similar to Joseph in chapter 2. However, in contrast to Joseph, I consider John's display of masculinity stronger and his negotiation of masculine concepts more explicit in that he uses his voice to challenge masculine authority, actively chooses asceticism while critiquing Herod Antipas's excess, and is praised by the Gospel for his divine service and prophetic similarity to Elijah.

Because there are number of references to John the Baptist and Herod Antipas scattered throughout the Gospel, I have compiled table 3.1 to identify key texts I discuss in this chapter that relate to the construction of John's masculinity and how they connect to the three criteria.

DIVINE SERVICE

In this first section, I discuss John's masculinity through the lens of his divine service, which I define as the behaviors and characteristics that establish alignment and congruency with the divine.[2] I argue that John demonstrates a very strong connection to God built around his prophetic speech, lifestyle, martyr's death, and relationship to Jesus. These behaviors are not unambiguous, and the case is not without problems. Overall, however, John's intimate and powerful connection to the divine makes a compelling argument for John's masculine status expressed in divine service, the strongest of the three discussed in this chapter.

The case for John's divine service is made in several key ways. First, John leads a lifestyle that conveys a reliance on God for safety and care, and a rejection of the material/physical world in favor of spiritual concerns. For example, the question from John's disciples in 9:14 indicates that John and his followers fasted, a spiritual discipline.[3] In addition, some see a spiritual aspect to John's diet described in 3:4. Carter, for one, notes that John's food choices highlighted in 3:4 illustrate "his commitment to and trust in God by not being distracted from the reign because of concern with daily food."[4]

Not all scholars agree on the significance of the locusts and wild honey. Citing other ancient sources, Kelhoffer questions the conventional conclusion that John's diet indicates asceticism.[5] Instead, Kelhoffer sees in Matthew's reference to John's diet a characterization of John as a "bonafide wilderness survivor," putting him in the company of other heroes such as Judas Maccabeus and Isaiah.[6] However, against Kelhoffer, both Judas Maccabeus and Isaiah are strongly committed to divine service in the wilderness, so the focus on spiritual dimensions is consistent among them. Comparing John's choices with theirs bolsters John's divine service and attention to spiritual matters through an ascetic diet.

John's location in the wilderness also signals a freedom from the expectations of conventional society and a freedom to focus on God.[7] This shift away from physical necessities is resonant with other areas of the Gospel where Jesus urges his followers not to dwell on concerns of the physical body but to

Table 3.1. Matthean references to John the Baptist and themes of masculinity

Text	Scene	Masculinity Issues		
		Divine Service	Control Over Self/Others	Wealth
Matthew 3:1–12	Introduction of John the Baptist: Isaiah reference, physical description, confrontation with Scribes and Pharisees	Prophetic behavior, association with Isaiah, announcing empire of heaven, preaching to question religious norms, baptizing and encouraging repentance	Ascetic physical description, public speech, popularity, challenging authority figures	Simple clothing and diet, physical location in wilderness
Matthew 3:13–17	Baptism of Jesus	Agent of God in baptism of Jesus		
Matthew 4:12–17	Reference to John's death and Jesus's decision to withdraw to Galilee	Reference to association of John with Jesus, especially Jesus's assumption in 4:17 of John's prophetic statement from 3:2		
Matthew 9:14–17	Disciples of John visit Jesus to ask about fasting	John's interest in and limited understanding of Jesus's movement, spiritual aspect of fasting.	Presence of John's disciples, physical aspect of fasting	
Matthew 11:2–6	Imprisoned John sends disciples to ask Jesus about his identity	John's awareness of and seeking clarity about Jesus's actions	Disciples visit at John's request while he is imprisoned	

Matthew 11:7–19	Jesus's speech about John to the crowds	John first called a prophet by Jesus, then "more than" a prophet, quotation of Malachi, explicit reference to Elijah, yet limited status in the empire	Described as "neither eating nor drinking" in contrast with Jesus, implicit contrast with Herod, who is later described as out of control	Contrasted with those who wear soft robes in royal palaces, implied contrast with Herod who is wealthy
Matthew 14:1–12	Herod, the dancing daughter, and the execution of John the Baptist	John's prophetic speech proclaims divine judgment on Herod. Is mistaken by Herod for Jesus, dies a martyr's death	Imprisoned, loses freedom and control over body, then loses head and life. Carried away by disciples for burial. No longer capable of public speech	Imprisonment and previous characterization contrasts with Herod's lavish lifestyle
Matthew 16:13–20	Simon Peter's confession at Caesarea Philippi	Association of John with Jesus as "John the Baptist" is disciples' first response to question "Who do people say that the Son of Man is?"		

Matthew 17:1–13	Transfiguration and conversation between Jesus and disciples about John the Baptist	John described by Jesus as Elijah, who is the forerunner to the Son of Man. Elijah also appears at Transfiguration with Moses, emphasizing both Elijah's and John's status, and linking Jesus to both	Reminder of John's suffering and loss of power, "they did to him whatever they pleased"
Matthew 21:23–41	Jesus questioned by chief priests and elders about authority	Divine authority of John's baptism subject of debate, "all" regarded John as a prophet according to chief priests and elders, Jesus criticizes them for not believing John's righteousness, likely reference to John in parable to slave the tenants kill in v. 35	John's ministry used by Jesus to deflect threat from authorities, public memory of him is still powerful

fix their minds on spiritual matters (4:1–4; 6:19–21, 25–34).[8] John is not distracted by material possessions or anxiety about meeting his physical needs. He is focused on God and God's mission in the world.

More than just an observer, John plays an integral role in communicating that mission. Preaching repentance, announcing the empire of heaven,[9] and pronouncing judgment on those who resist or ignore God's clear arrival, chapter 3 introduces him primarily in a prophetic role.[10] He is first described in 3:3 as the fulfilment of the prophet Isaiah, establishing his heritage and his identity. John is the one whose voice prepares the way of the Lord. His prophetic authority is further strengthened by the use of the phrase "For I say to you" in 3:9b (λέγω γὰρ ὑμῖν). Davies and Allison claim that Jesus's use of this phrase reflects his "implicit claim to be God's prophetic spokesman."[11] Yamasaki argues that John's use of the phrase should be taken the same way, identifying him as a divine spokesperson.[12]

John's prophetic status is also enhanced by the attention he receives. People come out to see and hear him, including those with both sympathetic (3:5–6) and critical (3:7–12) viewpoints. His impact extends not only to ordinary people but also to the authorities, the Pharisees and Sadducees who are the recipients of his critique. Their original motivation for visiting him is somewhat ambiguous. Matthew 3:7 says that the Pharisees and Sadducees were coming ἐπὶ τὸ βάπτισμα. There are various ways to translate the preposition ἐπί. Luz uses the more general "to," leaving the situation open to interpretation.[13] The NRSV translation "for" suggests a scenario in which the Pharisees and Sadducees coming to John in order to be baptized.

However, John's reaction to them, and the tenor of the section, make a friendly encounter seem less likely. He confronts the Pharisees and Sadducees in 3:7–10, calling them a "brood of vipers," (γεννήματα ἐχιδνῶν), commanding them to "bear fruit" (ποιήσατε οὖν καρπὸν), and calling into question their ancestral appeal to authority.[14] Therefore, I am prone to agree with Carter's argument for translating ἐπὶ as "against," indicating that they were opposed to John's prophetic message.[15] This makes more sense of John's response to them, as well as their continued conflict throughout the narrative.

For John, the impetus for repentance and baptism is the imminence of the empire of God, and the goal is awareness of and alignment with the coming of this empire (3:2). It is worth noting that the specific function of John's proclamation is open to question. The word "has come near" (ἐγγίζω), used here in the perfect tense, has both present and future aspects,[16] and it is unclear what precise relationship John's proclamation has with the arrival of the empire. This is especially the case because the phrase is repeated exactly by Jesus in 4:17, heightening the tension. Does John fully announce the empire's presence in 3:2? If so, what role does Jesus's later declaration play? If not, what is John's role in the earlier declaration?

Much of this is caught up in the relationship of John to Jesus, an issue that I explore more fully below. Complexities acknowledged, however, John plays a uniquely prophetic role that clearly aligns with God's purposes and calls others to attention. The connection between John and God's purposes is emphasized by Wink: "John is doing precisely what God desires, so much so that rejection of John's mission is tantamount to rejection of Jesus and the very purpose of God himself."[17]

It is no surprise, then, that John's prophetic preaching also involves challenging the societal authorities. John's prophetic critique of the authorities in chapter 3 is endorsed and extended by Jesus to the chief priests and the elders in 21:28–32. Their rejection of John, who announced the coming of

God's empire, becomes further evidence of their opposition to God's work. John's confrontative rhetoric communicates not only his powerful use of his own voice, but also his intimate knowledge of God's work and responsibility for making it known.

Likewise, in chapter 14, John speaks against the marriage of Herod Antipas to Herodias. The text indicates that this is an unlawful marriage, although the exact details of John's critique are not clear.[18] Whatever the reason, John considers this marriage a violation worthy of the risk of public criticism. In both cases, this example, and the previous one, John's prophetic voice speaks on God's behalf. It has authority and validity; Herod responds by imprisoning him, and people respond to John's wilderness preaching with repentance and baptism. This authority and validity underscore John's connection to God and his role in God's mission. Through his prophetic preaching, John prioritizes the divine reality over any human agenda.

If this story emphasizes John's connection to God, it also notes Herod's distance from God. More attention will be given to Herod Antipas in the next section on power, but here it is worth noting that John's role as divine servant is built, in part, upon a critique of Herod. It is Herod's disobedience that gives John the occasion to preach God's judgment. Herod's response, to have John imprisoned, further establishes his opposition to God and God's purposes (14:3). Unlike in Mark, the Matthean Herod does not find John compelling to listen to; John is a threat because the crowd reveres him.[19] From the perspective of divine service, Herod is at odds with God, while John is God's agent. In a Gospel that privileges divine service as an essential element of masculine status, this is a significant critique of Herod's masculinity and endorsement of John's.

John's role as divine servant is highlighted in a particularly important way for the Gospel in 3:13–17 when he baptizes Jesus. This scene is about Jesus's identity, which is revealed by the voice from heaven in verse 17. It is Jesus's baptism, performed by John, that prompts this revelation. Verse 13 positions John as already knowing something of Jesus's special identity; he tries to prevent Jesus from being baptized by him (διεκώλυεν, from διακωλύω), saying that it is Jesus who should baptize him (ἐγὼ χρείαν ἔχω ὑπω σοῦ βαπτισθῆναι).[20] But Jesus persists and John acquiesces.[21] Both his initial reaction to performing Jesus's baptism, and his role in the revelatory event, suggest that John is connected to God in ways that others are not.

Another way that John demonstrates divine service is in his death. Not only is his arrest related to a prophetic statement about Herod's marriage, but Herod's encounter with Jesus makes him think of John.[22] The association of John with Jesus in this story contextualizes John's death within the larger theme of acceptance or rejection of God's purposes and work that characterizes Matthew's Gospel. John's death, therefore, is understood to be the death of a martyr; he died for speaking God's truth to power.[23]

In addition to his own words and actions, references made about John by Jesus also contribute to his close association with the divine.[24] Before and after John's death, Jesus extols John's faithfulness and righteousness (11:7–15; 21:28–46). Concerning the first example, Murphy notes the strong contrast between John and others, claiming that, "Jesus affirms John without reserve."[25] Immediately after contrasting John with a reed shaken by the wind and those who wear soft robes, Jesus says that no one has arisen who is greater than John the Baptist (οὐκ ἐγήγερται ἐν γεννητοῖς γυναικῶν μείζων Ἰωάννου τοῦ βαπτιστοῦ). This is a dramatic statement; those "born of women" would appear to indicate all human beings. While this is not a claim explicitly about masculinity (presumably women are included in the reference), ancient assumptions about gender would suggest that men would occupy the "top spots." So, an argument stating that there is no one greater than John is an argument for John's masculinity.

In the second example, 21:23–46, Jesus first refers to John in arguing with the chief priests and elders and in diverting their questions (21:23–27). It is an effective strategy; the people's perception of John as a prophet—which Jesus endorses—prevents the chief priests and elders from answering Jesus's questions, which keeps Jesus from having to answer theirs. Then, Jesus moves into a pair of parables that implicate the chief priests and the elders (21:28–32, 33–41), punctuated by an overt pronouncement of judgment (21:42–26). Their judgment is based on their rejection of God's messengers, who are identified specifically as John in 21:32 and Jesus is 21:37–39. First they did not believe John; then, even when they recognized who John was, they still rejected Jesus.[26]

John's prophetic role in divine service finds specific focus in association with Elijah, another powerfully significant man who serves God.[27] His identification with Elijah is asserted early in chapter 3 and then explored by Jesus as the narrative progresses (3:4, 11:11–14; 16:13–14; 17:9–13).[28] First, John's initial physical description in chapter 3 evokes Elijah. His clothing is made of camel's hair (τὸ ἔνδυμα αὐτοῦ ἀπὸ τριχῶν καμήλου) and his food is locusts and wild honey (ἀκρίδες καὶ μέλι ἄγριον), recalling 2 Kings 1:8. Although they are not a perfect fit, the images clearly evoke Elijah.[29]

More direct associations follow. Elijah and John the Baptist are mentioned together by the disciples in company of Jesus in 16:13–14. When asked for their interpretation of Jesus's identity, the disciples state that people associate Jesus with John, Elijah, or Jeremiah. When seeking an identity for Jesus, John joins the big names. While these associations ultimately prove inadequate for conveying the identity of Jesus, they underscore the relationships of John and Elijah with the divine.

Then, when Jesus appears transfigured before the disciples in chapter 17, he is observed speaking with Moses and Elijah (vv. 1–4) just before the divine voice from the cloud claims Jesus as God's Son (v. 5). The combination of the presence of the heroes of the faith with the verbal declaration links Jesus unmistakably with the divine. Just after this, responding to the disciples' questions about the encounter, Jesus directly associates John the Baptist with Elijah in vv. 10–13, bringing John into the mix.[30] Jesus talks specifically about John's role in delivering God's mission, comparing him to Elijah who is a prophet, a spokesperson for the will of God, and the doer of miracles who came to restore all things.[31] The juxtaposition here of Jesus, Elijah, the divine claim, and John the Baptist underscores the connections among them and argues for John's status in divine service.

This association is effective not just from the Gospel's perspective, but also in the wider context. While the dominant Roman imperial culture may not recognize the full theological import of the comparison to Elijah, the "turn to the past" was an important way of constituting Roman identity. From a Roman perspective, evoking the presence of Elijah would be understood as an attempt to bolster John's claim to divine service and enhance his masculinity.[32]

Beyond the association with Elijah and the more general prophetic behavior language, there is one other curious reference to consider. In 11:9, responding to his own rhetorical question, Jesus calls John "more than a prophet" (καὶ περισσότερον προφήτου).[33] This intriguing phrase appears to set John apart even further. As Yamasaki notes, "While John has just been granted profound significance through his characterization as a prophet, this addition indicates that his significance transcends even that status."[34] But what does "more than a prophet" really mean? Does it also refer to John's identity as Elijah? Or might it elevate him even higher? Where does John's status as "more than a prophet" put him in relation to Jesus? To other human beings? To the divine?

Although it is not immediately clear what "more than a prophet means," the possibilities are thought-provoking. Luz sees in this phrase an additional connection to Elijah; John is not only a prophet, he is Elijah who has returned.[35] Wink claims that John's singularity is found in the content of his prophecy; he is uniquely important because he "announces the imminent arrival of the Coming One."[36] Among some other interpreters, including Carter, Davies and Allison, and Yamasaki, there is a common theme that John transcends the identity of prophet by being "himself the object of prophecy."[37] The references to Malachi 3:1, Exodus 23:20, and Isaiah 40:3 in verse 10 position John as (1) God's messenger, who (2) prepares the way.[38] Placing his behavior in this context identifies John's prophetic role as itself a fulfilment of scripture.[39] While each has its nuance, these interpretations focus on the unique status John has with respect to divine service, enhancing his masculinity.

Finally, it is important to acknowledge the close relationship between John and Jesus as a means for enhancing John's divine service. Previously I mentioned John's baptism of Jesus as an indicator of his prophetic role in the empire of God as well as Jesus's testimonies about John. Beyond these aspects of the relationship, however, parallels between John and Jesus indicate a unique closeness. Both have disciples (4:18–22; 9:14; 11:2; 14:12). Both preach the same news ("Repent, for the empire of God has come near"), John in 3:2 and Jesus in 4:17.[40] Both are enemies of Herod Antipas, who mistakes one for the other (14:1–2). Both have confrontational conversations with the Judean leaders (3:7–12; 21:23–46). Both lose their lives (14:9–12; 27:33–50). Wink calls this a "parallelism of destinies," a connection that "indicates a parallel purpose served by both in God's redemptive purpose."[41]

Each of these references—John's ascetic lifestyle, his prophetic words and behavior, his role in Jesus's baptism, his death, Jesus's words about John, John's explicit association with Elijah, and his close parallel connection to Jesus—strengthens the relationship between John and the divine, emphasizing John's divine service; not only does John act and speak in a way that associates him with God, others who are trustworthy think and speak about John that way, as well.

Such examples are only part of the picture, however. Merely arguing that John's relationship with Jesus enhances John's divine service is an oversimplification. While the examples above illustrate how John's relationship with Jesus strengthens his relationship with the divine, this relationship also reveals problematic power dynamics that subordinate John to Jesus, undercutting his power and status. More than John, Jesus exhibits behaviors that can be described as hegemonic, accentuating his power in more conventional terms and arguing for ideal status. In her work on the masculinity of Jesus in Matthew, Conway notes that while some of Jesus's behavior reflects a more marginalized masculinity, other behaviors correspond with hegemonic masculinity, where "Jesus' ideal masculine status is accentuated."[42]

With respect to John, Jesus's hegemonic behavior is exhibited in the encounters between them. Jesus is the authority, who determines what is right, necessary, and important. By contrast, John's knowledge and power are limited. This hegemonic behavior puts John in his place, limiting his power and influence as well as his status with respect to the divine. For example, while John announces God's mission in the world, plays a pivotal role in the announcement of Jesus's identity, and is used as an example of faithfulness by Jesus, his resistance to baptizing Jesus suggests that he lacks certain information.[43] Further, his hesitation is immediately challenged and overcome by Jesus's authoritative response. Even if it is resolved rather quickly,

John's instinct to demur and Jesus's assertion of power introduce tension into the scene.

In another example, John's disciples visit Jesus in chapter 9:14–17 in order to ask him why his disciples do not fast. John and his disciples do fast, something they share with the Pharisees, and fasting is considered an outward expression of devotion or attention to God.[44] John's assumption that fasting is a good spiritual practice is challenged by the behavior of Jesus and his disciples. Jesus's response (9:15–17), significantly, centers on his disciples' awareness of and proximity to him. They are closer to Jesus, both physically and spiritually, than John is. This familiarity renders the traditional practice of fasting unnecessary.[45] Here again, Jesus asserts his authority both with respect to John and with respect to fasting. This challenges John's understanding of Jesus as well as the notion that John is uniquely related to Jesus in a way that others are not.

In a subsequent exchange, John sends his disciples in 11:2–3 to ask whether Jesus is truly the Messiah, the "one who is to come." (ὁ ἐρχόμενος). This is perhaps strange or surprising, as this takes place well after the baptism in 3:11, where John is described as the one who bears witness to Jesus and insists that Jesus should baptize him. Luz suggests that it reflects a historical reality of ambivalence between those who followed Jesus and those who followed John.[46] Yamasaki contends that, as a plot device, it re-emphasizes the understanding of Jesus as eschatological judge, which has been John's consistent understanding of him since the beginning.[47]

It is possible to interpret the question positively. While others are no doubt missing the meaning of Jesus, John is attentive enough at least to inquire. Still, the scene casts doubt on John's immediate access to the divine and reinforces Jesus's hegemonic authority. Even if John is connected enough to ask, he doesn't already know everything.[48] Jesus's command to John's disciples, itself a power move, is to respond with a message highlighting eschatological-anticipating deeds of power as evidence of what "the Messiah was doing" (11:2).

This ambivalent rhetoric about John continues into the next section. In 11:11, Jesus asserts that "among those born of women, no one has arisen greater than John the Baptist."[49] This seems to be extremely high praise. And yet, in the very next phrase, Jesus claims that "the least in the empire of heaven is greater than he."[50] Perhaps this is meant to elevate the status of those who are the least in the empire of heaven; if John is great, then the least ones are even greater. This is supported by Jesus's association in verse 14 of John with Elijah as well as his identification of John as "more than a prophet." And yet, there is a sense that if others are greater than John, then John cannot be that great.[51] Again, the role of Jesus in naming John's significance is not insignificant; it underscores Jesus's hegemonic power and subordinates John to Jesus.

The next section does not clarify. Verses 12–13 seem to suggest that John's arrival coincides with a fundamental change in the history of God's work and that "he stands at the fulcrum point."[52] The details of John's role in this event, however, are not clear. Does he inaugurate that change? If so, does he participate in it once it arrives?[53] These confusing verses speak to the important role that John plays in the Gospel of Matthew as a whole, as well as the ambiguity concerning his role. Taken as a group, the references to John in Matthew's Gospel indicate that John plays a unique and powerful role in announcing God's mission (recall the parallel statements of 3:2 and 4:17), but then shows limited understanding of it when it arrives and does not play a large role in its continuing development. This section underscores this ambivalence.

Much of this ambivalence can be contextualized within the larger discussion of the relationship between John and Jesus, and the need—both literary and theological—for Jesus to increase in importance as the narrative progresses. John's role in divine service is clearly subordinate to Jesus's role, and Jesus's hegemonic masculinity asserts its power over John. John and Jesus discuss important matters, but Jesus is the authority and he has power over John's behavior (baptism) and John's disciples. Like Jesus, John dies, but unlike Jesus, John is not raised; Jesus's death and resurrection is the climax of the story. After John's death, Jesus takes over the task of proclaiming the empire of God, but he has a much higher profile and louder voice than John ever had.

The question is whether John's limitations qualify his status as divine servant *as a whole,* or just in relationship to Jesus. The evidence presented in this section (positive contrast with Herod and other human beings, negative contrast only with Jesus, parallels with Jesus, and positive praise from Jesus) argue for the latter. The concerns highlighted in this section contextualize John, but do not necessarily diminish him. It is possible to prioritize Jesus without rejecting John.[54] In fact, it may be argued that both the comparisons with and contrasts to Jesus strengthen John's character, because of the characterization of Jesus that emphasizes his ideal status.

John's relationship with Jesus in Matthew is multifaceted. The Gospel highlights not only points of connection but also potential disconnection with God's mission. John is connected favorably with Jesus in many respects, but is also clearly inferior. Overall, however, I consider John's connection to Jesus to be an argument for his divine service rather than against it. Even if that connection is limited, such limitations are not surprising, and John still retains special status in the Gospel in terms of his access to and role in proclaiming the mission of God. This is especially the case when one considers the contrast with Herod Antipas. John's prophetic identity is built, in part, on a critique of Herod and an establishment of Herod as an enemy of God. This contrast of John with Herod, who possesses other conventional aspects of masculinity, undermines the masculine status of Herod while elevating John.

This poses an interesting situation for a conversation about masculinity. If ancient masculinity is a public competition with winners and losers, then John both wins the competition for divine service over Herod and loses it to Jesus.[55] Yet, if John has to lose a masculinity competition, a loss to Jesus is perhaps one with minimal damage to his masculinity. As argued in chapter 2, one of the complexities of the human male's assertion of masculinity is his relationship with a masculine God.[56] There is no way for a human to win that competition, so expecting a perfect performance of divine service is unrealistic for anyone. According to Conway, in some ways the Matthean Jesus comes close, as he is described in "decidedly imperial masculine terms."[57] In contrast to this hegemonic masculine behavior, John cannot compete. And yet, the hegemonic male himself declares that among humans, there is none greater in Matthew than John.

I have argued in this section that a relatively strong argument for John's masculinity is made by the Gospel in terms of divine service. However, from a Roman perspective, this masculine claim is insufficient in some important ways. Rather than demonstrating the kind of hegemonic power asserted by Jesus, John is more in the company of the Hebrew Bible prophets who speak truth to power, but who do not wield it themselves. So, even if one perceives a relatively strong argument in favor of John's divine service, would this translate to an enhanced sense of masculinity from an ancient perspective?

In some respects, it would not. John's lack of earthly power coupled with his extreme ascetic behavior might be interpreted more as madness than as masculine power accessed through divine relationship. And the means of his death, which I explore in the next section, further emasculate him. And yet, there is enough other evidence to say that John enjoys divine favor and that his divine service is valued. His tie to the prophetic past, his obvious role in announcing God's rule, his contrast with Herod, his close association with Jesus, his death claimed as martyrdom for his faithful witness to God, and the identification of John's enemies as God's enemies all closely align him with divine purpose in an unmistakable way. The rhetoric about John's divine service, then, is compelling, if not univocal. Even if it's different from the norm, the claims to divine service may be intelligible, if not precisely conventional.

DOMINATING CONTROL OVER SELF AND OVER OTHERS

In this next section on dominating control over self and over others, I argue that John mostly fails to exhibit the kind of control assumed by ancient rhetoric on masculinity. In response, the Gospel emphasizes an alternative understanding of control as an important part in the construction of John's masculinity. Because of John's social status, this alternative construction of control is marked by ambivalence where the same event or behavior can be interpreted in terms of both loss and demonstration of power. John's control over self and over others emerges as a combination of mimicry and reinterpretation that includes asceticism, rejection of social and cultural expectations, reconsideration of death, and exhibition of both direct and indirect power and influence over others.

The ambivalence present in the Gospel's construction of John's control over self and over others is similar to other non-elites, including Jesus and Joseph. John is not afforded the same privilege as elites to protect his own body from imprisonment and execution, but he does control his own physical and social location and chooses alternate locations and behaviors from the norm. Likewise, while he does not have the kind of social location or positional power to dominate the movements or choices of others to the extent that would have been ideal, John's words and actions affect people—his own disciples, Herod, Pharisees, and scribes—more than might be assumed, and his influence extends even after his physical presence is removed.

In other words, I see John's character asserting power and influence in a way that enhances his masculinity, if incompletely or unconventionally. In its alternative construction of John's control, therefore, the Gospel neither rejects power itself nor considers John a failure as a man. Control over self and over others remains a core value for Matthew's construction of John's masculinity, even as the way that control is asserted based on the options open to John is quite different from the assumed elite norm. The alternative understanding of masculine control embodied by John opens the way for critique and re-imagination of power as it relates to masculinity even as it retains the risks of dealing with dominating control.

I first consider John's ability and inability to exercise control over himself and the potential impact of these dynamics on his masculinity, followed by his control with respect to others, both where he is subjected to them and where he exerts power over them. First, John exhibits control over his physical needs. The reference to fasting in 9:14 indicates that John and his followers exercised control over their appetites. As previously noted, the reference in 3:4 can be read to emphasize his ascetic lifestyle as one who does not require elaborate, or even standard, food and clothing. Even if the diet reference is not interpreted this way, however, Jesus's description of John in 11:7–8 makes a similar point by contrasting John with an elite and powerful male, "someone dressed in soft robes" (ἄνθρωπον ἐν μαλακοῖς ἠμφιεσμένον). Such elite and powerful people, Jesus says, are to be found in royal palaces (ἐν τοῖς οἴκοις τῶν βασιλέων), not in the wilderness with John.

Just prior, in verse 7, John is also contrasted with "a reed shaken by the wind" (κάλαμον ὑπὸ ἀνέμου σαλευόμενον). Here there are a variety of interpretative possibilities.[58] The prevalence of reeds near the Jordan may suggest that John is contrasted with something common, i.e., one can see reeds shaking in the wind every day, but John is worth coming out to the wilderness to see. Or, as Luz suggests, the shaking reed might make one "think of an inability to form independent judgments, or of an easy conformity that shows a lack of character . . . or in a more general sense of weakness."[59]

Either of these interpretations places John on the good side of a contrast; the shaken reed is the negative image and John is the positive. Both Carter and Luz, however, suggest that the reed may be a reference to Herod Antipas, who used the image on his coinage.[60] If this is the case, then it adds a layer of significance to John's asceticism, extending the critique of Herod's non-awareness of and opposition to God's purposes mentioned in the first section of this chapter.[61] Not only is John a prophetic spokesperson for God, his life is characterized by simplicity. Not only is Herod an enemy of God's servant, his life is characterized by excess.

These three references suggest that John rejects many of the comforts that other people desire or require. He is not a glutton, and is not interested in fancy clothes. When taken with the wider criticism of Herod Antipas in this Gospel, which I will continue to explore in this section, John's ability to control his own desires becomes an important part of his Matthean characterization. With masculinity in mind, the question is whether these ascetic behaviors qualify as "self-control." In Roman imperial ideology, self-control is an important marker of masculinity; Conway calls it "among the most important keys to ideal masculinity" in the first century.[62] Demonstration of self-control includes "mastery of the passions, especially lust and anger, but also self-restraint in eating, drinking, and luxury in general."[63]

John's rejection of earthly comforts comports with this understanding of self-control in some important ways. He does not exhibit lust, and he certainly shows self-restraint in "eating, drinking, and luxury in general."[64] Two considerations complexify the picture. First, John does demonstrate anger, an emotion which reveals, in Conway's words, the "cultural contradictions" of gendered discourse.[65] While anger is generally to be avoided, certain expressions of it can still be considered manly; the key seems to be the object or cause of the anger. If the anger is righteous anger directed at unrighteous people or situations, then it makes men stronger, rather than weaker.⁶⁶ While John's speech in 3:7–12 may contain elements of anger, its subject matter is a warning toward righteous behavior, and its purpose is to demonstrate John's important role in announcing God's mission. In terms of the narrative's point of view, then, it is possible to say that John's anger here strengthens his masculinity rather than weakens it.

Second, there is an emphasis on moderation with self-control, what Williams calls the "golden mean of masculinity."⁶⁷ This included sexual practice, emotions, eating and drinking, and even personal appearance. Excess on either end, too much or too little, could compromise masculinity. In this respect, perhaps John's expression of self-control is problematic. While preferable to Herod's gluttony or greed, John's lack of sexual behavior and asceticism are unusual and challenge the value of moderation. Certainly, if John's claim to masculinity rests on his expression of self-control, then his asceticism alone does not guarantee increased masculine status.

Then again, as demonstrated in the previous section, the Gospel also emphasizes John's connection to God's plan. This connection is not described explicitly as "righteousness," as it is with Joseph. But John is repeatedly associated with God's words and God's work in the world, bolstering his identity as a righteous person. If this is the case, then John's connection to the divine may supersede or contextualize his other behavior. This logic already applies to anger; perhaps it can extend to other aspects, leaving room to reinterpret excessive behavior. Roman masculinity is a slippery and multifaceted concept, where rankings aren't always solid or obvious.

Further, if the issue for Matthew is one of contrast, then more extreme may be better. For example, if self-control is an ideal, then John not only beats Herod but other elites by taking it to its logical extreme. If Herod is gluttonous, emotional, and avaricious, and John is the opposite, then John wins the masculinity competition in part by how different he is from Herod. For Matthew, the contrast doesn't work as well if John is only moderately better than Herod, even if that more comfortably fits the ancient narrative of masculinity, because an extreme approach to service of God is a Gospel value (Matthew 16:24). John's asceticism is not a perfect fit for the category of self-control from an elite masculine perspective. But there are enough shared values, and a clear enemy who lacks them, to say that John's masculinity is not undermined by his asceticism.

Apart from ascetic self-control, one intriguing aspect of John's ability to control his own body comes in his location, physical and social. In 3:1, John is introduced as appearing in the wilderness of Judea (παραγίνεται . . . ἐν τῇ ἐρήμῳ τῆς Ἰουδαίας). This location puts him far from the center of power in Jerusalem. And yet, people came out to see him, from Jerusalem and all Judea and all the region of the Jordan (Ἱεροσόλυμα καὶ πᾶσα ἡ Ἰουδαία καὶ πᾶσα ἡ περίχωρος τοῦ Ἰορδάνου). On the one hand, his physical location marginalizes his power with respect to traditional authority. On the other, if his physical and social locations are his choice, then it is possible to understand John's removal of his own body from society as a defiant gesture. It is worth asking whether his physical and social location means that he is asserting power and/or gaining freedom by extricating himself from the social expectations of community, family, and religion.[68] Carter says that the simplicity of John's life means that "He is indebted to no one."[69] This is true financially, but in many other respects, as well.

Also pertinent to the discussion about John's control over his own body is his use of his voice. Gleason argues for the prominence of public speech in the assertion of masculinity in the ancient world.[70] While the context is certainly different from the public debates of Favorinus and Polemo, the phenomenon of John speaking publicly and appearing to best his enemies is striking. Murphy asserts that "Herod felt threatened not only by John's rhetorical skill but also by his political power."[71] From a masculinity standpoint, the two are related. If one of the criteria for establishing masculinity is the privilege of public speech that is uncontested or triumphant in the face of challenges, then John's speech in chapter 3 is a strong argument in his favor.[72]

Of course, John's public speech in the wilderness gets him into trouble, and ultimately limits his ability to control the fate of his own body, a key value of Roman elite masculinity.[73] John is arrested and imprisoned for both his words and his actions that are a threat to Herod Antipas personally and politically (14:3–5).[74] When the time comes, he is not able to keep from dying (14:9–10). These events show a tragic lack of control over his own body and an inability to ward off threats of physical violence.

Beyond this aspect of lack of control, there are further implications to his death that threaten John's masculinity. Feminist interpreters, as well as those interested in masculinity, have pointed out the problematic agency of Herodias in the story. She is the reason for John's critique of Herod, and she calls for John's death in 14:8.[75] Benny Liew, for example, discusses how the agency of women has a feminizing effect on the men around them.[76] Liew argues that "a woman who raises herself to masculine status is inevitably lowering men to feminine status."[77]

Interestingly, Liew focuses on the way that the agency of Herodias feminizes Herod Antipas, but not John the Baptist.[78] While John the Baptist is a tangential part of Liew's discussion, his masculinity is not discussed. Similarly, Glancy argues that "Mother and daughter effect not only the death of the Baptist but the revelation of masculinity as a front."[79] For Glancy, this revelation is achieved through the depiction of Herod as bound to social expectations (14:9 says "out of regard for his oaths and for the guests" διὰ τοὺς ὅρκους καὶ τοὺς συνανακειμένους), which forces him to go against his own prior decision not to execute John.

While I would agree with both interpretations' assessments of the impact of Herodias's actions on Herod, I would argue that there is more to the story in terms of masculinity. Both Herod and John are emasculated by the agency of Herodias; Herod loses face and John loses his life. Not only can John not prevent an assault on his body, he is killed at the request of a woman.[80] In some ways, the focus on Herod and Herodias in the narrative (and in its interpretation) further marginalizes John and his claim to masculine status.[81]

This is particularly important because John doesn't just die; he loses his head.[82] As Janice Capel Anderson states, "The head is also a trope or figure of speech that represents the phallus. In patriarchal cultures the phallus often symbolizes male personhood and power. The severing of heads (decapitation or decollation) and castration are figures for each other."[83] The detail of John's head being brought to Herod on a platter does several things (including providing an unforgettable image), but one of the things it does is rob John of his masculine power. The euphemism underscores the emasculation that takes place in his death.

John's emasculating death is significant for his role in the narrative as it moves him from activity to passivity. John begins the narrative speaking and moving freely in public. After the baptism, he next appears in prison, an event which is not recorded in the Gospel.[84] Then, his death is told in retrospect as Herod reflects on the reports about Jesus. Finally, in 14:12, his disciples carry his body out for burial, drawing attention both to his lack of head and lack of agency. His final movements in the Gospel are to be carried. Further, as Glancy notes, the loss of his head takes away John's traditional masculine role as the subject who gazes upon others. After his death, "no longer can the Baptist see and condemn Herodian activities; the severed head can no longer gaze, but is the object of other gazes, including that of Herodias."[85]

The complex dynamics of this section clearly illustrate the ambivalence surrounding John's control over his own body. For example, after his death, John is mentioned several times during the course of the Gospel by others. On the one hand, this points to his importance in God's mission. But, on the other, it points to his lack of control, as he is talked *about* and does not speak for himself any longer. If at first John is identified by public speech, then after his death he is notable not for his ability to speak, but for being the subject of conversation and subjected to the evaluations of others. He becomes Elijah *redivivus* (17:9–13), an anonymizing move that redefines him as another and invisibilizes his particular identity and existence. He becomes for Jesus an example of faithfulness and of simplicity (11:16–19), and a symbol of the authorities' cruelty and their ignorance of or deafness to God's work in the world (21:23–41). While he starts with considerable agency, eventually he ends up with none. Jesus uses him frequently as a positive example, demonstrating his lasting influence, but John is not in charge of that legacy.

Even here, though, one suspects that John's death as depicted in the Gospel does not simply fit neatly into Rome's dominant discourse. John identifies himself as a forerunner to Jesus, and their stories have parallel experiences of arrest and execution. Given these narrative connections, it is unrealistic to expect that John will survive. Even if John's death is a failure from the perspective of the imperial authorities, it is not necessarily the case for the viewpoint of the Gospel. In 4:12, Jesus receives word of John's arrest. This news, however, does not prompt Jesus to quit, and there is no indication that John has failed. Rather, 4:17 transfers John's words in 3:2 to Jesus. This is the moment Jesus takes up the cause. For Matthew, John's death is tragic, but not the end of the mission.

John's death is also not a cause for shame for his followers, or for Jesus. Rather, Jesus argues that John's death says something negative about those who killed him (17:10–13; 21:23–27). There is a relationship between John's words and actions, the response of the authorities, and God's will that assigns meaning to John's death beyond simple defeat. Jesus's references to John's death not only condemn those who kill John, they associate John's death with Jesus's death. Both of them are regarded as prophets, and both of their deaths somehow signal the coming of God's empire and the rejection of it by the authorities.

John's death is not interpreted by the Gospel primarily as a failure, but as an inevitability, a consequence of his devotion to divine service and an indictment of those who reject God and Jesus. If his death, like the death of Jesus, is in some ways a foregone conclusion, then it is not something shameful, but instead something potentially powerful. In divine service, John's death exposes the enemies of God for who they are, and helps to usher in God's reign. In this scheme, John's death is not simply a failure to exert control, although those inadequacies are real. Rather than only undermining John, however, his failures to control what happens to his own body make a statement about the pointlessness of the structures that lead to his death and the power of God to work despite real threats from earthly authorities. John's death, thoroughly marked by ambivalence, may be less about his inability to control his own body and more about his ability to use his body—in death and in life—to proclaim and advance God's empire in service to the divine.

John is not able to express control over his own body in very many ways that would adhere easily to dominant Roman imperial values. That being said, he does show some control that could potentially be seen as positive in his asceticism and his public speech. More interestingly, though, John's character expresses control over himself in ways that take elements of dominant cultural values and stretch or reinterpret them for the Gospel's purposes.

His dramatic asceticism stretches imperial notions of self-control as well as moderation. His physical placement on the margins appears to reject the social structures that would limit him, freeing him to act according to his convictions and his insight into and commitment to the divine will. And, his death may be understood as a means by which God's enemies are exposed and God's empire is advanced. Even if this reinterpretation can be understood primarily as mimicry, such mimicry pulls apart the fabric of ancient understandings of power and masculinity, exposing inconsistencies and leaving holes for other potential constructions.

Shifting now to John's control over others, there is a similar pattern of ambivalence, achieved through both imitation and reinterpretation. John's alignment with the Hebrew Bible prophets positions him as one who is to speak the word of God and to elicit change in people's behavior.[86] This he accomplishes in a variety of ways, some overt and others subtle. In response to John's faithfully prophetic behaviors, people are affected. First, John exhorts his hearers to make a change on account of the advent of the empire of heaven. The Gospel indicates that people were receptive to John's preaching, being baptized by him, and confessing their sins (καὶ ἐβαπτίζοντο . . . ὑπ'αὐτοῦ ἐξομολογούμενοι τὰς ἁμαρτίας αὐτῶν).[87] John's preaching elicited a change in his hearers.[88]

Second, prophets bother the authorities, and John also carries out this expectation by speaking his mind and challenging their assumed leadership. His words and actions in the wilderness prompt the Pharisees and Sadducees to come out to oppose him and they endure harsh criticism from him (3:7–12).[89] John dominates them and the discussion; the Gospel does not record a retort from them. Rather, John's next act is to baptize Jesus, fulfilling the prophecy he just announced. Later in the Gospel, Jesus uses John as an effective example when he argues with those authorities (21:23–46).

John also challenges another authority, Herod Antipas, who represents conventional power and wealth as Rome's client ruler. In Matthew 14:3–4, Herod Antipas is first threatened by John's preaching against Herod's marriage, which leads to John's arrest. Also, in the flashback that introduces the scene, Herod's reaction to Jesus stems from his fear that the stories about Jesus signal John's return from the dead (14:1–2). In this second example, John exerts control over Herod even after his death, as the mere memory of him and a potential reappearance creates a fearful reaction in Herod.[90]

John's powerful influence is also noted outside the biblical tradition in the works of Josephus, who attributes Herod's decision to kill John to fear of John's popularity.[91] He wanted to stop the spread of John's message.[92] Josephus and Matthew understand Herod's motivations differently. However, they both understand John's arrest and execution to be the result of a situation where his words and actions have proven challenging to the authorities.

Third, John does exhibit dominating control over his disciples. The fact that he, like Jesus, has disciples suggests that his impact extends beyond prophetic encounters at the Jordan to leadership in a community of followers. These disciples come to Jesus twice, in 9:14–17 and 11:2–6, to ask him questions. The second visit is to deliver John's question to Jesus about Jesus's identity. At this point, John is imprisoned, and yet he can expect the loyalty and obedience of his disciples. This loyalty extends even to death; 14:12 notes that his disciples came and claimed John's body, honoring him with burial after his beheading.[93]

Again, there is considerable ambiguity in these assertions of control. From an elite Roman point of view, John's control does not closely resemble the kind of direct, dominating power that Romans associated with masculinity. Rather, it may be more accurate to say that the above examples qualify more as influence, where John demonstrates significant agency that affects others. Herod and the Pharisees are not under John's physical control, even if they are influenced by him. This is also true of those who are baptized by him and those who follow him; while he is a captivating, influential figure, the decision to be baptized or to become John's disciple is theirs. This kind of influential power is limited in its ability to physically control others. Like many prophets, John's influence is strong, but his control over others is not such that he can demand their obedience, save his own life, or direct the actions of those around and above him.

Still, John's ability to elicit reactions or changes in behavior is noteworthy and identifies a sense of control that is different from the ideal, but nonetheless effective. A comparison here with Joseph is helpful. In some ways, John's status is similar to Joseph; they are both non-elites. However, John's economic status is even less stable than Joseph and Mary because he is not described as having a trade or means for an income. Yet, John shows more agency and control than Joseph does. Joseph's primary sphere of influence is more private, "down" toward Mary and Jesus. He evades King Herod but does not actively criticize or confront him. John's primary sphere is more public, "out" and "up" toward the crowds and the societal and political leaders. Not only does Joseph not speak, but his actions are largely directed by an angel, and are in response to the actions and words of others. John speaks boldly and publicly and uses his physical agency to place himself on the margins, where he nevertheless continues to affect the actions of others.

Perhaps this departure from conventional notions of control reflects the non-elite status of the early Jesus-believers and is largely imitative. That is, John's style of power is indicative of the limitations of his economic status and would more closely resemble Roman elite power if given the same status.

Or it may constitute somewhat of a rejection of the imperial value of overt domination. In this case, the Gospel could be understood to challenge Rome's authority by claiming that Herod Antipas's power is dangerous, but not cosmic. Because of John's connection to God, his death does not compromise his power in the same way that it might otherwise. Most likely, there is a combination of the two.

In this section, I have considered various examples of John's control over self and over others as a potential expression of his masculinity, behaviors and events notable for their ambiguity. With these examples in mind, I conclude that Matthew's case for John's masculinity is built on an altered or redefined sense of control that both challenges and co-opts elements of the conventional. A focus on power remains, but its execution is not synonymous with the larger cultural understanding of power that dominates discourse on masculinity.

An essential aspect of the redefinition of control in Matthew is the contrast of John the Baptist with Herod Antipas. Throughout this section, I have noted places where John is elevated at Herod's expense, or where Herod is critiqued both subtly and overtly. And, as noted above, feminist discourse has long understood chapter 14 to emasculate both John and Herod, the former by his feminizing death and the latter by being outwitted by the women in the story. But despite this similarity, the narrative makes a clear distinction between the two, elevating John above Herod. Herod is John's enemy, and thereby God's enemy, and his power over life and death is real. And yet, the Gospel finds ways to critique Herod's dominating control by highlighting the roles of Herodias and the guests, and by refusing to define John's death in terms of failure. As with divine service, the aspect of Herod's masculinity defined by physical power is undermined.

One who approaches the story with assumptions grounded in ancient masculinity would expect that Herod ought to be the ideal male. He is wealthy, he represents Roman authority, and he has the power to control others' bodies and lives. However, this is not the case. Herod not only is critiqued, he is critiqued by John, who does not meet conventional masculine expectations. A positive assessment of John and a critique of Herod Antipas appear to work hand in hand in the Gospel's attempt to negotiate masculine control in favor of those who are in divine service.

An altered sense of control raises several important questions. What is the relationship between this kind of power and non-elite expressions of masculinity? Is a different sense of control the result of a perspective that is influenced by non-elite status, early Christian convictions, or a mixture? In turn, what impact does this kind of "sideways" or influential power have on early Christian concepts of masculinity? Does early Christian masculinity change the understanding of control enough to interrupt the association with domination? Or does the idea of "power over" remain as the unattainable ideal, and the more negotiating or influential style remain the preferred one for those of lower economic status?

When viewed through the lens of dominating control over self and over others, John is a slippery figure. He is not conventionally dominant, but influential in a way that makes conventional power nervous. He does not fit into a traditional social scheme, but has influence on it. Ambivalence permeates John's associations with control. And yet, Matthew's emphasis on John's influence and importance, paired with his death at the hands of the enemies of God, seems to argue for a strong claim to masculinity, if mitigated or altered somewhat based on economic status. John's approach to dominating control contributes to an overall construction of masculinity that is marked by deviance, and yet conforms in many respects to imperial values. The Gospel's construction of dominating control over self and over others present in John the Baptist leaves the door open for an uncoupling of power and domination, but that process is not realized within the Gospel itself.

WEALTH

In this final section, I consider wealth as an aspect of John's characterization. I argue that the Gospel's treatment of John's lack of wealth is a component of the larger effort to redefine status in terms of divine service. The Gospel acknowledges John's lack of wealth (in some cases even highlighting it) and uses him to critique those who do have it. Despite a conventional focus on wealth as an indicator of masculine status, John's lack of wealth does not preclude a claim to masculinity in Matthew's Gospel. Rather, in keeping with the emphasis on divine status outlined above, John's characterization interrupts the automatic association of masculine status with wealth, challenging its importance. This rejection of wealth is not a rejection of status itself, but part of an attempt to make room for an alternative interpretation that privileges divine service.

Indications of this characterization begin with the Gospel's introduction to John in chapter 3, where John is introduced appearing in the wilderness, a place far from the centers of powerful wealth. The description of John's diet and clothing in 3:4 carries many connotations already noted, but these include the poverty associated with asceticism.[94] John, like Elijah, is not the type of person to prioritize creature comforts, or to hesitate speaking truth to power for fear of losing his monetary resources. Rather, John is defined by his lack of resources, needing only simple food and clothing to sustain him.

Based on this description, which is the major narrative material directly focused on John's characterization, it is difficult to place John in Friesen's poverty scale.⁹⁵ He is not associated with a trade, and the narrative shows no means of income and no integrated role—social or familial—in the larger community. This means he would not qualify for the status of P6. He is not exactly or necessarily a beggar, one of the categories for P7, although he is a prisoner for a time, which would qualify him for that status.⁹⁶ In general, John does not fit neatly in the categories outlined by Friesen, but based on the information provided in the narrative, it is accurate to say that John does not display traits of economic or social stability exhibited by those who claim masculine status.

Jesus's contrast in 11:8 between John and "someone dressed in soft robes" (ἄνθρωπον ἐν μαλακοῖς ἠμφιεσμένον) who belongs in a royal palace underscores this depiction of economic simplicity.⁹⁷ While not all people of wealth live in palaces, palaces are full of people of wealth. Wealthy people do not belong in the wilderness with John. Contrasting John with these figures of power and privilege places him, physically and socially, with those who do not have wealth. Carter goes so far as to say that Jesus' remark here "mocks any thought of John's alliance with the elite."⁹⁸ The contrast is intentionally stark. Also, if the reference in verse 7 to "a reed shaken by the wind" (κάλαμον ὑπὸ ἀνέμου σαλευόμενον) is interpreted as a contrast with Herod, then this further separates John (and all he represents) from the wealthy and political elite.

Another important contrast is made between John and Herod Antipas in chapter 14, with an implicit critique of Herod's excess in favor of John's simplicity. While the daughter of Herodias dances to entertain the guests at Herod's presumably lavish birthday celebration (14:6), John sits in prison.⁹⁹ His imprisonment is mentioned both at the beginning of the story (v. 3) and when Herod's verdict is carried out in the midst of the party (v. 10). John's head is placed on a platter in the midst of Herod and the guests eating food on platters. It is obvious that the poor, imprisoned, prophet is the sympathetic victim in this story; the rich ruler is the villain. Here again, Herod's masculinity is undermined. The Gospel does not argue that he does not have wealth. Instead, the importance of that wealth is challenged in the context of God's purposes.¹⁰⁰ Herod's wealth does not help him; it makes him an enemy of John and of God.

A preferential distinction between John the Baptist and those who have wealth resonates with a larger Matthean preference for the poor and critique of the rich. In 11:4–6, when John's disciples ask Jesus if he is the one who is to come, Jesus's response includes good news brought to the poor (πτωχοὶ εὐαγγελίζονται) as evidence of God's action.¹⁰¹ John's practice of fasting, highlighted in 9:14, 6:16–18, and 11:18, points to a simple lifestyle that rejects gluttony and excess. In the teaching material, Jesus talks about the dangers of wealth and the care of God for those who do not have it (6:19–21, 24–34; 19:16–30).

This larger rejection of wealth provides an important interpretive context for an assertion of John's masculine status despite his lack of wealth. At first glance, this characterization would indicate a departure from presumed norms. John's lack of financial resources ought to compromise his masculinity, in part because it diminishes his ability to exert power over himself and others. However, considering the perspective of this Gospel, I contend that, in this respect, Matthew does not share or appropriate the values of the imperial world. Rather, the Gospel asserts another form of masculinity that both values freedom from wealth and emphasizes divine service as a means to status. The latter point has been addressed in the first section of this chapter; I now address the former.

Like its treatment of Joseph, the Gospel's preference for John the Baptist and his distance from those who have wealth indicates a critique of this facet of Roman masculinity. A typical Roman perspective would have understood John's masculinity to be inferior because of his relative lack of wealth.[102] His characterization as a "real man" who doesn't have a lot of "stuff" challenges those normative assumptions and is an example of how the Gospel uncouples wealth and masculinity.

While John does not have a discernible trade to make money, he also may not need or want one. His simple diet and apparel choices indicate that this may not be a necessity or goal for him. Carter notes that John's "food denotes poverty," but also freedom from distraction.[103] John's lifestyle, then, including his marginal location, is significant because it appears he is outside the system by his choice to respond to a divine call. He is not just a person of limited means. He chooses a different way of life altogether, placing himself on the margins where there is a measure of freedom.

Herod Antipas provides an important contrasting illustration. Herod is the one who has wealth, but he is not respected in the Gospel narrative. In some ways, his wealth actually limits him, as it puts him in a position to react in a certain way to his guests, even against his own instincts.[104] The narrative makes clear that John the Baptist is in prison, but the story suggests that he is not the only one whose movements and decisions are limited. The critique here makes John the victim of Herod's imprisonment to wealth, dominating control, and status.[105] Herod imprisons John, but Herod's wealth also imprisons himself. Here again, Herod's masculinity is undermined by the Gospel in favor of John. Wealth does not provide the kind of respect, freedom, or status for Herod that is usually assumed.

By contrast, even though John is actually imprisoned in the narrative, it's his message and his actions that have power. John's lack of wealth does not hold him back. People of wealth and power come out to see him in the wilderness; he bests them in rhetorical exchange. His popularity does not provide him with wealth, but he has disciples nonetheless. In 11:7–10, Jesus speaks of John's importance in the same breath as he contrasts John with those who have wealth. While he does not establish a causal relationship between the two, their juxtaposition suggests that Matthew's Jesus is connecting those two ideas: distance from wealth *and* status as a great man.

It is clear that the Gospel does not consider John's lack of wealth to be a problem for a claim to his masculinity. It downplays and problematizes the role of wealth, and redefines status in terms of divine service. For an ancient audience, the rejection of wealth as an indicator of status is a radical claim, but an emphasis on divine service is familiar. The deviant construction of masculinity present in John, then, does not immediately eliminate a claim to a kind of masculinity that would have been at least somewhat recognizable to an imperial audience. As a result, we must consider, as we did with Joseph, whether the Gospel is making a truly different claim to masculinity than the dominant conception or just working with the same pieces from the perspective of those with limited social capital.

If there is a character whose construction of masculinity can be construed as disruptive, it is John the Baptist. He is a destabilizing force, unsettling the structure, and challenging the status quo theologically, socially, and financially. John challenges the status quo in his initial preaching, in his baptism of Jesus, in his lifestyle, in his threat to Herodian power, and in his rejection of wealth. The challenge to the dominant masculine paradigm is significant in terms of the Gospel's rejection of wealth. However, the shift in emphasis from wealth to divine service as the primary source of status blunts any larger critique of masculine control and preserves a kind of masculinity that prioritizes competitive status determined by the sanctioning of a divine male authority. Wealth is critiqued in this Gospel, but it also loses importance as an indicator of masculinity.

CONCLUSION

In this chapter, I have considered the masculinity of John the Baptist through the lens of three conventional aspects of ancient masculinity: access to the divine, dominating control over self and over others, and wealth. Because their stories are connected, I have also included observations about the masculinity of Herod Antipas. I have shown how both contribute to an alternative form of masculinity that privileges divine service, rejects wealth, and both mimics and redefines control over self and over others.

John's masculinity is primarily grounded in divine service. His prophetic identity, contrast with Herod, connection to Jesus, and significant role in conveying God's purposes and exposing God's enemies (even after death) establish him as a divine servant without human equal. Although John is not perfect, his imperfections are mostly in comparison to Jesus, who *is* the very presence of God (1:23). In a Gospel that privileges adherence to God's work, John meets the expectation, and this quality becomes the dominant expression of his masculinity.

The other two characteristics of masculinity discussed in this chapter are negotiated within this framework. The Gospel retains an emphasis on control, despite the obvious limitations for someone like John the Baptist. When it is possible, John demonstrates control over his own body and the bodies of others. When that is limited, the Gospel reinterprets power in a way favorable to John. The result is a deeply ambiguous portrayal of John's control that nonetheless argues for his masculinity. Likewise, the Gospel does not shy away from John's poverty. Rather, it rejects wealth and its automatic association with masculinity. Status itself is not rejected but redefined in terms of divine service. But the significance of wealth for both masculinity and for divine purposes is strongly challenged.

An integral part of building the case for John's masculinity as outlined here is a continual contrast with and critique of Herod Antipas. In each of these categories, John and Herod are juxtaposed with John as the victor. Like his father, Herod Antipas ought to be the default supreme male, the one with dominating control, wealth, and divine service. Instead, Herod's power is questioned, his wealth devalued, and his distance from—and opposition to— divine purpose emphasized. A key part of establishing John's masculinity is undermining Herod's.

The construction of John's masculinity sets him apart in the Gospel. Like Joseph, John represents an example of non-elite masculinity negotiating the expectations of the ancient imperial world. But John's example of non-elite masculinity is quite different. Both John and Joseph figure out their masculinity with predictable limitations; they are held back in similar ways. But John is engaged in masculine competition and comparison in ways that Joseph is not. John takes up physical and theological residence on the margins, but is simultaneously involved in far more human interaction than Joseph, who is quite isolated.

The Gospel never records Joseph speaking to another human being, even Mary. He listens to the angel, he acts, presumably he talks to his wife even if we don't see it. But he does not speak in the text, which is a key component of competitive masculinity. John does speak, and his speech is actively engaged in challenging those with political and religious authority, asserting and challenging masculine status: his, Jesus's and Herod's. Joseph's connection is primarily centered around his identity as a righteous man. While John may also be described as righteous in his words and deeds, his connection with God is both broader and deeper.

John is a figure marked by controversy, and his masculine status is actively contested by language in the Gospel itself. This is unsurprising, as all masculinity is inherently unstable. His masculinity is asserted and mitigated several times in the course of the Gospel. In some cases, he wins. In others, he loses ground. When he loses, the Gospel offers another interpretation of events in light of God's purposes that mitigates the damage to his masculinity. John is as much of a man as can be expected for someone in his position, but he's actually far more of a man than should be possible.

In the eyes of the Gospel, John is a model for others. Faithful people are to listen to him. Those who reject him do so because they reject God's purposes. This is critically important, as it means that John's masculinity both challenges and supports traditional understandings of masculine power. Language by and about John in Matthew's Gospel establishes a kind of alternative, non-elite masculinity that challenges imperial values, but nonetheless uses some of the same categories (control, divine service) as dominant masculinity and speaks in the same familiar terms. Because John is so closely aligned with God's mission, both the challenging and the conventional aspects of his masculinity become embedded in the Gospel's sense of divine purpose. For those interested in questioning or dismantling the automatic association of God's purpose with masculine power, John presents a daunting challenge and a redefined model.

NOTES

1. See Graham N. Stanton, *A Gospel for a New People: Studies in Matthew* (Louisville: Westminster John Knox, 1993), 77–84.

2. I discuss masculinity and divine service further in chapter 1 and 2. A full account of scholarship focusing on John the Baptist is not within the scope of this project. However, a review of recent scholarship reveals that work on John is frequently interested in questions of history and theology, often vis à vis Jesus, as well as John's relationship with the Judaism of his time. Some of this research is quite different from my approach, but some does overlap with the questions I am asking in this project, particularly those works interested in power, in John's status relative to Jesus, and his role in the proclamation of God's mission. Representative works that include both categories include Carl R. Kazmierski, *John the Baptist: Prophet and Evangelist* (Collegeville: Liturgical Press, 1996); Catherine Murphy, *John the Baptist: Prophet of Purity for a New Age* (Collegeville: Liturgical Press, 2003); W. Barnes Tatum, *John the Baptist and Jesus: A Report of the Jesus Seminar* (Sonoma, CA: Polebridge Press, 1994); Joan E. Taylor, *The Immerser: John the Baptist within Second Temple Judaism* (Grand Rapids, MI: Eerdmans, 1997); Robert L. Webb, *John the Baptizer and*

Prophet: A Socio-Historical Study (Sheffield: Sheffield Academic Press, 1991); Walter Wink, *John the Baptist and the Gospel Tradition* (New York: Cambridge University Press, 1968); Gary Yamasaki, *John the Baptist in Life and Death: Audience-Oriented Criticism of Matthew's Narrative* (Sheffield: Sheffield Academic Press, 1998).

3. This practice of fasting by John and his disciples, which is a conventional spiritual discipline, is subsequently rejected in some sense by Jesus in 9:15–17. This rejection does not appear to be about fasting itself, however, but about proximity to Jesus. If the point of fasting is to be connected to God and not distracted by other things, then when Jesus is there with you, fasting loses its purpose. So John's fasting is not rejected on principle, but the purpose and practice of fasting is somehow impacted by the presence of Jesus. See Warren Carter, *Matthew and the Margins: A Sociopolitical and Religious Reading* (Maryknoll: Orbis, 2000), 222–23; W. D. Davies and D. C. Allison, *A Critical and Exegetical Commentary on the Gospel According to St. Matthew*, 3 vols, International Critical Commentary (Edinborough: T&T Clark, 2004), 2: 108–9; Ulrich Luz, *Matthew 8–20: A Commentary*, trans. James E. Crouch, ed. Helmut Koester, Hermeneia (Minneapolis: Fortress Press, 2001), 2: 36–37.

4. Carter, *Matthew and the Margins*, 95. Carter here also lists a number of examples of others, Jews and Gentiles, who eschew food and drink to focus on serving God.

5. James A. Kelhoffer, *The Diet of John the Baptist: "Locusts and Wild Honey" in Synoptic and Patristic Interpretation* (Tübingen: Mohr Siebeck, 2005).

6. Kelhoffer, *The Diet of John the Baptist*, 128.

7. See Carl H. Kraeling, *John the Baptist* (New York: Scriber's Sons, 1951), 28. Scholars differ on their interpretation of John's choice to preach in the wilderness. It is possible to understand John rejecting the priesthood or redefining it. There are potential connections to Qumran, but the exact relationship is unclear. For a helpful summary of historical perspectives, see Tatum, *John the Baptist and Jesus: A Report of the Jesus Seminar*, 142–43.

8. Despite this focus on spiritual matters, it is important to note that the Gospel also shows a concern for the hungry. The feeding of the 5000 in 14:13–21 and the 4000 in 15:32–39 speak to physical hunger and God's role in alleviating it. So also, 12:1–8 advocates for the disciples eating when they are hungry. That story is more about the decision to pluck grain on the Sabbath than about fasting itself. And, regardless, ascetic living is not the same as starvation. Fasting serves a purpose for a time but people are still supposed to eat.

9. Following the emphasis on Roman Empire in this study, I use the translation of "empire" for βασιλεια rather than "kingdom."

10. John's credibility and authority is also supported by the narrative itself. Yamasaki states that, from a literary perspective, "John exhibits a degree of omniscience" in verse 9 when he presumes to know what his opponents are thinking. For Yamasaki, this enhances his reliability as a character in the narrative, making his claims about them credible. Yamasaki, *John the Baptist in Life and Death,* 88.

11. Davies and Allison, *The Gospel According to Saint Matthew*, 1:490. There are a few variants of the phrase, with or without the "Amen;" Davies and Allison consider them to be functional equivalents.

12. Yamasaki, *John the Baptist in Life and Death,* 89.

13. Ulrich Luz, *Matthew 1–7: A Commentary,* trans. James E. Crouch, ed. Helmut Koester, Hermeneia (Minneapolis: Fortress Press, 2007), 1:133.

14. Yamasaki emphasizes the potentially negative characterization that this aorist imperative implies. Rather than an ingressive aorist, which would imply a change of behavior, Yamasaki advocates understanding the imperative as "a command with a punctiliar sense." This interpretation turns the imperative into "a sarcastic taunt that adds significantly to the negative characterization of the Jewish leaders." Yamasaki, *John the Baptist in Life and Death,* 88. Both possibilities underscore John's boldness.

15. Carter, *Matthew and the Margins,* 96–97. See Frederick W. Danker, Walter Bauer, William F. Arndt, and F. Wilbur Gingrich, *Greek-English Lexicon of the New Testament and Other Early Christian Literature,* 3rd ed. (Chicago: University of Chicago Press, 2000), 366.

16. Robert F. Berkey, "ΕΓΓΙΖΕΙΝ, ΦΘΑΝΕΙΝ, and Realized Eschatology," *Journal of Biblical Literature* 82, no. 2 (Jun 1963), 177–87.

17. Wink, *John the Baptist in the Gospel Tradition,* 19.

18. Perhaps John speaks out about the marriage because it violates Lev. 18:16 and 20:21. Davies and Allison, *Gospel According to Saint Matthew,* 2:470; Luz, *Matthew* 2:306. Additionally, as Carter notes, perhaps John "resists a consolidation of the center's power" represented by a political marriage such as this one. Carter, *Matthew and the Margins,* 303. The conflicts between the Synoptic and historical account of whose wife Herodias was before she married Herod Antipas do not help matters. See Carter, *Matthew and the Margins,* 303; Davies and Allison, *The Gospel According to Saint Matthew,* 2:469–70; Murphy, *John the Baptist: Prophet of Purity for a New Age,* 62.

19. There is some inconsistency in Herod's portrayal in Matthew; v. 5 says that he wanted to put John to death, but v. 9 states that Herod "was grieved" (λυπηθεὶς) at the thought of beheading him. Perhaps this is due to an inconsistent redaction of Mark, where Mark 6:20 is left out in the Matthean version but Mark 6:26 is retained in Matthew 14:9. The omission of Mark 6:20 and addition of Mark 14:5 suggest that this is a significant aspect of Matthew's portrayal of Herod, but the inclusion of 14:9 complicates things a bit.

20. The text does not specify what John thought or knew about Jesus prior to his baptism. Yamasaki identifies tension here in the characterization of John that undercuts his reliability. Yamasaki, *John the Baptist in Life and Death,* 95–98. The incomplete or perhaps inaccurate perceptions of John are important and will be addressed shortly. However, despite initial incomplete or imperfect knowledge, John shows an awareness of Jesus's importance, and an eventual willingness to obey him.

21. Jesus's persistence and power over John here suggests a construction of masculinity marked by more solidly hegemonic behaviors and characteristics than John's. I will explore this more hegemonic construction, and John's relative subordination, in the subsequent discussion about John's relationship with Jesus.

22. It is not necessarily the case that Herod associated John with the divine; 14:5 says that Herod feared the crowd, because they considered John to be a prophet. But when taken with all the other Matthean references to Elijah and prophecy, John's association with Jesus in this story fits into the Gospel's larger association of John with divine purposes.

23. For Wink, Matthew's emphasis on John as Elijah is especially significant here, making "his murder all the more inexcusable." Wink, *John the Baptist in the Gospel Tradition,* 41.

24. Because Jesus has been established as a reliable character, his positive words about John can be trusted. Further, they underscore John's reliability as a source of information, as well. Yamasaki, *John the Baptist in Life and Death,* 79–80.

25. Murphy, *John the Baptist: Prophet of Purity for a New Age,* 68.

26. ὑμεῖς δὲ ἰδόντες οὐδὲ μετεμελήθητε ὕστερον τοῦ πιστεῦσαι αὐτῷ. Murphy compares this passage to Luke 7:29–30, noting that for Luke the issue is John's baptism. Those who were not baptized by John rejected the purpose of God. Matthew does not mention baptism here and is more interested in whether they believed and accepted that John is from God. Murphy, *John the Baptist: Prophet of Purity for a New Age,* 79.

27. Carter, *Matthew and the Margins,* 90–94; Yamasaki, *John the Baptist in Life and Death,* 81–84.

28. It is Matthew who makes this connection between John and Elijah more explicit and explores its meaning. The association is suggested by Mark, "but whereas Mark is somewhat cryptic and allusive about the relationship . . . Matthew bluntly equates the two figures." Murphy, *John the Baptist: Prophet of Purity for a New Age,* 80–81.

29. For discussions of the references to both 2 Kings 1:8 and Isaiah 40:3, see Carter, *Matthew and the Margins,* 95; Luz, *Matthew,* 1:135; Davies and Allison, *The Gospel According to Saint Matthew,* 1:295–96.

30. Wink calls this the "Elijianic Secret," the rapid resolution of which is characteristic of Matthew's desire to make the connection between John and Elijah direct and explicit. Wink, *John the Baptist in the Gospel Tradition,* 31.

31. See 1 Kings 17–19:21; 21:17–27; 2 Kings 1:1–2:12 for the stories of Elijah. He delivers God's judgment to the rulers Ahab and Jezebel who have strayed from the God of Israel, defeats the prophets of Baal, meets God in the sheer silence, pronounces God's sentence on Ahab, denounces Ahaziah, and ascends to heaven having passed his mantle to Elisha.

32. The Roman "turn to the past" is exemplified in *The Roman Antiquities* of Dionysius of Halicarnassus. Josephus brings the Jewish and Roman contexts together with his emphasis on Jewish heritage in *Jewish Antiquities.* His use of the ancient traditions is intended to bolster the status of Jews within Roman society, asserting their relevance because of their longevity and heroic leaders of the past. Josephus highlights Jewish leaders, sometimes even embellishing or altering their stories in order to underscore that theme of antiquity and power. For an extensive discussion of this phenomenon and an example of how it potentially functioned in the context of early Christian texts, see Warren Carter, *John and Empire: Initial Explorations* (New York: T&T Clark, 2008), 93–122.

33. Not insignificantly, this declaration is preceded by the prophetic formula "I say to you" mentioned above, indicating divine authority.

34. Yamasaki, *John the Baptist in Life and Death,* 111.

35. Luz, *Matthew,* 2:138.

36. Wink, *John the Baptist in the Gospel Tradition,* 19.

37. Davies and Allison, *The Gospel According to Saint Matthew*, 2:249.
38. Carter, *Matthew and the Margins*, 252.
39. Yamasaki, *John the Baptist in Life and Death*, 111–12.
40. Yamasaki sees in this parallel discourse not only a continuity between the two, but evidence of John's importance. "It is interesting to note the tenacity of this character," he says. "John has just been removed as a character at the story level of the narrative (4.12), and yet he still makes himself useful at the discourse level, as the target of introspection." Yamasaki, *John the Baptist in Life and Death*, 102.
41. Wink, *John the Baptist in the Gospel Tradition*, 28.
42. Collen M. Conway, *Behold the Man: Jesus and Greco-Roman Masculinity* (Oxford: Oxford University Press, 2008), 108.
43. Yamasaki claims that is particularly strange from a literary point of view. The story has obviously led to this moment, and yet John demonstrates ignorance of his role in the drama. Yamasaki, *John the Baptist in Life and Death*, 95–98.
44. The connection here with the Pharisees is especially interesting given John's earlier judgment of them.
45. It is possible that Jesus intends for fasting to cease for all who know him during his time with them, including John and his disciples. That seems to be the message of 9:16–17, where new practices are contrasted with old ones. But that is not made clear in the encounter. Again, it does not seem that he is criticizing fasting in general. It will return when the bridegroom goes away again (v. 15). But John's ignorance of this change, or maybe even the reason for the change, disrupts the characterization of him as one uniquely connected to God's purpose. On the one hand, he announces the reign of God. On the other, he seems to miss it when it arrives.
46. Luz, *Matthew*, 2:132. Murphy also argues for the story's historicity but stops short of grounding it in ambivalence or conflict. Murphy, *John the Baptist: Prophet of Purity for a New Age*, 66.
47. Yamasaki, *John the Baptist in Life and Death*, 104–5.
48. Another possibility is that something has happened between the baptism and the scene in chapter 11 to make John doubt Jesus's identity, but the narrative doesn't give us any information that would support or explain that change.
49. Οὐκ ἐγήγερται ἐν γεννητοῖς γυναικῶν μείζων Ἰωάννου τοῦ βαπτιστοῦ.
50. ὁ δὲ μικρότερος ἐν τῇ βασιλείᾳ τῶν οὐρανῶν μείζων αὐτοῦ ἐστιν.
51. For a review of interpretive options, see Davies and Allison, *The Gospel According to Saint Matthew*, 2:251–53.
52. Murphy, *John the Baptist: Prophet of Purity for a New Age*, 68.
53. Davies and Allison, *The Gospel According to Saint Matthew*, 2:252–59.
54. Wink argues that the distinction between the two is necessary partly because they are so alike. "Precisely because of their extensive assimilation the need arises to maintain the necessary boundaries." Wink, *John the Baptist in the Gospel Tradition*, 36. See also Davies and Allison, who recognize 3 outstanding features of John the Baptist in Matthew: 1) his identity as the forerunner of Jesus, 2) his utter subordination to Jesus, and 3) a high degree of parallelism between John and Jesus. This combination of qualities produces the somewhat confusing portrayal of John in Matthew

without resorting to negative judgment about John. Davies and Allison, *The Gospel According to Saint Matthew*, 1:289.

55. Incidentally, the common theme of "competition" between John and Jesus among biblical scholars begs the question of whether some of the implicit assumptions about masculinity in the ancient world are shared by modern interpreters.

56. See my discussion on Joseph's divine service in chapter 2, as well as Howard Eilberg-Schwartz, *God's Phallus: And Other Problems for Men and Monotheism* (Boston: Beacon Press, 1994).

57. Conway, *Behold the Man*, 125.

58. See Carter, *Matthew and the Margins*, 251; Davies and Allison, *The Gospel According to Saint Matthew*, 2:247–48; Luz, *Matthew*, 2:137–38.

59. Luz, *Matthew*, 1:138.

60. Carter, *Matthew and the Margins*, 251; Luz, *Matthew*, 1:138.

61. Further, if a reference to Herod Antipas is intended here, the reference to "soft robes" may also be a critique of him that connects soft clothing to sexual passivity and control over one's body. See Catharine Edwards, *The Politics of Immorality in Ancient Rome* (Cambridge: Cambridge University Press, 1993), 77.

62. Conway, *Behold the Man*, 24.

63. Conway, *Behold the Man*, 24.

64. John is a relatively straightforward case, as he is not defined in terms of sexuality at all. For most people, it is far more complex. For more on the details of sexual behavior relative to masculine status, see Conway, *Behold the Man*, 24–25; Craig Williams, *Roman Homosexuality: Ideologies of Masculinity in Classical Antiquity*, 2nd ed. (Oxford: Oxford University Press, 2010), 177–245.

65. Conway, *Behold the Man*, 26.

66. Conway, *Behold the Man*, 26–28.

67. Williams, *Roman Homosexuality*, 143.

68. This is an important distinction from Joseph, whose choices are limited by social convention, and who participates in the cultural and economic life of his community. John's choices communicate a desire to separate himself from that kind of community.

69. Carter, *Matthew and the Margins*, 95.

70. Maud Gleason, "Elite Male Identity in the Roman Empire," in *Life, Death, and Entertainment in the Roman Empire*, ed. D. S. Potter and D. J. Mattingly (Ann Arbor: University of Michigan Press, 1999), 67–84 and *Making Men: Sophists and Self-Presentation in Ancient Rome* (Princeton: Princeton University Press, 1995).

71. Murphy, *John the Baptist; Prophet of Purity for a New Age*, 6.

72. Neyrey makes this point about Jesus, saying that Jesus's frequent public speeches that include confrontation with enemies contribute to his masculinity. Jerome Neyrey, "Jesus, Gender and the Gospel of Matthew," in *New Testament Masculinities*, ed. Stephen Moore and Janice Capel Anderson (Atlanta: Society of Biblical Literature, 2003), 43–66. John is not the subject of Neyrey's analysis, and he does not meet the rest of his criteria for use of public space, but Neyrey does also acknowledge John's public voice in chapter 3. Neyrey, "Jesus, Gender, and the Gospel of Matthew," 61.

73. See chapter 1.

74. Matthew's version of the story names Herod as John's chief enemy rather than Herodias. Wink groups the Herodians together, calling them "a single rank of opposition" to God's agents, John and Jesus. Wink, *John the Baptist in the Gospel Tradition*, 28.

75. Janice Capel Anderson, "Feminist Criticism: The Dancing Daughter;" in *Mark &Method: New Approaches in Biblical Studies*, 2nd ed., ed. Janice Capel Anderson and Stephen D. Moore (Minneapolis: Fortress Press, 2008), 103–34; Jennifer Glancy, "Unveiling Masculinity: The Construction of Gender in Mark 6:17–29;" *Biblical Interpretation* 2, no. 1 (Mar 1994), 34–50; Tat-siong Benny Liew, "Re-Mark-Able Masculinities: Jesus, the Son of Man, and the (Sad) Sum of Manhood?" in *New Testament Masculinities*, ed. Stephen D. Moore and Janice Capel Anderson (Atlanta: Society of Biblical Literature, 2003), 93–135. These interpreters work with the Markan version of the story, which is slightly different. The Matthean version is tamer; for example, it omits the reference to Herodias's desire for revenge (Mark 6:19), as well as the claim that Herod considered John to be a holy man and liked to listen to John (Mark 6:20). Yet, despite these differences, enough of the gender analysis rings true for the Matthean version to consider it here.

76. Liew, "Re-Mark-Able Masculinities," 122–23; 132–33.

77. Liew, "Re-Mark-Able Masculinities," 123.

78. Liew's argument is that Herod is outwitted by Herodias while Jesus is not similarly outwitted by the women he encounters.

79. Glancy, "Unveiling Masculinity," 42.

80. The question, "Who killed John the Baptist?" is a complex one. Glancy, for example, is attempting to counter years of interpretation that assigned blame to Herodias. While acknowledging the agency of Herodias and the daughter, she also underscores Herod's power in the story. "Herod the king, not Herodias, not the child, retains power in the scene." Glancy, "Unveiling Masculinity," 41. Matthew 14:5 indicates that Herod wanted to put John to death but had decided against it because of the crowd. Although he is the only one who can give the order for John's death, the death would not have happened without the request by a woman.

81. This is evident from the scholarly literature cited here that reflects on the gendered implications for Herodias, the daughter, and Herod, but not (until now) for John.

82. Pushing the English metaphor, if Herod loses "face" then his head is also adversely affected!

83. Anderson, "Feminist Criticism: The Dancing Daughter," 133–34.

84. Yamasaki emphasizes the importance in having John "shackled off-stage." For Yamasaki, this fits the narrative's larger purpose of deemphasizing John and emphasizing Jesus. From this perspective, John is chained by both the narrative and by Herod. Yamasaki, *John the Baptist in Life and Death*, 101.

85. Glancy, "Unveiling Masculinity," 42, note 23.

86. Of course, many of those prophets failed at their endeavors to change people's behavior. This does not necessarily discredit them but points out the unfaithfulness of the hearers. God sent a prophet; the prophet did his job; the people didn't listen.

87. While repentance is not a new concept for the people of Israel, here it represents not only a personal change but a challenge to the dominant religious and political authorities of the time. On a macro level, the idea of repentance and returning to God is a conventional and consistent theme in the history of the people of Israel. Often, however, this involved repenting from the ways that their religious leaders and institutions strayed from God. John fits into this tradition.

88. Although they share many characteristics, in this respect, John is not exactly like Elijah. They both bring God's judgment on the authorities, they both spend time in the wilderness, and they wear similar clothing. But Elijah's attack goes directly to the top, while the people, both powerful and ordinary, come to John. John's time in the wilderness attracts a crowd; Elijah's time spent in the wilderness is spent alone and with the widow of Zarephath.

89. Again, the alternative translation of ἐπὶ as "against" emphasizes the antagonistic relationship between John and the Pharisees and Sadducees, as well as John's identity as an agitator of the status quo. See Danker, *Greek-English Lexicon,* 366 and Carter, *Matthew and the Margins,* 96–97.

90. This is true in the Matthean account as well as that of Josephus. See Murphy, *John the Baptist: Prophet of Purity for a New Age,* 6.

91. Interestingly, Josephus describes John as "a good man." (ἀγαθὸν ἄνδρα) See Josephus, *Jewish Antiquities, Volume VIII: Books 18–19*, trans. Louis H. Feldman, Loeb Classical Library 487 (Cambridge, MA: Harvard University Press, 1965), 80–84. Feldman's translation is as follows: "But to some of the Jews the destruction of Herod's defeat is attributed to his murder of John the Baptist. Herod's army seemed to be divine vengeance, and certainly a just vengeance, for his treatment of John, surnamed the Baptist. For Herod had put him to death, though he was a good man and had exhorted the Jews to lead righteous lives, to practice justice towards their fellows and piety towards God, and so doing to join in baptism. In his view this was a necessary preliminary if baptism was to be acceptable to God. They must not employ it to gain pardon for whatever sins they committed, but as a consecration of the body implying that the soul was already thoroughly cleansed by right behavior. When others too joined the crowds about him, because they were aroused to the highest degree by his sermons, Herod became alarmed. Eloquence that had so great an effect on mankind might lead to some form of sedition, for it looked as if they would be guided by John in everything that they did. Herod decided therefore that it would be much better to strike first and be rid of him before his work led to an uprising, than to wait for an upheaval, get involved in a difficult situation and see his mistake. Though John, because of Herod's suspicions, was brought in chains to Machaerus, the stronghold that we have previously mentioned, and there put to death, yet the verdict of the Jews was that the destruction visited upon Herod's army was a vindication of John, since God saw fit to inflict such a blow on Herod." For a discussion of this passage, see Webb, *John the Baptizer and Prophet,* 31–46.

92. This is different from Matthew, where Herod's fear convinces him *not* to kill John, and from Mark, where Herod is described as a somewhat sympathetic listener to John. For Josephus, Herod's motivation is tactical.

93. cf. Tobit 1.

94. Luz, *Matthew*, 1:135–36, Carter, *Matthew and the Margins*, 95.

95. Steven J. Friesen, "Poverty in Pauline Studies: Beyond the so-Called New Consensus," *Journal for the Study of the New Testament* 26, no. 3 (Mar 2004), 341.

96. In the ancient world, punishment fit not the crime but the social status of the accused. It was one way of keeping social order and political power. Crucifixion is an example. The imprisonment and beheading of John, therefore, says something about his lack of wealth and status. See Carter, *John and Empire*, 6, 139–40.

97. Describing the work of Roman moralizing writers, Edwards notes that, "Criticising the size and luxury of an emperor's house could constitute a resonant attack on the extent and arbitrariness of his power." Edwards, *The Politics of Immorality in Ancient Rome*, 139. So, while having a palace or large home could be seen as a mark of power, it could also be grounds for criticism. John's words here, while drawing a contrast, may also outline a similar critique.

98. Carter, *Matthew and the Margins*, 251.

99. Carter notes that Herod's guests would have included "the political and social elite, predominantly male, though high-status women are present." Carter, *Matthew and the Margins*, 303.

100. Edwards is again helpful here, noting that ancient writers attacking the elite's morals often focused on what they determined as "an improper distribution of wealth," where wealth itself was supposed to be a marker of status, but there were those who had wealth who did not "deserve" the regard afforded the elite. Edwards, *The Politics of Immorality in Ancient Rome*, 140.

101. Matthew's examples here are taken from various references in Isaiah but arranged here in a specifically Matthean order. Carter, *Matthew and the Margins*, 250; Davies and Allison, *The Gospel According to Saint Matthew*, 2:242–43. This is Q material that Matthew and Luke use slightly differently. Luz, *Matthew*, 2:130.

102. As noted in chapter 1, the presence of wealth alone was not a guarantee of masculine status in the ancient world. As with sexual desire, excess wealth that is misdirected could compromise masculinity. But the presence of substantial wealth used in appropriate ways was a key component in facilitating the kind of benefaction and status display that was required to establish masculinity. John lacks this.

103. Carter, *Matthew and the Margins*, 95.

104. Jillian Engelhardt explores the role of oaths in Herod's actions in the Markan version of this story, drawing on the work of James Scott in public and hidden transcripts to explain the role of the guests in Herod's decision to kill John against his own instincts. Jillian Engelhardt, "Performing Power in the Public Court of Reputation: Capital Punishment, John the Baptist, and Julius Jones," *Review and Expositor* 119, 3–4 (2023), 303–14. For another approach to this topic, see Liew, "Re-Mark-Able Masculinities," 132. While Liew is interested in the role that Herodias plays in John's death, he also discusses the "delicate and volatile social dance" between Herod and his guests, as well as Herod and John the Baptist, that negotiates for masculine status. In the end, Herod loses the competition.

105. This banquet is an example of what Edwards calls "competitive entertaining," an integral part of establishing social power, including masculinity. Edwards,

The Politics of Immorality in Ancient Rome, 202. This private space that functions in a very public way both asserts and limits Herod's power according to the cultural expectations placed upon him. John has no such burden.

Chapter 4

Peter

In this chapter, I argue that Peter's masculinity in Matthew is primarily constructed with a combination of dominance and ambivalence, present in each of the three categories of masculinity in focus in this study: divine service, dominating control over self and over others, and wealth. Narratively, Peter is the most prominent of the disciples. From this prominence, he exhibits some classic behaviors of hegemonic masculinity: asserting his dominant status by speaking for the group, demonstrating a privileged connection with Jesus, receiving authority over forgiveness described in monetary terms, and showing passion for the expectations of discipleship. However, Peter's characterization is marked by unmistakable ambivalence, as it also includes a lack of control over his own passion and action, submission to Jesus that relativizes his dominance, failure to remain loyal to Jesus, conflicting attitudes about wealth and status, and failure to comprehend the mission of God. These failures and inconsistencies significantly undermine his masculine status, and contribute to an overall picture of Peter that is marked by both power and weakness.

The ambivalence surrounding Peter's masculinity manifests itself in two important ways. One, despite some attempts to mimic or redefine markers of masculine status, Peter's low economic status and limited control over self and others compromise his masculinity from a Roman perspective. Two, the demanding Matthean expectations of discipleship, emphasizing loss and submission to Jesus, present an inherent conflict for Peter's masculinity. In other words, Peter's attempts to preserve masculinity (especially with respect to status and control over self and other others) lead to failure as a disciple. Likewise, attempts to prove his discipleship (divine service) lead to compromising his masculine status. This irreconcilable conflict results in a conflicting portrayal of Peter both as a disciple and as a man. It also potentially exposes a fundamental tension between masculinity and discipleship that is embedded into ancient and contemporary understandings of masculinity and Christianity.

The ambiguity present in Peter's character in Matthew has been noticed and addressed by biblical scholars from a variety of angles. One perspective resolves the tension in Peter's favor. Within this group, there is a range of engagement with the shadow sides of Peter's character. Some interpreters claim Peter's prominent status as community-builder or teacher overwhelms the negative portrayals, while others directly acknowledge the tension in Peter's character, but contextualize that tension somehow within his larger roles of discipleship or leadership.[1]

When Peter is positioned as a representative disciple, his negative characteristics are understood as evidence of Peter's humanness, and therefore God's willingness to accept other flawed humans as disciples. Some works combine these elements or emphases. These rehabilitative approaches often take place in combination with other texts, including New Testament presentations in Acts and other Gospels, and also early Patristic texts. The composite picture of Peter retains its multifaceted nature to varying degrees, but the tension is resolved to Peter's benefit.

On the other end of the spectrum, a smaller number of scholars have focused on the negative depictions of Peter. Arlo Nau, for example, understands Peter's characterization as "encomiastic dispraise," the result of conflict over Peter's role and an attempt to undermine his power and authority.[2] Kari Syreeni's literary analysis argues that the ambiguity in Peter's depiction leaves him a "dubious symbol," whose character is marked by irony and scandal.[3] And Robert Gundry argues that the negative portrayals are the definitive lens for interpreting Peter as an apostate, and that they outweigh any positive depiction that Peter receives in Matthew.[4] Rather than seeing Peter as teacher, builder of the church, or model disciple, Gundry argues that he is apostate and a failed disciple.

What the present analysis contributes to this phenomenally large body of work is a new lens through which to view the fundamental tension in Peter's characterization. It provides a new understanding of the conflict within this character, as well as the interpretive efforts to resolve it. Contrary to depictions that either harmonize his roles as a prominent male leader and model disciple or focus on one to the exclusion of the other, prioritizing issues of masculinity suggests that the ambiguity in Peter's character is the result of an irreconcilable tension between masculinity and discipleship. Peter's (actually quite conventional) construction as a hegemonic male is at odds with the Gospel of Matthew's values of submission to Jesus and resulting loss of status, wealth, and control; the expectations of Peter's discipleship compromise his masculine status.

Later Gospels, as well as countless interpreters, have worked to resolve this tension. But the tension is not resolved in Matthew, and it is not in this study. Rather, I consider this tension to be evidence of the challenges that early followers of Jesus faced in trying to reconcile their commitment to discipleship with the expectations of the ancient world around them. Matthew's depiction of Peter shows that the expectations for Jesus-followers largely, but not consistently, run counter to expressions of imperial masculinity.[5] Some of these characteristics may be reconcilable, but many may not be.

Exposing this tension provides a window into early attempts to make sense of discipleship marked by suffering and loss in a world where masculine power is prized. On the one hand, this suffering and loss emphasized in Matthew can be understood to imitate the traditions of noble suffering and death in the ancient world.[6] However, the rhetoric about discipleship in Matthew can also be seen as a challenge to masculine power and an alternative way of understanding worth in terms of valuing submission to Jesus and participation in his mission (10:7–8, 24–25). Early communities of believers faced many challenges in integrating their beliefs with the values and practices of the world around them. The conflict in Peter's characterization suggests that masculinity was one of those sites of imitation, redefinition, and contestation.

DIVINE SERVICE

A connection with the divine that demonstrates alignment or congruence with divine purposes establishes power and virtue, which are critical elements of masculine status. In this section, I explore Peter's divine service, which is defined as discipleship, highlighting both positive and negative aspects of his portrayal. Peter's dominance, combined with the emphasis this Gospel places on discipleship, creates a potential expectation that Peter will be a hegemonic male and a dominant disciple. The reality, however, is much more complex and ambiguous both in terms of masculinity and in terms of discipleship.

Peter's dominance as a disciple is evident both in the way that he is set apart from the other disciples and how he functions as their spokesperson. This prominence makes him a force to be reckoned with, and the most dominant masculine figure among the disciples. The many positive depictions of Peter's divine service in Matthew argue for his importance as a disciple, and later Christian interpretations certainly describe him in this way. Peter is the first called (4:18–22), the first named in the list of male disciples (10:2–6), the only one to walk on water (14:28–31), and the one who receives a special blessing and commissioning from Jesus (16:13–20). He shows great passion for discipleship and for participating in the mission of Jesus and the empire of heaven, even claiming that he alone will stay faithful when others desert Jesus (26:33).

However, the significant negative aspects of Peter's character also present in the Gospel interrupt this portrayal as model disciple, complicating his claim to masculinity. Peter is called Satan by Jesus (16:23), walks on water briefly then sinks (14:30), frequently misunderstands the divine situations he experiences, and denies Jesus after his arrest (26:69–74). Rather than a model or ideal figure, Peter emerges as a prominent and eager disciple showing dominance and passion, but also serious flaws and betrayal of Jesus. This complicated picture makes contradictory claims concerning Peter's masculinity through divine service.

After returning from the temptation in the wilderness and withdrawing to Galilee at the news of John's arrest, Jesus echoes John's words (3:2) and announces the empire of the heavens (4:17; ἡ βασιλεία τῶν οὐρανῶν). The announcement of the empire of the heavens is showcased or illustrated in his next act of calling the disciples (4:18–22).[7] In the initial interaction (4:18), Peter is named first, and Andrew is called his brother (τὸν ἀδελφὸν αὐτοῦ). Peter is first called by the name Simon, and then his nickname is used. Both the order and use of the nickname indicate Peter's relative importance over Andrew, as well as over anyone who comes after them.[8]

Jesus himself calls them and indicates that they will enter a special relationship; if they follow him, Jesus will change their livelihood, their life's work, and their identity.[9] In the empire of the heavens, Jesus will now reign over their lives. This establishes the close ties that Peter, as a disciple, will have with Jesus.[10] The Gospel indicates that they showed no hesitation, but immediately (εὐθέως) followed (ἠκολούθησαν) him, suggesting their eagerness to participate in divine service.

Peter's "firstness" is also highlighted in chapter 10. After summoning the disciples (μαθητὰς), the names of the twelve—now called apostles (ἀποστόλων)—are listed. Again, Peter is first, and both names are used. Some have read Peter's "firstness" to indicate his primacy in terms of authority and power; others interpret that primacy in terms of order in salvation history.[11] Gundry interprets it as a sign of falseness since "the first will be last" (19:30; 20:16).[12] While these interpretations differ, they each acknowledge the dominance of Peter as a disciple, and thus of his masculinity. As one who is set apart to be a disciple, a critically important theme in Matthew, and one who is then set apart from that group of disciples, the importance of Peter's divine service is established from the outset.

The story of Jesus healing Peter's mother-in-law (8:14–15) also suggests a certain closeness in Peter's relationship with Jesus. Perkins understands this closeness to establish a "prominent place" for Peter and his family.[13] For Cassidy, "the import of the passage for suggesting a privileged relationship between Jesus and Peter is not negligible."[14] Others downplay Peter's role in this story, arguing that he is incidental to the story, and the focus is on Jesus as a powerful healer. Luz, for example, argues: "All biographical or novelistic interest is missing, even here where Peter's family is involved. The only thing that matters is Jesus' deed."[15] Still others note that while the story might not indicate anything in particular about Peter's status as a disciple, it does say something about Peter's economic status, something I will explore in the section on wealth.[16]

In this section on discipleship and divine service, it is enough to note that Peter has first-hand experience with the healing powers of Jesus in his own house and among his own family members, and his is the only house mentioned of the disciples where Jesus enters.[17] While this story may not play a large role in the construction of Peter's dominance as a disciple, those aspects just named underscore Peter's close relationship with Jesus and support assertions of his prominence.

One scene that does focus on Peter is 14:28–33, where Peter follows in the footsteps of Jesus and walks on water. Subsequently, Peter begins to sink and is rescued by Jesus. Parts of this story, including Jesus walking on water in the midst of a storm, have parallels in other Gospels (Mark 6:45–52, John 6:16–21). Peter's part in the story, however, is unique to Matthew (14:28–31). This striking story argues for Peter's dominance in terms of divine service (and thus his masculinity) even as his sinking and lack of faith compromise it.

In the ancient world, walking on the water is usually reserved for God and emperors.[18] As Luz says, ancient texts reveal that such walking "is impossible for human beings and is reserved for God, unless humans are in a special way sons of God or achieve divine powers by magic—or unless in their audacity they invade dimensions that are reserved for the divine."[19] In biblical texts, there are very few references to walking on water, and they are reserved for God alone.[20] With respect to emperors, claims of lordship or sovereignty over the sea are made on behalf of many rulers, including Julius Caesar, Augustus, Tiberius, Gaius Caligula, Vespasian, Titus, and Domitian.[21] This persistent theme places dominion over the waters in the hands of only the most powerful men in the imperial world.

Peter is neither God nor emperor; he is a provincial man who depends on access to the sea for his living. Now he dominates the sea, demonstrating power over it. He is a subjugated non-elite who mimics the imperial center's power. Walking on the water not only exerts his dominance over the sea, but also speaks to his status as a disciple and his unique relationship with Jesus. Although all of the disciples witness Jesus walking on water, Peter is set apart from them as the only one who joins Jesus on the water. His excursion results from his own request (14:28–29), which may suggest several things: eagerness to be a disciple, faith, desire to be like Jesus, or hubris.[22] Jesus's affirmative response validates the request and enhances Peter's connection with Jesus, and therefore his divine service.

This episode is also important in terms of divine service because it prompts the first confession of faith, which is made by all the disciples together: "Truly you are the Son of God" (ἀληθῶς θεοῦ υἱὸς εἶ). As Davies and Allison argue, "if Peter walks on the sea at Jesus's bidding, then Jesus must wield divine authority."[23] Jesus's show of control over the elements, including his ability to make Peter walk on water and to save him when he sinks, demonstrates divine power that all the disciples recognize and confess together at this significant moment. Peter participates in a unique way in making this known.

Peter's sinking can be read in multiple ways. Jesus calls him "little faith," (ὀλιγόπιστε) which is surely a critique. Even as he witnesses the divine power of Jesus, Peter's faith is inadequate and his doubt is disappointing. Davies and Allison suggest that Peter's problem is not that he loses his faith, but that "he never knew or believed that Jesus could save him from sinking in the waters."[24] The fact that he steps out at all surely demonstrates some faith. Peter's enthusiasm, however, appears to be hubris, as he loses his faith very quickly.

Comparison to the ideal is not the only criteria available for evaluating Peter's sinking faith. When compared with the other disciples, it hardly seems fair to say that Peter is less faithful than they are, because they didn't even ask to try. He fails because he tries; others aren't given the same opportunity. In Matthew's Gospel, discipleship is incredibly demanding, and Jesus repeatedly raises the expectations. This mitigates the judgment a bit, although the result is still that more is expected of Peter than he can deliver.

We will return repeatedly to this dynamic in this chapter, where Peter fares relatively well in comparison with other disciples but fails to live up to the ideal of discipleship in Matthew. Peter's demonstrations of dominance, such as walking on the water, enhance his expression of masculinity, especially when compared with other disciples. But Peter's failures, in this case his sinking, limit his expression of masculinity through discipleship as divine service. Because masculinity in the ancient world is agonistic, the lack of ideal is significant. But so is the establishment of relative status over peers. When it comes to divine service in the empire of heaven, no disciples even come close to Peter, even as he fails to meet expectations of ideal discipleship.

Peter's next appearance, in 15:15, is in the context of Jesus's teaching about defilement. Here, Peter serves as a spokesperson for the disciples, asking a question about this teaching. There are two other texts where he plays a similar role (18:21 and 19:27), the first about forgiveness and the second about rewards for having left everything to follow Jesus. In addition to these three, there is a fourth story (17:24–27) where Peter serves as a spokesperson for Jesus and a representative of their community. In subsequent sections of this chapter, I will address additional aspects of these stories, including the issues of power inherent in Peter's public speech. Presently, I am interested specifically in how Peter's consistent role as spokesperson speaks to his prominence as a disciple and his divine service.

The role of spokesperson, what Luz calls Peter's "first function," prompts a few observations.[25] Peter's role as spokesperson can argue for enhanced status in divine service, claiming that he inhabits a dominant, privileged, position that allows him to speak freely *with* Jesus and *for* others. Looking at these texts as a group within the entirety of the Gospel, Peter is the only disciple to serve as a spokesperson and this dominant role sets him apart from the others. At the same time, Peter's speech is intended to represent the group, which indicates their like-mindedness as much as his difference from them. While Peter is the only one who speaks, he doesn't speak for himself but on behalf of the collective mind of the group. Peter's role as spokesperson makes him dominant, but not necessarily different or better than the others.

Also qualifying the argument for a privileged position is the fact that although Peter is engaged and encouraged by Jesus in 19:27–29, he is also criticized for not understanding (15:16), and corrected when he misspeaks (16:22–23; 17:25–27; 18:21–22). Peter's lack of understanding questions an automatic conclusion of his connection with the divine.[26] In some ways, Peter's inability to comprehend Jesus's teaching resembles John the Baptist, who also sent word by his disciples for clarification and showed limited understanding of the mission of Jesus (11:2–6). In that case, I argued that although John's limitations compromised his masculine status somewhat, they did not negate his overall argument for divine service. I see a similar dynamic here. While Peter's limitations in understanding the mission of Jesus are real, other aspects of his character explored in this chapter will more significantly undermine his role as divine servant than his lack of understanding.

Here again, comparison plays a role. When compared with what might be called "ideal discipleship" championed by the Gospel, Peter does not universally impress, especially in his moments of limited understanding. However, Peter's role as a spokesperson in and of itself argues for his dominance, connecting him to Jesus and to the empire of heaven in a unique way. No other disciple in Matthew demonstrates the kind of familiar relationship with Jesus, personal engagement with the issues of discipleship, or expectation to interpret or ask for the group, that Peter does.

Chapter 16 contains what is likely the most important text about Peter in Matthew, if not the whole biblical tradition. It would take an entire study to deal with the extensive, detailed, treatment that 16:13–20 and 16:21–23 have received in Gospel interpretation. In this chapter, I am interested in the way that these texts function in the construction of Peter's dominance in his divine service. I consider 16:13–20 to be the strongest argument for both the quality and ambiguity of Peter's divine service in the Gospel of Matthew, as well as for Peter's dominance. With the previous discussions of "firstness," walking on/sinking into water, and speaking for the group in view, this text extends and expands Peter's dominance, articulating a special status for Peter in the empire of heaven that no one else receives.

The story opens with Jesus positing a question of the disciples, and their group answer (vv. 13–14). The next question in verse 15 is also asked of the group (ὑμεῖς δὲ τίνα με λέγετε εἶναι), but it is Peter who answers alone in verse 16 with the confession, "You are the Messiah, the Son of the living God" (σὺ εἶ ὁ χριστὸς ὁ υἱὸς τοῦ θεοῦ τοῦ ζῶντος). Peter is not the first or only disciple to make this kind of confession; the disciples as a group voice a similar one in 14:33 (ἀληθῶς θεοῦ υἱὸς εἶ) and agree with God's statement in 3:17.[27] But Peter's confession here is important and interesting because it is made in the context of a larger conversation with Jesus where Peter is privileged.[28] So I understand Peter's confession to assert his dominance and elevate his status among the disciples.

This interpretation is supported by Jesus's response to Peter. Jesus blesses (16:17) as well as commissions him (16:18–19). Both set Peter apart from the other disciples, giving him authority and responsibility in the community. As with the confession, this is not the only blessing Jesus gives; in 11:6, he blesses those who do not take offense to him, and in 13:16–17 he blesses the disciples for their ability to hear and see what others have not. But the blessing in 16:17 draws particular attention to Peter as dominant within the group of the blessed disciples. Even the second half of verse 17, which can be read to reduce Peter's authority by placing the revelation in the hands of the divine, can also infer an increase in his status.[29] While Peter does not come to these conclusions on his own, he is the recipient of a revelation that corresponds with an individual blessing. If anyone among the disciples is going to receive a revelation from the Father in heaven, it is Peter.

Evaluating the interpretation of the many nuances of the commissioning given to Peter in 16:18–19 is beyond the scope of the discussion here.[30] Some scholars have read verse 18 to refer to Peter's words, others Peter himself. Verse 19 may infer authority with respect to forgiveness, or inclusion in the community, or some relationship between the two. Again, as with the confession and the blessing, a similar commission to this one is subsequently given to all of the disciples in 18:18–19. As is the case of the other two, the repetition of this commission both spreads out the authority to the disciples and also singles Peter out as the only individual who is given this responsibility by name.

In summary, while there are multiple potential implications, there is a singularity in this exchange and a sense of power and authority given to Peter that establishes his dominance. While the most expansive interpretations of Peter's influence in these verses may not be endorsed by all interpreters, even those that advocate for a more limited or moderate interpretation still set

Peter apart from his colleagues. In terms of divine service as an expression of masculinity, no other disciple participates in this combination of personal confession, blessing, and commissioning, underscoring Peter's dominance.

Interestingly, this text is followed immediately by one that undermines Peter's role in divine service. 16:21–23 includes Jesus's first prediction of his suffering, death, and resurrection. Peter responds to this prediction by rebuking Jesus (ἐπιτιμᾶν), passionately denying that this should ever happen to him (οὐ μὴ ἔσται σοι τοῦτο). Carter sees in this rebuke a lack of knowledge of "the specifics" of Jesus's language about his role, which Peter thinks he understands.[31] Syreeni calls Peter "a worried and deeply involved friend."[32] Luz allows for both interpretations, also suggesting that Peter is resisting his own suffering as a disciple whose life is to resemble that of Jesus.[33]

Whether from compassion, ignorance, fear, or a combination, Peter challenges Jesus's pronouncement. The fact that he feels comfortable to do so can underscore the closeness of the relationship I have posited previously, arguing for Peter's status among the disciples.[34] Alternatively, Peter's rebuke may reveal a disconnect in Peter's connection to the mission of Jesus. Jesus's response to Peter validates this sense of separation or disconnect. He tells Peter in verse 24 that his mind is not on the things of God (τὰ τοῦ θεοῦ) but the things of human beings (τὰ τῶν ἀνθρώπων). This lack of attention to the things of God means that Peter cannot accept what will happen to Jesus, and suggests that he has not truly understood what the empire of heaven is about.

The accusations Jesus makes in verse 23 intensify the critique. Peter is called both a "tempter" (σατανᾶ) and an "offense" or "cause of sin" (σκάνδαλον), meaning that his rebuke is not just a reflection of him, but potentially an impediment of the work of Jesus.[35] This language connects Peter to the tempter in 4:1–11; like that tempter, Peter is resisting divine purposes.[36] Just as Jesus overcomes and dismisses the tempter in 4:10, he does so again with Peter in 16:23. The comparison of the two texts puts Peter in very bad company as one working against the purposes of God, on the wrong side of the cosmic divide Jesus speaks of in 12:32.

Jesus continues in verse 24 with a description of discipleship that emphasizes self-denial and suffering. This is significant, as it connects the suffering of Jesus in verse 21 with the fate of the disciples. Peter's rebuke of Jesus's suffering suggests that he will not willingly accept his own, although that is the expectation of discipleship.[37] This puts Peter's commitment to discipleship in question. To be sure, the silence of the other disciples means others may have similar struggles. But because of his prominence, it is Peter's credibility as a disciple that is decentered here.

The resulting picture from the juxtaposition of 16:13–20 and 16:21–23 is one of dramatic dominance, both positive and negative. As Brown, Donfried, and Reumann observe, "It is significant that, despite the way Matthew has magnified Peter in the special material he has inserted into the Marcan scene of Peter's confession, he has also kept and indeed heightened the rebuke of Peter at the end of the scene."[38] Peter is dominant both in his confession, blessing, and commissioning as well as in his challenging rebuke of Jesus's discourse on loss, both his own and that of the disciples.

What does this mean for Peter's masculinity? Meeting the expectations for divine service is an important part of masculine status in the ancient world dominated by Roman imperial thought. However, Roman imperial concepts of divinity did not generally include loss, suffering, and crucifixion as indicative of the divine. Rather, men proved their connection with the divine in order to appropriate the associated power, status, and virtue and establish masculine status.[39] With Jesus's predictions of his own suffering and death, and the expectation that his disciples will experience the same, the Gospel interrupts an automatic association between divinity and power.

That being said, those associations are not necessarily automatic or universal. Within this same section predicting loss and death, 16:21 and 16:27–28 also emphasize resurrection and parousia. If the result of Jesus's suffering and that of his disciples is divine reward, then this potentially undercuts the import of the suffering and reifies notions of power. And ancient imperial thought on masculinity considered noble death and courage in suffering to be potential demonstrations of masculine power and identity.[40] Someone who then refuses courageous service, even if it involves suffering, is not masculine. It is difficult in the ancient world to separate ideas about the divine from other ideas of life. So, if noble death and courage are part of ancient masculinity, then they may also be related to notions of divinity. If so, then the relationship among divinity, power, and suffering is far from clear-cut.

While acknowledging these nuances, I contend that the emphasis on loss with regard to Jesus and the disciples makes a significant statement that is distinct from other ancient discourse. Peter's resistance to Jesus's prediction in 16:21 suggest that Peter does not see Jesus's suffering and death as something that will enhance Jesus's status, but something to be avoided. And Jesus's response in verse 23 that Peter's resistance is rooted in human concerns reinforces the idea that what Jesus is expecting from himself and his disciples is different from what other perspectives would expect. I continue to explore these issues in other sections of this chapter. At present, I highlight the dissonance in order to argue that the tension between masculinity and discipleship is helpful in understanding Peter's contradictory behavior in these two juxtaposed scenes. The tension created by contradictory expectations is an important part of the depiction of Peter's discipleship and contributes to the overall ambivalence in Peter's masculinity in Matthew.

Despite the conflict between Peter and Jesus in 16:21–23, six days later Jesus takes Peter along for the Transfiguration (17:1–8). He is neither rejected nor shamed by Jesus, but rather included in a select group along with James and John; Peter's brother Andrew is not included. This scene repeats some of the themes of dominance and prominence already highlighted, including a close connection to Jesus and being set apart from the disciples.[41] It also contains familiar ambivalence in terms of Peter's (non)understanding of and commitment to discipleship. Nevertheless, Peter's dominance in divine service here remains a consistent expression of his masculinity.

To this consistent expression of dominance, this story adds a dimension of divine access that Peter has not experienced before. The disciples as a whole have seen Jesus perform healings, do acts of power, and walk on water. But, in the Transfiguration, not only is Jesus changed in appearance into something they have never seen, he is joined by Moses and Elijah, the two most prominent leaders in their religious tradition.[42] The story not only links Jesus to these heroes of faith, but Peter, James, and John have the privilege of witnessing the connection.

It is presumably Peter's knowledge of the importance of this connection that prompts him to suggest in verse 4 that he could make three dwellings (σκηνάς) for them. Matthew does not include Mark's aside that Peter makes this suggestion out of fear and not knowing what to say (Mark 9:6); the omission leaves Peter's motives up for discussion.[43] However, despite the inappropriateness of Peter's suggestion, he does understand that Jesus is to be treated in the same way as Moses and Elijah.

God's voice interrupts the scene to clarify Jesus's identity and role. Recalling Matthew 3:17, the voice identifies Jesus as God's beloved Son and exhorts the hearers to listen to him.[44] This statement asserts divine status and demands divine service; not only does it solidify the connection between God and Jesus, but it pulls the three disciples present directly into the conversation. The scene is thoroughly marked by the assertion of divine masculine status, from the presence of the heroes to the father/son dynamic. The disciples respond to God by falling to the ground to worship (v. 6), conveying again the power of the divine encounter from their perspective.

Here, after the voice, is where Matthew mentions fear (ἐφοβήθησαν σφόδρα) and it is experienced by all of them, not just Peter. In the presence of divine masculine power, the disciples are put in their place.[45] In this case, fear may be appropriate in relation to the overwhelming divine presence, indicating an awareness of divine service. The goal of the fear appears to be further action as disciples. In verse 7, Jesus tells them not to be afraid and to get up, meaning that they do not have to take a prostrate position and hide their faces. The next section continues with more discussion on the nature of divine service.

On the whole, this scene argues for Peter's dominance in divine service in a way that is consistent with the other texts I have addressed. He not only sees Moses and Elijah in the company of his own Lord, he hears the voice of God addressing him. The presence of the other two disciples limits Peter's prominence somewhat; he is not the only disciple to witness this display of divine power. But his confidence in speaking out in such auspicious company and unusual circumstances again sets him apart and above the others.

The divine interruption telling the disciples to listen to Jesus is potentially important given Peter's either inability or unwillingness to listen to Jesus's prediction of his death in the previous chapter. Still, Peter is included in the gathering, so the assumption is that he *can* listen to Jesus, even if he hasn't shown that ability or desire yet. And Matthew refrains from explaining Peter's actions with fear, leaving room for a potentially more positive construction of his request. Jesus's reassurance in verse 7 tells the disciples that they do not have to be afraid, even in the presence of the voice of God.

Peter's presence here remains relatively dominant, even in a context where divine power is on display. Although he makes a potential misstep in suggesting the dwellings, Peter's presence in the inner circle, and his willingness and ability to speak in the presence of Moses and Elijah, point to his continued dominance as a disciple. Within the larger context of Matthew, this is significant. Given the conflict with Jesus portrayed in the previous section, 16:21–23, it is striking that Peter's status has not been compromised. While there may be challenges or difficulties, Peter is still the dominant disciple in the emerging mission of Jesus.

After a healing story and another passion prediction, Peter appears again in 17:24–27, a brief story about paying tax.[46] I address other aspects of this story, specifically power and wealth, in more detail in the next sections of this chapter. In terms of discipleship dominance, this story is unique in that people outside the movement come to Peter as a spokesperson for Jesus, asking for clarification on Jesus's practices with respect to the tax. In verse 25, Peter answers in the affirmative. The text indicates no hesitation on Peter's part. In these verses, others treat Peter as a spokesperson not just for the other disciples but for Jesus, and he accepts the role.

Jesus brings up the issue with Peter after returning home (17:25b–27). While there may be an element of rebuke or correction in this exchange, most scholars see explanation or instruction.[47] I find this convincing because while Jesus explores the nuances of the act of paying taxes with Peter, he ultimately does not disagree with Peter's first answer. There is no language of rebuke here. Even if the disciples are building a reputation in Matthew for showing a lack of full understanding of Jesus's mission, Peter is worth teaching and capable of accurate perception. Here, as before, Peter remains the most prominent of the disciples, and the only one who is engaged by Jesus in exploring the details and implications of this form of divine service.

A further example of this exploration is the next text involving Peter, 18:21–35, which focuses on forgiveness. This section continues Peter's role as prominent disciple and arbiter of forgiveness presented in chapter 16, and now expands that conversation to include forgiveness in community. 18:15–17 sets the stage with Jesus's teaching about how to resolve conflicts among members of the community. In verses 18–20, Jesus continues with a further commissioning of the disciples that echoes the commissioning given to Peter in 16:19.

After Jesus finishes, Peter, not any of the other disciples, asks in verse 21 how often he should forgive a member of the community. His suggestion is seven times, which is generally interpreted by scholars to be a generous number.[48] Jesus's response, however, is far more than seven; while some traditions have translated this seventy times seven, others prefer seventy-seven times.[49] In either case, it is far more than seven, and can be understood to imply limitlessness.[50]

Taken as a whole, this text is rather mixed in its portrayal of Peter's divine service understood as dominance in discipleship. Peter initially appears to grasp the importance of forgiveness for the community, but seriously underestimates how often it should be used. As Syreeni observes, "Obviously Peter himself thinks he is liberal enough, but again his judgment is premature."[51] Of course, if Peter thinks he is being generous in his original suggestion, then perhaps this text extends the theme from 16:17 that such an expansive understanding is not possible for any human without divine revelation. The repetition of the "binding and loosing" language from 16:19 in 18:18 can be seen as evening the playing field between Peter and the other disciples; a commission that was originally given first and only to Peter is now extended to the rest. However, immediately afterward, Peter again asserts his singular role as dominant spokesperson.

The content of the commission also has a mixed assessment of Peter's divine service. Forgiveness is a critical function of divine service, containing the power to release people from divine judgment or place it upon them. If the disciples are given the responsibility of forgiveness, then Peter's role as their spokesperson gives him significant status. However, he is told specifically how to carry out this task, including a command essentially not to withhold it. This command not only subjugates Peter, it also mitigates the power associated with this responsibility, further limiting Peter's power.

The subsequent parable (18:23–35) further complicates the picture. Although the phrase "for this reason" (διπὰ τοῦτο) ostensibly connects the two sections, Carter observes that "while these verses exhort repeated forgiveness, the parable does not."[52] Instead, this parable introduces an element of threat and considerable limits on forgiveness into the discussion, as the king reneges on forgiveness originally offered. Comparing the king with

God, as the connective phrase suggests, portrays God not as a benevolent ruler, but an unforgiving tyrant.[53] What does this mean for Peter as a disciple responsible for forgiveness? Verse 35 in particular seems to imply that if he and the other disciples do not forgive as Jesus commands, there will be divine consequences.[54] Peter remains the dominant disciple, tasked with important roles in divine service, but the overall picture of masculine power expressed in divinity is problematic and Peter's true power and status uncertain.

The final appearance of Peter before the entry into Jerusalem comes in 19:27. After the story about the rich young man in 19:16–22, Jesus comments to the disciples in 19:23–26 how difficult it will be for the wealthy to enter the empire of heaven. Performing his dominance, Peter, and not any of the other disciples, replies in verse 27 with a question: "Look, we have left everything and followed you. What then will we have?" (ἰδοὺ ἡμεῖς ἀφήκαμεν πάντα καὶ ἠκολουθήσαμέν σοι. τί ἄραἔσται ἡμῖν;). Jesus's reply to Peter in verse 28 indicates divine reward for those disciples who have done what Peter said, including sitting on thrones (ἐπὶ θρόνου) to execute judgment (κρίνω) over the twelve tribes of Israel. Verse 29 expands the reward circle to include all who have followed Jesus; the promise is made that they will receive "a hundredfold" (ἑκατονταπλαςίονα) as well as eternal life (ζωὴν ἔσψατοι). The last verse in this section, however, contains what sounds like a warning as Jesus tells them that the first will be last and the last will be first.

Peter's claim to divine service is certainly bolstered by this promise of reward, what Luz describes as "an incredible exaltation that is out of all proportion to their present sacrifice."[55] Jesus's response in verses 28–29 indicates divine approval for their choices and their behavior. In this respect, Peter has met the exacting demands of discipleship, and will be honored along with the other disciples by God for his sacrifice. There is also a sense of divine investment in and commitment to their well-being in the future, a promise of eschatological abundance, even if they now sacrifice the comforts of life. It is a strong endorsement of the disciples, with Peter as always their dominant spokesperson.

This strong endorsement is unsettled by the final theme of reversal in verse 30. It is unclear whether this verse is meant to question the certainty of the divine reward or merely to discourage complacency.[56] The subsequent parable (20:1–16), which ends with a similar statement about the first and the last (20:16), seems to suggest that the reward is intact. The difficulty comes when the ones called first feel slighted when the latecomers are treated equally (20:10–12).

But the ambiguity of the warning seems intentional, raising the possibility that "if the twelve are examples of the last becoming first, they need beware, lest they likewise become examples of the first becoming last."[57] For Peter, the one who was literally named "first," the prospect cannot be dismissed quickly. Even when the demands of discipleship are met, the bar is then continually raised. These complex nuances of discipleship continue to infuse instability into Peter's characterization as a dominant disciple, problematizing his masculinity expressed in divine service.

As the narrative turns to the arrest, crucifixion, and resurrection of Jesus, Peter's prominence continues, and the tension around his discipleship intensifies. At the end of the meal Jesus shares with the disciples, Jesus predicts that they will all desert him. (26:31). In a familiar pattern, it is Peter who responds to Jesus. In this case, he speaks in the first person (ἐγὼ οὐδέποτε σκανδαλισθήσομαι), contradicting Jesus.[58] He contrasts himself with the others, at some level personally setting himself apart.[59] Peter is clearly asserting dominance; Davies and Allison—perhaps recognizing the masculinity on display—go so far as to say that he is "crowing like a proud cock."[60]

In addition to his behavior, the content of his claim makes a very strong statement. As in chapter 16, he argues with Jesus's prediction, but this time he strongly and emphatically asserts his faithful discipleship, embracing the kind of loyalty he rejected in chapter 16. The verb used in 26:33 (σκανδαλισθήσομαι) is related to the noun that Jesus uses when rebuking Peter in 16:23 (σκάνδαλον). Peter claims he will not be what Jesus earlier called him; instead, Luz says, "Peter now appears to have learned his lesson. He is ready to die with Jesus."[61] After Jesus intensifies the prediction, personalizing the denial and adding detail specific to Peter, Peter doubles down, replying again in verse 35 with another protest. Here the word choice, the negated "deny" (ἀπαρνήσομαι) recalls 16:24, where Jesus exhorts the disciples to deny (ἀπαρνησάσθω) themselves in following him. Peter will not deny Jesus, he will deny himself as Jesus as taught him to do.

At the end of verse 35, Peter extends his commitment even unto death, a statement that is echoed by all the followers. This scene begins and ends with the larger group, and Peter's dominance is asserted in between. Luz observes that Peter's "self-inflating words . . . are not the exception; the others speak the same way."[62] But even if they all share in the arrogance or eagerness, it is Peter who asserts dominance by making the claim first and in the first person, and Peter who receives the personal prediction of denial by Jesus. He is the dominant disciple, whether positively or negatively.[63]

Given the previous contradictions in Peter's expressions of discipleship, in the course of the narrative this scene has the potential to be a definitive statement. Perhaps Peter has finally "gotten it," accepting the realities of discipleship and committing himself to following Jesus, even when it means great personal loss. On the other hand, Peter has never lacked for initial zeal or enthusiasm, even as he has remained limited in understanding and in follow-through, so perhaps this sets up another cycle of disappointment.

As the action unfolds, it is the latter that comes true. The repeated pattern of zeal and failure heightens the disappointment in what immediately follows.[64]

In the very next scene, Jesus takes Peter, James and John, along with him, separating them from the larger group (26:36–37). The group is the same as in 17:1–9, but this time they go to Gethsemane.[65] Jesus goes on further alone, leaving the trio together, so he can pray. By the time he gets back in verse 40, they are sleeping. Peter's dominance is again assumed in that Jesus addresses him in verses 40–41, chiding them for sleeping and calling them to remain awake to avoid "the time of trial" (πειρασμόν). The contrast between Jesus's grieving prayer and Peter's slumber could not be more striking. After just claiming he would follow Jesus to the death, he does not even stay awake long enough to keep vigil. The two sons of Zebedee are ignored.

The pattern repeats two more times. The second time Jesus returns after praying, he finds them asleep, but he does not speak to them (v. 43). The third time he speaks to the group, not just to Peter (v. 45). At this point, they have not only failed to keep Jesus company during serious spiritual distress, they have failed to notice that the arresting party has arrived. A few chapters earlier in Matthew, Jesus encourages the disciples to keep awake (24:42–44; 25:1–13). The emphasis in these parables is awareness as much as being awake.[66] Further, this lack of awareness is translated into a lack of obedience; Luz describes the sleep of the foolish bridesmaids in 25:5 as that of those who "do not obey the Lord and his command."[67] In this text, Peter and the other two disciples are neither awake nor aware.

Jesus's direct address to Peter in 26:40 also underscores the moral implications of falling asleep, as he exhorts Peter to stay awake in order that he might not fall into the hour of trial. A sleeping disciple is vulnerable to doubting God's "plans, goodness, faithfulness, and ability" and prone instead to despair.[68] While all three are guilty of this lack of faith, Peter is the one singled out by Jesus, just as he has been singled out throughout the Gospel. His inability to stay awake and aware is amplified, both by Jesus's question and by his own strong statements in the previous scene.

After Jesus is arrested, 26:58 says that Peter followed him "at a distance" (ἀπὸ μακρόθεν) and stopped in the courtyard of the high priest, waiting "to see how this would end" (ἰδεῖν τὸ τέλος).[69] Peter's action here is ambiguous.[70] He is truly singled out, no other disciple is described as following this far. He intends to stay until he knows Jesus's fate. And yet, he did not give his life in the confrontation at the garden; instead, Matthew says that "all the disciples" (τότε οἱ μαθηταί) abandoned Jesus (26:56). And when he does follow, he does so at a distance and stops short of following Jesus all the way into the hall, waiting outside. Peter remains both dominant and ambiguous.

This lingering ambiguous tension concerning Peter's discipleship reaches a climax in 26:69–75. Here, after vacillating between earnest desire to follow

Jesus and incomplete understanding, acceptance, and performance of the expectations of discipleship, Peter's last named appearance in the Gospel is his repeated denial of Jesus and his subsequent grief. He is identified by two different servant-girls and then a group of bystanders as a follower of Jesus; all three times he denies it. The final time he even swears an oath (26:74), contradicting Jesus's teaching in 5:33–37. Following the third denial, the cock's crow reminds Peter of Jesus words earlier in 26:34. He leaves the courtyard, the place where he had been waiting to see what would happen to Jesus, and weeps bitterly (26:75). This is the last time Peter is mentioned by name in the Gospel.

The word for Peter's denial in 26:70, 72, ἠρνήσατο, is used elsewhere in the Gospel; these previous statements about denial indicate the severity of Peter's actions. First, it is related to the word used in Jesus's prediction of the disciples' abandonment (ἀπαρνήσῃ), including Peter's own protest in 26:34–35. In addition, the same word (ἀρνήσηταί) is mentioned by Jesus in 10:32–33 in the context of teaching about persecution. The temptation is to fear earthly power, but Jesus tells his disciples instead to fear divine power (10:28), because those who deny Jesus will be denied by Jesus before the Father (10:33). Finally, in his discourse on discipleship (16:24–28), he instructs the disciples to deny (ἀπαρνηςάσθω) themselves and follow him (16:24).

The use of the same word in 26:69–75, as well as its repetition within this section, drives home the point. Peter has done what Jesus has repeatedly warned against. He has done the opposite of what disciples are supposed to do. The implications of this denial vary from interpreter to interpreter. For some, the severity of Peter's denial is enough to speak of his divine condemnation.[71] For most, it is a clear indicator of Peter's abandonment of discipleship.[72]

Peter's bitter weeping in verse 75 indicates that he grasps the severity of his choices. Most interpreters use this verse to argue for Peter's redemption, or indicate remorse.[73] But in terms of Peter's masculine dominance, his bitter tears are consonant with the multifaceted sketch of Peter's divine service in discipleship. Throughout the Gospel, he has remained the most dominant disciple both positively and negatively, his dominance only emphasizing the inherent contrast in his character. Verse 75 continues this characterization, highlighting the instability inherent in Peter's masculinity expressed in divine service. I will discuss another aspect of Peter's weeping that affects masculinity, namely the connection to passions, in the subsequent section on control.

Indeed, Peter's dominance has played an important part not only in the construction of Peter's character but in the narrative of the entire Gospel. This makes his disappearance after 26:75 all the more striking. The only remaining scene where Peter is assumed to be present is at the very end in 28:16–20. Here, "the eleven" do as Jesus requests and return to Galilee. Since Judas is gone, this includes Peter. But Peter is not named, the group is addressed as one, and there is no response from a spokesperson. Peter is no longer the dominant disciple.

What does this mean? Some interpreters simply assume Peter's place is restored and the omission is insignificant. Others have suggested that the choice is intentional and may reflect Peter's compromised status as a disciple or even that he might be among the doubters referenced in 28:17.[74] Or, given his personal commission in 16:17–19, perhaps there is no need to draw attention to Peter here. From the perspective of masculinity, the omission is striking because it signals a change in the dominant status that Peter has asserted and enjoyed throughout the narrative.

Perhaps this indicates that Peter has finally accepted what it means to be a disciple in terms of the loss of status required to truly follow Jesus. Or, perhaps he and the other disciples have finally understood what Jesus's mission was about and do not require any more clarification or training, which was part of Peter's role as spokesperson.[75] In either case, Peter's expression of masculinity has changed; he is no longer defined in terms of dominance in divine service. While he may now be a true disciple, his divine service is no longer expressed in a way that conveys masculine dominance.

Thus far in this chapter, I have traced the texts where Peter is involved in order to argue that Peter's masculinity in terms of divine service is constructed on his identity as a dominant disciple. I have established Peter's dominance as a disciple in terms of his "firstness," his role as a spokesperson, his unique relationship with Jesus, and his eagerness to follow. I have also noted the areas of tension and friction in this characterization where Peter's prominence and discipleship are at odds (including his rebuke in 16, his denial of Jesus in 26, and the loss of his prominence in 28), suggesting that this tension reveals a fundamental conflict between masculinity and discipleship.

I want to suggest further that this fundamental conflict speaks to a potential redefinition of masculinity in the Gospel in terms of divine service. A continued emphasis on domination and power, despite language about discipleship and loss, suggests that some element of power remains central to the understanding of discipleship. They key to obtaining it is not acquiring divine power, but loyalty and submission to Jesus. In addition to the texts already cited in this chapter, Jesus's words in 12:46–50 speak of a reconstituted household constructed around obedience to Jesus. Submission to Jesus through discipleship brings the great privilege of being in this household.[76] I contend that the Gospel is redefining masculinity in terms of the patriarchal dividend, whereby the good man aligns with Jesus in submission and obedience, and that this good choice will be rewarded eventually with power and status.

With these ideas in mind, I next move to the other two categories of masculinity, control and wealth, filling in this picture of Peter's masculinity and further identifying examples of this fundamental conflict with discipleship and potential redefinition of masculinity.

DOMINATING CONTROL OVER SELF AND OVER OTHERS

I turn now to the concept of dominating control over self and over others, integral parts of masculine status. For ancient masculinity, control over passions demonstrates self-mastery while preservation of one's body from outside attack establishes status. Control over others through speech and action extends one's sphere of power. In this section, I argue that control over self and over others is an important part of Peter's role as a dominant disciple, but one that is also marked by ambiguity and conflicting expectations.

Peter enhances his status through behaviors like public speech and forgiveness of others. At the same time, his control over both himself and others is limited in some important ways: he falls asleep in the garden, nearly drowns, exhibits passions that are extreme, is rebuked by Jesus and interrupted by the voice of the divine, and is publicly revealed to be Jesus's disciple by those in the courtyard only to deny it. Further, the expectations of discipleship outlined by Jesus involve a loss of control, obedience, and submission, creating a difficult paradox. Some of Peter's behaviors to preserve his own body or exert control over others, which are traditional expectations of masculinity, now limit his faithful performance of submissive discipleship. And, vice versa, his attempts to follow Jesus require him to relinquish control over himself and others.

As outlined in the first section, Peter's primacy and "firstness" are an important part of his dominance as a disciple. His prominence sets up an expectation of control over others. From the very beginning, however, this control is ambiguous.[77] For example, in the fishing scene in Matthew 4:18–22, Jesus's call both gives Peter more control and also causes him to submit to another male. Jesus becomes the hegemonic male, and Peter transfers his skills to something called "fishing for people."[78] The implication of this calling is that Peter has power over others' eschatological destiny as well as how they spend their days. However, in order to do this, he paradoxically gives up his own means of providing for himself and his family, and becomes a disciple, someone who lives under the instruction and control of another.

The power of Peter's master, Jesus, is emphasized in 8:14–15, when he heals Peter's mother-in-law. The location of the story in a series of healing narratives emphasizes Jesus's power over physical illness. Luz calls this "a pure Jesus story," where Peter's role is almost incidental and "the only thing that matters is Jesus's deed."[79] Carter points out that the woman's response of service is meant to "denote a life of doing the will of God."[80] While she is not explicitly identified as a disciple, her action reiterates Jesus's power and that service and obedience are the proper response to it (cf 12:46–50). This is the life to which Peter has been called. So, while Peter may exercise some power over others in his new calling, the focus is on Jesus's power.

Verses 28–31 of chapter 14 illustrate the same combination of forces. After witnessing Jesus walk on the water, Peter asks to walk on the water himself, a request that Carter calls "submissive yet daring."[81] At Jesus's command, Peter is able to walk on the sea, demonstrating significant power and performing a physical act that sets him apart from others. This act, though, is not attributed to Peter's power, but focused on Jesus's power to make Peter's walk possible.[82] It is Peter's personal weakness, not strength, that is highlighted in the story as his doubt and fear cause him to sink, requiring Jesus to rescue him.[83] From the perspective of ancient imperial masculinity, this is a complex scene. Peter's ability to walk on water puts him in divine company. However, proximity to the divine should enhance power, not diminish it. And yet, here, proximity to Jesus and the performance of powerful acts elevates Jesus and puts Peter in danger.

Also, given the emphasis on preservation of life and limb that accompanies masculinity, Peter's attempts to save his own life make some sort of sense; protecting his body is a logical and important part of masculinity. This scene is not about the kind of "noble death" that I previously noted which Conway points out can enhance masculinity. Rather, what is operative here for me is Traister's work on protecting the body from violation or damage.[84] Masculine status affords the privilege of protecting or defending the body. Here, Peter's desire to follow Jesus jeopardizes his body.

Yet, from the perspective of discipleship, this reaction of self-preservation is cause for criticism (v. 31) as his panic over his physical safety overcomes his trust in Jesus. The emerging message of the Gospel is that relinquishing safety and self-protection is necessary for true discipleship. In other words, becoming a disciple means giving control over one's body to Jesus, which diminishes masculinity.

This tension finds particular focus in Peter's response to Jesus's prediction of his suffering and death in 16:21–23. Having received a blessing and commission from Jesus, Peter now rebukes Jesus's teaching about his fate.[85] Immediately, however, he is strongly rebuked in return. If Peter's rebuke is an attempt to assert status, then Jesus's response thwarts that attempt. Further, because of the content of Jesus's rebuke, Peter's challenge is not evidence of his strength, but "showing the kind of weakness that will lead him to deny Jesus."[86] In verse 23, Jesus accuses Peter of having his mind not on divine things but on human things (οὐ φρονεῖς τὰ τοῦ θεοῦ ἀλλὰ τὰ τῶν ἀνθρώπων). What are the human things Peter is considering? He rejects the idea of Jesus suffering and dying, experiencing physical violation and loss of control over his body and his life. Peter exerts his own power in order to resist this loss, but his assertion is associated with weakness and humanity, rather than divine power.

In his rebuke of Peter, Jesus doubles down, extending the loss of physical control and jeopardized bodies beyond himself to the disciples. Now it is Peter's loss that is described. 16:24–25 speaks of denying oneself, taking on suffering, and dying. To be a disciple means Peter will die as Jesus does, and will live as Jesus does, which Carter describes as "a call to a life of marginalization, to identify with the nobodies like slaves, foreigners, criminals, and those understood to be cursed by God."[87] Part of Peter's limitation in terms of discipleship is his focus on the "human things" of bodily safety and expressing physical control over self. Here, the Gospel advocates for loss of physical control, living and dying as the marginalized do, in order to embody discipleship.

From the perspective of Peter's masculinity, this is difficult and confusing. On the one hand, fulfilling the expectations of discipleship is essential for a figure whose masculinity is constructed as the dominant disciple. On the other, fulfillment of these expectations means sacrificing another essential element of masculinity, control over self and protection of one's body. While Peter's masculinity is enhanced by his relative status over others and his unique status with respect to Jesus, this status is compromised by his lack of understanding of the divine work being done in Jesus, and his inability and/or unwillingness to sacrifice his own body.

Peter's exchange with Jesus in this scene also points to the larger dynamic of public speech as a marker of ancient masculinity in the Gospel's presentation of Peter's power over self and others. As argued in chapter 3, free public speech is the prerogative of males, so Peter's speaking role is an important aspect of his dominance. Peter is the disciple who feels free to speak for himself, even in dramatic moments; he talks to Jesus both at the Transfiguration (17:1–9), and while walking on the water (14:22–33). In addition, as argued in the previous section, there are several scenes where Peter asks questions on behalf of the group or representing the group (15:15, 17:24–27, 18:21, 19:27). Speaking for others is accomplished masculinity.

As noted above, however, Peter's conversations with Jesus both contribute to and compromise his masculinity. His confidence at being able to speak to Jesus in all circumstances speaks to his status. He feels free even to argue with Jesus, in both 16:21–23 and 26:31–35. That being said, Peter never wins an argument with Jesus, and often speaks inappropriately or errantly. Jesus is the master and Peter the disciple. While Peter is permitted to speak on behalf of the group, even in public (17:24–27), Jesus always maintains superior status to Peter.

The Transfiguration story in 17:1–9 provides a further example of these power dynamics at work. With the rebuke still fresh in the narrative, Jesus takes Peter along with James and John to the mountain.[88] Peter tries to take action in verse 4, offering to build booths for Jesus, Moses, and Elijah. It is striking that Peter thinks that something needs to be done, and that he thinks he is the one to do it.[89] This reinforces the assumptions about both Peter's authority and his public speech. In this story, Jesus does not rebuke him, but "God talks Peter down."[90] Interrupting Peter, the divine voice in verse 5 urges neither speech nor action, but listening. This command points again to Jesus's words just prior that characterize discipleship in terms of loss of status, bodily sacrifice, and death. Active masculine behavior is replaced by acts of discipleship, putting the two in conflict once again.

Peter's next scene in 17:24–27 approaches the tension of control over self and others from a slightly different perspective. Peter is again the spokesperson, but this time not just for the disciples but also for Jesus in the company of outsiders who ask about Jesus's tax-paying habits.[91] His public speech supports the construction of Peter's masculinity as dominant over self and others, but that is not the point of the text. Indeed, verse 25 emphasizes Jesus's power, not Peter's, as Jesus knew about Peter's response even though he wasn't there.[92]

Instead, Peter's positive response to the question of paying the tax becomes part of a larger lesson by Jesus. Jesus does not rebuke or correct Peter, but the emphasis on Jesus's authority continues as he instructs Peter, expanding his understanding of the power dynamics inherent in the act of paying tax. Jesus simultaneously argues for acquiescence and for resistance to Roman rule, recognizing that the power of the "kings of the earth" is inevitable, but that all things originate with God. In this way, he redefines the significance of the tax. The implication of Jesus's teaching resonates with the larger statement of the Gospel about Peter's compromised status; as a non-elite male under Roman rule, his control over self and others is relative and tactical.

A final set of examples of gendered speech where Peter's status is at stake are the accusations that prompt his denial. Here, Peter's public speech is reactive and defensive, and causes him to reject his identity as a disciple. He is forced into this speech by not one, but two, women in the courtyard. It is their public speech that brings him to deny Jesus. From the standpoint of masculinity, it is significant that two women who are slaves exhibit control over him in those moments.[93] Not only do they force him to make a choice between his body/life and Jesus, they do it by public speech, a masculine act. Peter is emasculated by their words, and then further emasculates himself by denying Jesus.

Another element of control over others that shapes Peter's masculinity is the control Peter and the other disciples have over forgiveness. In Jesus's commissioning of Peter in 16:19, Peter is given proverbial keys by Jesus. While there is some discussion among interpreters about the exact meaning of the keys, they clearly symbolize power.[94] The second half of the verse appears to associate that power with the interpretation of the law and judging its adherence.[95] For a Gospel focused on a radical understanding of discipleship in light of the empire of heaven, this is important power with significant consequences. This same phrase about binding and loosing is later used with the larger group of disciples in 18:18, giving them the same authority. But it begins with Peter in 16:19, and the first part of the verse concerning the keys to the empire is unique to Peter.

The authority of Peter and the disciples over judgment and the interpretation of the law is echoed in the later conversation about forgiveness in 18:15–35. This discussion, however, complexifies the association of forgiveness with power, both in terms of the use of forgiveness and in terms of the use of force. Peter's question about the extent of forgiveness in 18:21 assumes that forgiveness is his right and responsibility. Jesus does not argue that point, but in 18:22 he clearly pushes Peter beyond his assumptions about how to use that power, suggesting that the power of forgiveness is meant to be given away, not retained.

Immediately after, Jesus tells the story of the unforgiving servant, which is full of troubling elements. Although the context is forgiveness, physical control and safety are the themes as the unforgiving servant tries to use his power over his debtor to extract payment and is then subject to the power of the king. There are references to physical dominance, bodily force, and punishment. In 18:25, the king orders the slave and his family to be sold, reducing their bodies to property and taking away their control over their own fates. In response, the slave falls to his knees in a submissive physical posture, communicating the dominant power of the king. In his subsequent interaction with his fellow debtor slave in verse 28, the unforgiving slave seizes the other by the throat (κρατήσας αὐτὸν ἔπνιγεν). And, in 18:34, the unforgiving servant is imprisoned and tortured (βασανισταῖς), both limiting his movements and violating his body.

The explicit identification of the king with God in verse 35 amplifies the unease, associating God with destructive assertions of power in the form of slavery, imprisonment, and torture. This is especially unsettling within the context of teaching about forgiveness. Forgiveness becomes a threat rather than a comforting promise, for "God will act as a tyrant king if God's will to extend forgiveness is not done."[96] While elsewhere in the Gospel, God is contrasted with the ways of empire, here the power is in the comparison. In this parable, the Gospel does not challenge, but rather perpetuates, the association of violence and physical control with masculinity and with divinity.

The implications for the disciples in terms of their authority over forgiveness are problematic. Do the disciples really have control over forgiveness if their incentive is to avoid punishment from someone else? Then again, if the forgiveness of the king is so easily reversed by the actions of the slave, then that suggests a different kind of power. If Jesus's response to Peter in verse 22 endorses extravagant forgiveness, the subsequent parable reinforces the role of physical control in relationships both among humans and with God.

The discussion in 19:27–30 continues the theme of control over others. In response to Peter's question about rewards for having left everything, Jesus promises the disciples that they will sit on twelve thrones, judging the twelve tribes of Israel (19:28).[97] This striking image of power expressed in thrones and judgment takes place not in this life, but "at the renewal of all things" (ἐν τῇ παλιγγενεςίᾳ) and presumably continues without end. There is a reward for having sacrificed earthly possessions, and it is power and dominating rule over others.[98] Here, forgiveness is not emphasized, but judgment. This reifies the connection between masculinity and control over others, even in the empire of heaven, and reassures Peter and the others about their masculinity, despite their current sacrifice of control.

Then, as the section closes, Jesus issues the warning about the first and the last (v. 30), leaving the previous expression of control and structure again unsettled. Does this verse undercut the promise of power expressed in verse 28? Or does it merely admonish the hearers not to take it for granted? Jesus's next parable in 20:1–16 about the laborers in the vineyard reinforces God's power to give equal reward to those to arrive late and to those who arrive early. This indicates that the promise of control is valid, but that God distributes the control in unexpected ways. This reminds the disciples and Peter, the original questioner, that their control over others is not ultimate, and may not be exclusive.

Taken as a whole, these passages seem to suggest that while Peter and the rest of the disciples have significant control, including the responsibility of forgiveness, they are subject to the control of God, so are to use it according to God's direction and not to take it for granted. So, the power of judgment and forgiveness does enhance Peter's masculinity to an extent, but additional power dynamics limit his authority and emphasize that he is subject to the control of God, who is described as a hegemonic male. This tensive positionality of Peter's discipleship resonates with the larger themes of discipleship in the Gospel as a whole.

A final aspect of Peter's masculinity as expressed in control over self and over others is the depiction of his passion and exuberance. Conway's work outlines the expectation of control over one's passion as an expression of hegemonic masculinity, and the presence of passions that are out of control as evidence of compromised masculinity.[99] Throughout the Gospel, Peter is described as having strong emotions and enthusiastic reactions. While his enthusiasm can sometimes be understood to be a positive aspect of his discipleship, at other times his lack of control is the cause of his failure as a disciple. Overall, Peter's characteristic exuberance endangers his masculinity as well as his discipleship.

An early instance of this lack of control is found in 14:22–33. While Peter's eagerness to walk on the water like Jesus can be construed as boldness or trust, his rapid shift to sinking and cries for help suggest that there is also an element of recklessness or lack of control present. Specifically, verse 30 attributes Peter's sinking to his fear, which he is not able to overcome on his own. Rather, it overtakes him, and he cries out to be saved. Jesus's response in verse 31 chastises Peter for giving into his fear rather than trusting in Jesus.

The next example comes from the critical encounter with Jesus in chapter 16. After receiving the privilege and responsibility of Jesus's commissioning in 16:16–19, and continuing to describe the expectations of discipleship, Peter responds by rebuking Jesus in 16:22. Whether this rebuke shows a lack of acceptance of Jesus's mission or a challenge to Jesus's masculine status, it reveals a man overcome by his emotions who cannot help but blurt out a response.[100] This emotionally inappropriate response is repeated in the next scene, when in 17:4, Peter pipes up and offers to make dwellings for Moses, Elijah, and Jesus during the Transfiguration. The scene is described in dramatic terms, with heroes of the faith in conversation with one another. That Peter's suggestion is an emotional outburst is supported by verse 5, when the divine voice interrupts him and urges listening rather than speaking.

Peter's appearances in the story of Jesus's arrest, crucifixion, and resurrection also include some important references to the lack of control over his passions which relate directly to his failure as a disciple. The first of these comes in 26:36–46, when Peter is unable to stay awake in the garden. In verse 40, when Jesus returns from praying, he speaks specifically to Peter, criticizing him for not being able to stay awake. He is not able to control himself enough to keep vigil with a suffering Jesus. This foreshadows what will later take place when Peter is not able to keep vigil in the courtyard during Jesus's trial like he intends (v. 58). This physical weakness of falling asleep is emphasized in Jesus's words in verse 41, as he tells Peter that while his spirit may be willing, the flesh is weak. Jesus here critiques Peter's actions as unequal to his desire, but there is also an inherent critique of Peter's outsized passion.

Peter's lack of control over passions in the Passion Narrative also plays a role in the juxtaposition of 26:31–35 and 26:69–75. In the former scene, Jesus predicts Peter's denial, which Peter vehemently rejects. In verse 33 he says he will not desert Jesus; in verse 35 he says he is even willing to die for Jesus. Both of these show that Peter understands the expectation of discipleship, at least in theory, as well as showing his tendency to hastily blurt out his intentions. With both the prediction and his protest in mind, and after initially following Jesus at a distance, Peter then does exactly as Jesus says he will do in vv. 69–75. His denials build in intensity, culminating in him swearing an oath in verse 74. Peter's lack of control over his fear results in his denial of Jesus, and his failure as a disciple. The contrast is all the more striking given his exuberant claims made to Jesus in 26:33–35. Again, there is a gap between Peter's passionate declaration and his inability to act in concert with his claims.

Peter's immediate weeping in verse 75 upon hearing the cock crow signals that he, too, recognizes this failure. Weeping itself is extreme, showing another aspect of lack of control over passions.[101] From a discipleship standpoint, Peter's weeping has been understood by many as repentance and an opportunity for redemption. But even in this understanding, the goal is not to point to Peter at all, but to emphasize "Jesus's sovereign intervention."[102] Peter is subject to Jesus's power, both to predict his denial and to possibly redeem him. Thus, through the lens of masculinity, Peter's weeping demonstrates his lack of control over himself both in his excessive display of emotion as well as his dependence on Jesus for redemption.

As stated in the first section of this chapter, Peter's final appearance in the Gospel in 28:16–20 is notable for his lack of prominence or dominance. He is not named, and does not speak, when the disciples gather together and receive final instructions from Jesus.[103] While the construction of Peter's character in terms of control over self and over others has been both positive and negative, here he lacks any control at all. The wider narrative is not about Peter, it is about Jesus, so it is not wise to interpret this final scene as somehow definitive in terms of Peter's character. But it is still noteworthy. If Peter's masculinity has been defined by his dominant control, here he expresses no dominance and no control over self or over others. He is a silent, unnamed, member of the group.

In the Gospel as a whole, Peter's control over self and over others contributes an important perspective to the construction of his masculinity as the prominent disciple. His control over others is frequently asserted in his role as spokesperson, and in his unique status with respect to Jesus. In some ways, then, the Gospel accepts control over others as an inevitable and important part of both masculinity and discipleship. At the same time, Peter's control is not universal; he is also shown to be under the control of God, and subject to the rebuke of Jesus. Peter's authority to forgive others is honored but also limited in that he is expected to give away and not retain this power, and he is also shown to be a non-elite male negotiating imperial power (17:24–27); both of these instances are perhaps a subtle critique of control.

In terms of ancient masculinity, this means that Peter is able to establish relative control over others, but there are other hegemonic males more powerful than he, limiting the expression of his masculinity. As with divine service, the Gospel engages in a redefinition of masculinity in terms of control, aligning it with submission to God and Jesus, and providing the obedient males with power through the patriarchal dividend.

Other expressions of Peter's control, particularly over himself, are limited. Peter is consistently described in terms of his exuberant passions, and his inability to control or temper them compromises his masculinity and his discipleship. Not only that, but Peter's eager desire to follow Jesus is frequently tempered by the Gospel's expectations for physical loss, which is an aspect of ancient masculinity. His overemotional resistance to physical loss compromises his performance of divine service, which is the primary aspect of the construction of his masculinity. In the end, after his denial of Jesus, and Jesus's death and resurrection, Peter recedes from prominence, leaving a sense of ambiguity around both Peter's masculinity and his discipleship.

WEALTH

In this third and final section, I engage the question of Peter's masculinity through the lens of wealth. A marker of status, wealth generally associates men with power and authority, enhancing masculinity.[104] As with control over self and others, wealth is an important aspect of Peter's prominence as a disciple, which both argues for his status and further problematizes the conflict between discipleship and dominant cultural patterns of masculinity. Discourse from and about Peter deals with the expectation that disciples will eschew wealth, as well as the larger theme of loss associated with discipleship, the complex negotiation of taxation, and the barrier of wealth to salvation. Peter's question about forgiveness also leads into a parable where Jesus speaks of forgiveness in financial terms.

In this section I illustrate how Peter's masculinity in Matthew is diminished by his financial sacrifice, bolstered and reinterpreted by his promised reward in the Empire of God, and yet chastened by warnings against status. While Peter claims rightly to have met the expectation of giving up wealth for discipleship, his desire for status in the empire of the heavens is clear. This desire is both honored and challenged by Jesus, suggesting that while the Gospel critiques wealth, other expressions of status are not univocally troubled.

Congruent with the rest of the Gospel's expectations for discipleship, Peter is asked to leave behind financial power and security in order to follow Jesus

(4:18–22). As we have seen from both Joseph and John the Baptist, wealth is an area of critique in Matthew. In the case of Peter, this means giving up his livelihood. The first thing we know about Simon Peter in Matthew, besides his name, is his profession. 4:18 states that Peter and his brother Andrew were fishermen (ἁλιεῖς). While fishermen were not wealthy, particularly considering the heavily regulated and taxed fishing industry, they would have been able to provide for themselves and family members, especially if they were part of a family cooperative that possessed a boat.[105]

Just as important as income, fishing placed Peter in a community network. Hanson and Oakman list and illustrate the complex relationships of cooperatives, leases, brokers, processors, and merchants that characterized the ancient fishing economy.[106] Jesus calls Peter and the others to follow him, changing their occupation to fishing for people rather than fish. Significantly, verse 20 says that they immediately left their nets and followed him. There is no hesitation, so the income, contracts, equipment, and skills of their previous trade—all means of providing for a household (8:14)—are left behind. Peter is now defined not by being a fisherman, but by being a disciple.

Davies and Allison emphasize the economic impact of this choice for Peter and Andrew: "Their call is to homelessness. They are being ordered to deny self, to suffer the loss of their own lives and livelihood."[107] This sacrifice is significant, and brought up by Peter himself later in the Gospel when speaking to Jesus about status (19:27). Giving up his profession means that he has no income to depend upon. From a Roman imperial perspective on masculinity, such a decision makes little sense. One establishes masculine status by providing for self and others (such as a household, mentioned in 8:14), by having a means of making money that can support yourself and others. Greater wealth means greater power and status. Lack of wealth is emasculating; it decreases status.[108]

However, from the perspective of the Gospel, this does not seem to diminish Peter's masculinity. Rather, it enables his discipleship; he cannot be a fisherman *and* a disciple. And discipleship will be supported financially by others. Chapter 10 gives the instructions to the disciples, which is Peter's primary vocation now. Despite the order not to take any money with them, Jesus says that the laborers deserve to be fed (10:10). In fact, Jesus makes it sound like disciples shouldn't take money along with them precisely because they shouldn't have to pay anymore for food; their work is too important. And if they don't find hospitality in one place, they are told to move on until they do. The intention is not that they will starve. The intention is that other people will provide for them. As Carter points out, "they do not completely give up economic and household ties . . . [w]holehearted allegiance to Jesus also involves continuing participation in socioeconomic structures."[109]

This carries with it both a potential source of shame but also status. From a more traditional imperial perspective on masculinity, depending on the kindness of strangers could be seen as a weakness. But from the perspective of the Gospel, it is a demonstration of status. Their work is incredibly important, and their labor will be compensated. And, if the Gospel is interested in at least some disciples rejecting earthly wealth as belonging to the evil powers of this world, then not having to touch it or deal with it is a sign of privilege and status.

Such a construction inevitably raises questions about not just Peter, but the community surrounding him. If Peter and the other disciples are no longer able to support themselves, then it falls to others to do so. In chapter 8, Peter is said to have a house inhabited by his mother-in-law, where Jesus stays. One wonders what his family did if he wasn't working. In addition, the reference to others providing for the disciples acknowledges a reality check (if not potential hypocrisy) with respect to the Gospel's attitude toward wealth. While the Gospel's extreme demands for discipleship require the rejection of power from wealth, discipleship itself requires the support of those who continue to work in the world of imperial wealth and power. Certainly the impact of Peter's lack of income extends beyond himself to the ambivalence that marks the Gospel.

The loss of wealth combined with the retention of status repeatedly surfaces in the depiction of Peter. While he has certainly made financial sacrifices, this evidently does not mean giving up completely the kind of status that financial power is supposed to provide. From an imperial perspective, wealth is important because it is a means of dominance over others, determining what people can do, what they cannot do, and with whom they associate. Even after giving up financial security, Peter continues to exhibit power and status in his relationships (10:2; 15:15; 16:13–20; 17:1–9; 17:24–27) and receives a promise of even more power and possessions in the divine realm (19:16–30). Each of these markers is not without ambivalence, but the presence of even mitigated power argues that while Peter has given up wealth as a means of power and status, he retains it in other ways. In chapters 2 and 3, I have argued that the Gospel uncouples the association between wealth and status, combining an overall critique of wealth with an alternative construction of status. This has been true of both Joseph and John the Baptist, and now it is true of Peter.

Exploring further the examples cited above, the Gospel's rejection of wealth and redefinition of status is a common theme in texts about Peter. First, the fact that Peter is called to be a disciple *and* is identified as "first" is illustrative of this tension. On the one hand, Peter is called to give up his former identity and vocation, taking on a life of discipleship, which is characterized by the Gospel in terms of service to Jesus and loss of status. At the same time, Peter's status as "first" remains important (10:2), and his new, alternative, status is highlighted in 16:13–20 in Jesus's blessing and commissioning. His lack of wealth is not mentioned as a corollary here, but his status in the empire of heaven is raised.

Perhaps this insight helps to interpret the subsequent confrontation with Jesus in 16:21–3. In the previous section, I have argued that the loss of bodily control is at work in this scene. In addition, I see Peter resisting the loss of status that he has come to expect so far in the Gospel. If Jesus suffers and dies, then what happens to the status Peter has been gaining by association? If he has given up financial status for elevated status with Jesus in and over a community of followers, then Jesus's words are a threat to that arrangement.

The Transfiguration scene in 17:1–9 provides another example of this conflicting sense of status within the Gospel. Peter keeps auspicious company with Jesus, Moses, and Elijah, and his offer to build booths seems to grasp the importance of this company, even as it raises questions about the appropriateness of Peter's speech and initiative. The scene reveals the status of Jesus among the heroes of the faith, and Peter's presence there elevates his status. And yet, the divine voice interrupts Peter's suggestion to remind him of Jesus's words about sacrifice and discipleship.

The conflicting expectations about wealth and status continue in 19:16–30, where Peter specifically asks about his financial sacrifice and is told by Jesus that he and all who make such financial sacrifices will receive a substantial material reward for their commitment (19:29). Although Jesus is clearly capable of rebuking Peter (16:21–3), he does not do so here; the question is not inappropriate. Although Peter and the others will have to wait for their reward, it is promised, and their sacrifice of earthly possessions and relationships in the present is acknowledged. The story ends on an ambiguous note, however, when Jesus says in verse 30 that many who are first will be last, and the last will be first. This warning does not explicitly say that eschatological rewards are precarious. But, as argued previously, the subsequent parable does suggest that disciples shouldn't take their own status for granted and expect instead that God will distribute rewards in surprising ways that do not make sense from the perspective of imperial economics.

The connection between earthly and eschatological reward is also explored in 18:15–35. Here, the topic is forgiveness, but there is a potentially important connection between forgiveness and wealth. Whereas Peter's question to Jesus is about forgiveness of sin, the parable is about forgiveness of debt; Peter's authority to forgive sins is put in financial terms. The association of forgiveness with money is another indication that even though Peter might give up financial power in this life, he retains what amounts to financial power in the spiritual realm. Forgiveness is currency.

These examples demonstrate that while the Gospel questions the value of wealth and warns against assuming automatic status in the empire of heaven, it retains and redefines a relationship with status itself. This relationship, while unconventional, still fits an imperial scheme where power and authority are prized and wielded. In some ways, Peter's ability to retain them without financial resources is even more impressive, because he transcends earthly constraints. So, while the articulated rejection of wealth critiques that particular aspect of imperial masculinity, Peter's alternative expression of status means that much of the imperial scheme remains intact in the Gospel. This continues a theme in this project of recognizing that status and power retain their hold on the Matthean perspective, even as the role of wealth in that status is questioned.

One final story involving Peter where wealth is mentioned is 17:24–27, about paying tax. This story illustrates the power associated with wealth from an imperial perspective and reveals the Gospel's strategy for negotiating that power. While acknowledging earthly power by agreeing with Peter that the tax is to be paid, Jesus also argues for a different mindset behind paying the tax. Roman emperors were often associated with control over nature, as well as nature submitting to the Emperor's power; Jesus here does the same with God.[110] By connecting the payment of the tax with the fish, he separates power from Rome and associates it with God instead. God not only provides the fish, but also provides the means for the disciples to pay the tax.[111]

In terms of Peter's masculinity, this is an example of non-elites negotiating a place where masculine status can still be expressed even in an exploitative system. That being said, the system itself is not dismantled. The tax is still paid, and the imperial authorities are not directly challenged. Further, the role that God plays here and elsewhere in the Gospel (18:15–35) is that of a hegemonic male. So the emphasis here is on God's power being greater than imperial power, even as Peter and others are clearly subject to God. Here, as in the texts about forgiveness (18:15–35) and reward for leaving wealth (19:16–30), Peter's status is simultaneously established and relativized.

Because of discipleship, Peter's masculinity with respect to wealth is unconventional. He gives up his livelihood, which compromises his earthly power. However, the Gospel is able to reconcile Peter's rejection of wealth (a value consistent with the Gospel but not imperial masculinity) with his masculinity by emphasizing his retention of status as a disciple, especially related to forgiveness, which becomes Peter's new "currency." By becoming a disciple of Jesus, Peter enters a new system with its own rules about amassing status that do not require wealth, and he quickly builds status in that system. Peter is promised both earthly sustenance and eschatological material rewards, and his responsibilities in that system regarding forgiveness are couched in financial terms.

At the same time, these stories about wealth emphasize the authority of God who wields hegemonic power. Peter's status is relative, and the system of power itself remains intact. Obedience is expected, and power derived from the patriarchal dividend is promised. It is true that the Gospel consistently criticizes wealth, and even includes warnings against assumptions about eschatological status. Ambivalence remains, particularly in the Gospel's heavy language about loss and discipleship. However, the idea of status remains quite traditional with respect to empire, even as the Gospel replaces the language and concepts and warns against arrogance. It is redefined, but clearly imitative.

CONCLUSION

I have argued in this chapter that Peter is the dominant disciple, and his masculinity is constructed around this concept in all three categories of masculinity used in this study: divine service, control over self and over others, and wealth. In all three categories, Peter's expression of masculine power is partially effective. He functions as the group's spokesperson and is given unique access to Jesus. He has flashes of insight, like at Caesarea Philippi, where his words are met by blessing and commissioning. He does as Jesus commands and gives up the financial security of this world to depend on God and to follow Jesus.

But he also is clearly limited, both from the perspective of the Gospel and ancient masculinity. After briefly walking on water, he begins to sink, highlighting his incomplete faith. He falls asleep in the garden, indicating his lack of self-control. He doesn't fully comprehend what he's experiencing during the Transfiguration, and rebukes Jesus for talking about suffering and death, expressing a lack of control over his emotions and a lack of mastery over his master's words and plans. And, when it matters most, despite his protests to the contrary, he denies Jesus and flees the scene of his trial. In his final appearance in the Gospel, although he is presumably present and still an identified disciple, he is no longer dominant, a silent and unnamed member of the group.

From the perspective of masculinity studies, Peter's characterization is an important example of non-elites actively negotiating the expectations of masculinity in the midst of both compromised abilities and competing narratives. What makes Peter unique is the dual set of expectations of dominance and loss, masculinity and discipleship. While the constructions of Joseph and John the Baptist also deal with compromise and limits, the constructions of their masculinity are arguably more successful. Why? The argument for Peter's masculinity is more complicated, and ultimately incomplete and unsuccessful, because of the added dimension of submitting to and following Jesus. These requirements of discipleship compromise Peter's masculinity on all fronts. At the same time, a familiar imperial emphasis on hegemonic power remains, transferred now to Jesus or to God, elements of which are available to Peter through the patriarchal dividend.

What is remarkable about the construction of Peter's masculinity is that sometimes his expression of masculinity compromises his discipleship, and, in turn, the expectations of discipleship compromise his masculinity. Peter's understanding of, or participation in, the divine work in Matthew is problematic, limited, and compromised partially because of the conflicted relationship between "divine work" and hegemonic masculinity itself. It is worth asking whether the tension in Peter's character in Matthew is finally resolved in 28:16–20 in favor of Peter's discipleship, leaving behind his prominent masculinity. Although other Gospel traditions have worked harder to retain his prominence, in Matthew he loses his individuality and voice. If this is the case, then perhaps in this moment the Gospel chooses discipleship over the status and control inherent in masculinity. Alternatively, Peter's assimilation into the group could indicate a victory for the hierarchical, hegemonic, impulses of the Gospel, where he becomes one of a group of males under the authority of Jesus sanctioned for dominance in making other disciples.

The unfolding argument of this study claims, in part, that the Gospel is neither willing nor able to reject all forms of Roman masculinity marked by power and status. This is certainly present in this chapter, with the conflicting attitudes toward power and status. But Matthean discipleship with its extreme demands presents a daunting challenge to ancient masculinity, and, I suggest, lodges a permanent sense of tension between masculinity and discipleship that has remained a fundamental problem in Christianity through the centuries. Hegemonic males struggle to conform to the expectations of discipleship that emphasize suffering and loss. In diffusing the tension, sometimes the demands of discipleship are softened or altered. But they cannot really be reconciled, so fundamental tension remains.

The conflict exposed here, I argue, still lives on in Christianity. While there are many aspects to this issue addressed in multiple ways by various biblical texts, the figure of Peter is particularly interesting because he is (1) a disciple and (2) a leader. If one of the functions of a Gospel is to convey expected behaviors for other followers of Jesus, the tension in Peter's character conveys troubling and problematic expectations to other subsequent disciples, especially leaders. The fundamental conflict between self-sacrifice and expressions of power and status remains to this day in discussions of male discipleship and especially leadership in faith communities.

From a feminist perspective, the gap between the ideal disciple and the way the leadership in Christian communities has wielded power has created and perpetuated over the centuries a situation where women have been subjugated, abuse has been ignored, and the bodies and careers of men are privileged and protected. Feminists continue to challenge this troublesome gap, but it is stubborn. I am convinced that constructions of masculinity are a particularly potent contribution to the problem and a reason this system is not easily dismantled. The problematic tension and conflict that privileges male status and preservation of male bodies while at the same time valuing the loss of power is a toxic blend for the Church, and ends up targeting non-masculine bodies with those expectations while leaving the power structure intact. This tension goes all the way back at least to Matthew's characterization of Peter.

NOTES

1. Representative works include Francis Wright Beare, *The Gospel According to Matthew* (Oxford: Basil Blackwell, 1981); M. Bockmuehl, *Simon Peter in Scripture and Memory: The New Testament Apostle in the Early Church* (Grand Rapids: Baker Academic, 2012); Raymond Brown, *Biblical Reflections on Crises Facing the Church* (New York: Paulist, 1075), 63–83; Richard J. Cassidy, *Four Times Peter: Portrayals of Peter in the Four Gospels and at Philippi* (Collegeville: Liturgical Press, 2007); Oscar Cullman, *Peter: Disciple, Apostle, Martyr*, trans. Floyd V. Filson (Philadelphia: Westminster Press, 1953); W. D. Davies and D. C. Allison, *A Critical and Exegetical Commentary on the Gospel According to Saint Matthew*, 3 vols., International Critical Commentary (Edinburgh: T&T Clark, 2004); Craig A. Evans, *Matthew* (New York: Cambridge University Press, 2012); Larry R. Helyer, *The Life and Witness of Peter* (Downer's Grove: InterVarsity Press, 2012); Jack Dean Kingsbury, "The Figure of Peter in Matthew's Gospel as a Theological Problem," *Journal of Biblical Literature* 98, no. 1 (Mar 1979), 67–83; Daniel Patte, *The Gospel According to Matthew: A Structural Commentary on Matthew's Faith* (Minneapolis: Fortress Press, 1987); Raymond Brown, Karl Donfried, and John Reumann, eds., *Peter in the New Testament: A Collaborative Assessment by Protestant and Roman Catholic Scholars* (Eugene, OR: Wipf and Stock, 2002); Pheme Perkins, *Peter: Apostle for the Whole Church* (Columbia: University of South Carolina Press, 1994); Georg Strecker, *Der Weg der Gerechtigkeit*, Forschungen zur Religion und Literatur des Alten und Neuen Testaments 87, 2nd ed. (Göttingen: Vandenhoeck & Ruprecht, 1971); Timothy Wiarda, *Peter in the Gospels: Pattern, Personality, and Relationship*, WUNT 2, no. 127 (Tübingen: Mohr Siebeck, 2000).

2. Arlo J. Nau, *Peter in Matthew: Discipleship, Diplomacy, and Dispraise* (Collegeville: Liturgical Press, 1992).

3. Kari Syreeni, "Peter as a Character and Symbol in the Gospel of Matthew," in *Characterization in the Gospels: Reconceiving Narrative Criticism*, ed. David Rhoads and Kari Syreeni, JSNTSup 184 (Sheffield: Sheffield Academic, 1999), 106–52.

4. Robert H. Gundry, *Peter: False Disciple and Apostate according to Saint Matthew* (Grand Rapids: Eerdmans, 2015).

5. See Matthew 20:25–28, but also 19:28.

6. Colleen M. Conway, *Behold the Man: Jesus and Greco-Roman Masculinity* (Oxford: Oxford University Press, 2008), 29–31 and L. Stephanie Cobb, *Dying to be Men: Gender and Language in Early Christian Martyr Texts* (New York: Columbia University Press, 2008).

7. In Carter's words, Jesus's "words make available God's empire/reign and create for those who follow an alternative community and way of life with a different center, values, and structure." Warren Carter, *Matthew and the Margins: A Sociopolitical and Religious Reading* (Maryknoll: Orbis, 2000), 121.

8. Davies and Allison, *The Gospel According to Saint Matthew*, 1:396; Kingsbury, "The Figure of Peter in Matthew's Gospel," 70. Cullman makes a case for the importance both of the giving of the nickname, and its meaning. Cullman, *Peter: Disciple, Apostle, Martyr*, 17–21.

9. Daniel Patte notes, "Through the juxtaposition of the call of the disciples with the proclamation of the kingdom (4:17), the command 'Follow me' has special connotations. They proclamation of the kingdom, besides being a call to acknowledge God's kingship, also involves a reorientation of one's life toward the kingdom as the ultimate blessing." Patte, *The Gospel According to Matthew*, 57.

10. Cassidy notes that "Peter speaks to Jesus in eleven scenes, speaking twice in three scenes, and three times in one scene . . . Jesus speaks explicitly to Peter a total of nine times." Cassidy, *Four Times Peter*, 63.

11. For a review of these arguments, see Kingsbury, "The Figure of Peter in Matthew's Gospel," 67–83. Kingsbury balances the two, acknowledging Peter's primacy but arguing it is best understood in terms of his "firstness" in salvation history.

12. Gundry, *Peter: False Disciple and Apostate*, 9.

13. Perkins, *Peter: Apostle for the Whole Church*, 60.

14. Cassidy, *Four Times Peter*, 70. Bockmuehl, drawing on Hengel's work, also amplifies this scene but does so to argue for Peter's importance in the early Christian tradition, not his narrative relationship with Jesus. Bockmuehl, *Simon Peter in Scripture and Memory*, 24; Martin Hengel, *Saint Peter: The Underestimated Apostle*, trans. T. Trapp (Grand Rapids: Eerdmans, 2010), 103–34.

15. Ulrich Luz, *Matthew 8–20: A Commentary*, trans. James E. Crouch, ed. Helmut Koester, Hermeneia (Minneapolis: Fortress Press, 2001), 2:13.

16. Carter, *Matthew and the Margins*, 204.

17. Although it is not explicitly stated, it may also be the house Jesus returns to later in the Gospel, in 9:10 and 17:25. If so, it strengthens the connection in the relationship.

18. Luz provides a helpful overview of ancient texts that describe walking on water. Luz, *Matthew*, 2:319–20.

19. Luz, *Matthew*, 2:320. As an example of the latter, Luz notes, "as 'lord of the Sea' and 'god,' Caligula builds a bridge over the gulf of Puteoli (Josephus, *Ant.* 19:5–6)—a sign of his insanity." Luz, *Matthew*, 2:319.

20. Luz here is careful to delineate between references to passing through water and those about walking on water, noting only Job 9:8 and possibly Psalm 77:20 qualify. Luz, *Matthew*, 2:319.

21. For reference to Julius Caesar, see Plutarch, *Lives*, 7.38. For Augustus, see *Res Gestae Divi Augusti* 3, 13; Philo, *Against Flaccus* 1.104; Philo, *On the Embassy to Gaius*. 1.309. For Tiberius, see Philo, *On the Embassy to Gaius* 1.141. For Gaius Caigula, see Philo, *On the Embassy to Gaius* 1.44 and Josephus, *Jewish Antiquities* 19.6, 81. For Vespasian, see Josephus, *The Jewish War* 3.401–2. For Titus, see Martial, "On the Spectacles" 28. And for Domitian, see Philostratus, *Apollonius of Tyana*, 2.7.3; and Juvenal, *Satires* 4.83–84.

22. Luz sees faith here. Luz, *Matthew*, 2:320. Cassidy, on the other hand, sees a desire "to share in this startling expression of Jesus' exalted status." Cassidy, *Four Times Peter,* 72.

23. Davies and Allison, *The Gospel According to Saint Matthew,* 2:507.

24. Davies and Allison, *The Gospel According to Saint Matthew,* 2:509.

25. Luz, *Matthew,* 2:366.

26. While this is the prevailing viewpoint, for a counterargument see John R. Markley, "Reassessing Peter's Imperception in Synoptic Tradition," in *Peter in Early Christianity*, ed. Helen K. Bond and Larry W. Hurtado (Grand Rapids: Eerdmans, 2015), 99–108. Markley understands Peter's imperception to be an apocalyptic motif, something he calls "human imperception in the face of divinely revealed mysteries" Markley, "Reassessing Peter's Imperception," 108. In this case, these exchanges between Jesus and Peter would enhance his status, not detract.

27. The confession of Peter in Mark 8:29 is, "You are the Christ." The confession of the disciples in Matthew 14:33 is, "You are the Son of God." Here, Matthew combines the two and adds the modifier "living." The claim agrees with God's statement in 3:17: "This is my beloved son." The repetition of the language in agreement with God suggests its importance (also 17:5).

28. Brown, Donfried and Reumann put the contextual difference this way: "It is true that previously all the disciples have confessed Jesus as 'Son of God,' (14:33—in response to what Jesus did for Peter), and therefore Peter's confession is not so unique as it is in Mark. Nevertheless, Matthew has chosen not to focus the same attention on the previous confession by all the disciples that he focuses on Peter's confession because he records no laudatory reaction to the disciples' confession." Brown, Donfried, and Reumann, *Peter in the New Testament,* 106–7.

29. Markley's argument cited above would strengthen this case, but even without it, Peter is in a unique position as the one to receive "divinely revealed mysteries." Markley, "Reassessing Peter's Imperception," 108. Carter interprets this verse to be a statement in general about humanity's "inability to know God or God's ways." Peter is then an exception to others not because he already knows about Jesus, but because God chooses to reveal Jesus's identity and purpose to him. Carter, *Matthew and the Margins,* 334.

30. Davies and Allison comment that verse 18 "has been the object of much heated debate and much wasted ingenuity." Davies and Allison, *The Gospel According to Saint Matthew,* 2:627. A brief, helpful, summary of the dominant interpretative traditions of this text can be found in Ulrich Luz, *Matthew in History: Interpretation, Influence, and Effects* (Minneapolis: Augsburg Fortress, 1994), 57–63.

31. Carter, *Matthew and the Margins,* 342.

32. Syreeni, "Peter as Character and Symbol," 132.
33. Luz, *Matthew,* 2:382.
34. Their interaction also raises the issue of establishing masculine status through verbal challenge. I address this in the next section.
35. Luz uses "offense" for σκάνδαλον instead of "stumbling block." Luz, *Matthew,* 2:382. Carter uses "cause of sin." Carter, *Matthew and the Margins,* 343. Davies and Allison connect the two terms and use "temptation to sin." Davies and Allison, *The Gospel According to Saint Matthew,* 2:664.
36. Carter, *Matthew and the Margins,* 106–7.
37. Luz, *Matthew,* 2:382.
38. Brown, Donfried, and Reumann, *Peter in the New Testament,* 93.
39. See my discussions in chapter 1 and chapter 2 for more on divine service as a means to establish masculinity.
40. Conway, *Behold the Man,* 29–30. She draws particular attention to Suetonius's account of Otho, whose courageous suicide redeemed what had been a fragile display of masculinity in life.
41. It's true that Peter is here part of a small group, rather than on his own. But he is still the only disciple who speaks.
42. The biblical traditions potentially represented in this story are traced succinctly by Luz, *Matthew,* 2:395–97. For our purposes, the status of Moses and Elijah as dominant male religious figures is sufficient.
43. Luz (*Matthew,* 2:399) identifies two possible reasons for the inappropriateness of Peter's suggestion: (1) that Peter wants to treat heavenly beings in an earthly way, or (2) that Peter wants to keep the heavenly beings on the mountain. Also possible for Luz is this is related to Peter's desire to keep Jesus away from the suffering in Jerusalem.
44. In Matthew, an additional phrase "with him I am well pleased" (ἐν ᾧ εὐδόκησα) is added to Mark 9:7.
45. I return to the issues of dominating control in this scene in the next section of this chapter.
46. While some have favored a more spiritual or apolitical interpretation, I understand the story to be about paying the post-70 CE tax levied by the Romans on conquered Jews. For a review of these arguments, see Warren Carter, "Paying the tax to Rome as Subversive Praxis: Matthew 17:24–27," *Journal for the Study of the New Testament* 22, no. 76 (Apr 2000), 3–31.
47. Those who see instruction include Carter, *Matthew and the Margins,* 358; Davies and Allison, *The Gospel According to Saint Matthew,* 2:744–45; Luz, *Matthew,* 2:418. Here again, Markley's argument about Peter's role as the recipient of divine revelation is pertinent. Markley, "Reassessing Peter's Imperception," 108.
48. Luz suggests that the use of seven as the number of perfection gives Peter's question the sense of, "Is perfect forgiveness expected of me?" Luz, *Matthew,* 2:465.
49. Luz, *Matthew,* 2:465–66.
50. Carter, *Matthew and the Margins,* 369.
51. Syreeni, "Peter as Character and Symbol," 141.
52. Carter, *Matthew and the Margins,* 370.

53. Carter distinguishes here between discourse on God's *reign* and God's *forgiveness*, arguing that the parable is mostly about the former. When God's commands about forgiveness are not followed, then God's subsequent anger is justified. This resolves somewhat the literary tension between the two texts, if not the uncomfortable theological implications. Carter, *Matthew and the Margins,* 371.

54. Carter, *Matthew and the Margins,* 374–75; Davies and Allison, *The Gospel According to Saint Matthew,* 2:803; Luz, *Matthew,* 2:475.

55. Luz, *Matthew,* 2:517.

56. Carter, *Matthew and the Margins,* 393.

57. Davies and Allison, *The Gospel According to Saint Matthew,* 3:53.

58. For a history of interpretation of Peter's reaction here to Jesus, see Ulrich Luz, *Matthew 21–28: A Commentary,* trans. James E. Crouch, ed. Helmut Koester, Hermeneia (Minneapolis: Fortress Press, 2005), 3:390. Luz identifies two major "accents." One identifies Peter's sins as contradicting Jesus and asserting himself over the other disciples. The other attributes Peter's actions to faith, redeeming his intention; in this case, his sin is fragility and weakness.

59. Luz says here that Peter "breaks the group's solidarity by saying that all may stumble because of Jesus, but he will not. He will be the great exception!" Luz, *Matthew,* 3:389.

60. Davies and Allison, *The Gospel According to Saint Matthew,* 3:487.

61. Luz, *Matthew,* 3:389.

62. Luz, *Matthew,* 3:389.

63. Luz, *Matthew,* 3:389.

64. I discuss Peter's passion and emotions in the next section on control over bodies. It can be noted here that Peter's zeal as a disciple is out of balance with his ability to act in a corresponding manner.

65. Davies and Allison helpfully demonstrate the parallel structure of these two texts. Davies and Allison, *The Gospel According to Saint Matthew,* 3:495; Luz describes the similarities this way: "Here, as there, Jesus expects something special from the three disciples; both times they fail." Luz, *Matthew,* 3:395.

66. I focus more on the sleeping aspect of this passage and its implications for masculinity in the next section on control.

67. Luz, *Matthew,* 3:297.

68. Carter, *Matthew and the Margins,* 511.

69. Given Jesus's 3 passion predictions in 16:21, 17:22, and 20:17–19, Peter should presumably know Jesus's fate. If not, this would argue against Peter's status in divine service as he still is unable to understand Jesus's mission. However, it's also likely that Peter is simply there to witness the details of what he knows is a foregone conclusion.

70. Summarizing the history of interpretation, Luz determines that the reading of Peter's actions here have been "basically positive;" he does not immediately abandon Jesus, and tries to follow before failing. Luz, *Matthew,* 3:424. Davies and Allison echo this interpretation, adding also that, narratively, the verse keeps Peter in the reader's mind in preparation for the denial scene. Davies and Allison, *The Gospel According to Saint Matthew,* 3:522–23.

71. For some commentators, the severity of Peter's denial is enough to contemplate his status with respect to God. For representative discussions on the judgment of Peter, see Luz, *Matthew*, 3:455, and Gundry, *Peter: False Disciple and Apostate*, 43–52; 99–100.

72. Davies and Allison, *The Gospel According to Saint Matthew*, 3:547.

73. Representative are Davies and Allison, *The Gospel According to Saint Matthew*, 3:550; Luz, *Matthew*, 3:456; Brown, Donfried, and Reumann, *Peter in the New Testament*, 77. Against this scholarly consensus, Gundry argues that Peter's weeping is connected to the "weeping and gnashing of teeth" of those cast out into the outer darkness. Gundry, *Peter: False Disciple and Apostate*, 52. Gundry reviews the arguments for Peter's remorse and redemption in *Peter: False Disciple and Apostate*, 51–62.

74. Gundry traces the history of interpretation of this passage, noting those who explain it away and others who assign it significance. Gundry, *Peter: False Disciple and Apostate*, 63–67. For another view skeptical of Peter's continued dominance, see Syreeni, "Peter as Character and Symbol," 147.

75. There is no guarantee of this, however, as Matthew indicates in 28:17 that some of the disciples still doubted.

76. Although he is not a disciple, similar themes run through my discussion of Joseph in chapter 2. Obedience is key for Joseph's divine service, but that obedience affords him certain power and status available through the patriarchal dividend.

77. Syreeni observes that "Unlike John the Baptist, Peter appears as a character only through Jesus's action. He is a follower of Jesus; his childhood or pre-Gospel life has no bearing on Matthew's story. But from the very start of Jesus' public career, he occupies a prominent role among the followers." Syreeni, "Peter as Character and Symbol," 121.

78. Both Carter and Cassidy emphasize the compelling nature of Jesus's calling here. "One cannot volunteer to be a follower. Nor does one belong by birth, wealth, gender, or training. Jesus's call invades and challenges their everyday world" Carter, *Matthew and the Margins*, 121. Cassidy calls Jesus's calling "authoritative and decisive." Cassidy, *Four Times Peter*, 70.

79. Luz, *Matthew*, 2:13.

80. Carter, *Matthew and the Margins*, 205.

81. Carter, *Matthew and the Margins*, 311. Luz notes that Jesus's command to Peter in v. 29 is the foundation for Peter's request. "This foundation authorizes it and preserves it from self-grandeur. Thus Peter does not attempt to play the role of a guru or magician exploring or demonstrating his supernatural abilities; he obeys his Lord." Luz, *Matthew*, 2:320.

82. The emphasis in scholarship is on what this scene proves about Jesus's power, i.e., "Jesus works a miracle for Peter, almost as a proof." Brown, Donfried, and Reumann, *Peter in the New Testament*, 81. Davies and Allison note that the impossibility of humans walking on the water is the point. Since this is impossible for humans, then "if a man walks on the sea, he does so only by divine authority," proving that Jesus wields this divine authority. Davies and Allison, *The Gospel According to Saint Matthew*, 2:507.

83. Luz emphasizes Peter's fear and Jesus's power. Luz, *Matthew*, 2:320.

84. See my discussion in chapter 1 on Traister's article, "Academic Viagra."

85. Davies and Allison suggest that he is "emboldened" by the promise he just received, without understanding that the way forward is death. Davies and Allison, *The Gospel According to Saint Matthew*, 2:661.

86. Brown, Donfried, and Reumann, *Peter in the New Testament*, 94.

87. Carter, *Matthew and the Margins*, 344.

88. "Even within this innermost circle it is almost always Peter who stands in the foreground." Cullman, *Peter: Disciple, Apostle, Martyr*, 23. This prominence is nowhere more striking than here, juxtaposed with the previous scene of rebuke.

89. Davies and Allison, *The Gospel According to Saint Matthew*, 2:699.

90. Carter, *Matthew and the Margins*, 350.

91. Interpreters have noted that because of the timing of the Gospel, the context for this conversation is not the temple tax of Jesus's time, but the Roman tax following the destruction of the temple in Jerusalem. See Carter, "Paying the tax to Rome as Subversive Praxis."

92. Noting this phenomenon of "special knowledge" is present in other parts of Matthew (9:3–4; 12:14–15, 25; 22:18), Carter claims that Jesus's "mysterious knowledge enhances his authority." Carter, *Matthew and the Margins*, 358.

93. While making a similar point, Carter also noted that the servant-girl does have some status as the slave of the high priest. In this case, both her gender and her relative status emasculate Peter as she exposes him as a follower of Jesus. Carter, *Matthew and the Margins*, 519.

94. For the details of this discussion, see Davies and Allison, *The Gospel According to Saint Matthew*, 2:634–635 and Luz, *Matthew*, 2:364–65. Carter summarizes that "often keys indicate access . . . and authority or power." Carter, *Matthew and the Margins*, 336.

95. Davies and Allison provide a summary of possible interpretations. Davies and Allison, *The Gospel According to Saint Matthew*, 2:635–41. Luz here notes the twin responsibilities of teaching and judging. Luz, *Matthew*, 2:365. Carter's phrase "discerning an appropriate way of life shaped by God's empire" is helpful. Carter, *Matthew and the Margins*, 336.

96. Carter, *Matthew and the Margins*, 374.

97. Luz sees in 19:28–29 another juxtaposition of the few with the many; the twelve are set apart in 28, but the many who follow Jesus are included in 29. Luz, *Matthew*, 3:516–17.

98. Connecting this ruling activity with Jesus's words in 20:20–21, Carter suggests that the kind of ruling done by the disciples may be different from what is experienced in the empire, marked by a lack of dominating behavior. Carter, *Matthew and the Margins*, 392. However, the preceding parable about the unforgiving king cautions against redeeming the image too quickly. Even if there is a difference, the power dynamic and the association with masculinity remain.

99. Conway, *Behold the Man*, 21–30.

100. While the text does not use this language, Peter's emotion here may be interpreted as anger. Conway notes that, in excess, "anger is associated with women."

Conway, *Behold the Man*, 27. If Peter demonstrates excessive anger here, that anger is gendered.

101. The verb used here, κλαίω, is only used once in Matthew; elsewhere in the Gospels it is often used when women are mourning the dead or those marked for death (Luke 7:38, John 11:31, 33; 20:11, 13, 15). Some examples of men weeping include John weeping in Rev. 5:4 because no one is worthy to open the scroll, and Jesus weeping over Jerusalem in Luke 19:41. The most common reference to Jesus in terms of this verb is when he tells others not to weep (Luke 7:13, 8:52; 23:28; Mark 5:38.) While not univocal, the use of this verb connects Peter at least somewhat with weeping women, suggesting another aspect of compromised masculinity.

102. Cassidy *Four Times Peter*, 80.

103. Syreeni's description states the issue clearly: "the narrative silence around Peter is remarkable in comparison with the expectations the reader has been led to have about Peter's central role. . . . Why did he lose his voice in the first triumphal scene?" Syreeni, "Peter as Character and Symbol," 147.

104. As previously noted, there are exceptions, including those who are self-indulgent or freedmen whose wealth did not secure elite status. See chapter 2, note 8 about the freed slave Trimalchio. Wealth itself was not a guarantee of masculine status, but it could be used to perform masculine behaviors, and its absence was prohibitive to establishing elite masculinity.

105. For helpful discussions of the fishing economy during Jesus's day in Galilee, see K. C. Hanson and Douglas E. Oakman, *Palestine in the Time of Jesus: Social Structures and Social Conflicts*, 2nd ed. (Minneapolis: Fortress Press, 2008), 106–10; and K. C. Hanson, "Galilean Fishing Economy and the Jesus Tradition," *Biblical Theological Bulletin* 27, no. 3 (Fall 1997), 99–111.

106. Hanson and Oakman, *Palestine in the Time of Jesus*, 107–8.

107. Davies and Allison, *The Gospel According to Saint Matthew*, 1:399–400.

108. As mentioned in chapter 3, the Cynic renunciation of wealth is an important exception to the general statement made above where a man may reclaim some power by exerting self-control and valuing discipline. But while such a comparison might be made with John the Baptist, Peter is a different type of figure. He is not called to an ascetic life, but to give up his financial independence in favor of dependence on others.

109. Carter, *Matthew and the Margins*, 122–23. 8:14–17 illustrates this with Jesus's healing of Peter's mother-in-law in her home.

110. For example, Vespasian's destiny to be Caesar is foretold by an oak tree, an ox bowing to him, one eagle triumphing over another, and a dog bringing to him at dinner a human hand (a symbol of power). Suetonius, *Lives of the Caesars*, 38.5. Similarly, in his "On the Spectacles celebrating the opening of the Coliseum in Rome," Martial recounts how the animals honored Domitian and his entertainment demonstrated mastery over nature.

111. Carter, "Paying the tax to Rome," 27–29.

Chapter 5

Judas

In this chapter, I view the controversial figure of Judas through the lens of masculinity. Of the three categories highlighted in this study, the following analysis shows that Judas's masculinity is primarily constructed in terms of dominating control over self and over others, and not in relation to wealth or divine service.[1] In some respects, Judas's attempts to establish masculine authority are successful. He asserts control over Jesus by turning him over to the authorities, gaining some wealth—one of the other measures of masculinity—in the process. However, these masculine actions put him at odds with God's purpose and in line with the enemies of Jesus, exposing tension between control and divine service expressed as discipleship. This tension extends to Judas's suicide, where he loses control over himself. Judas's story ends tragically in remorse, failure, and death. Ultimately, his attempt at asserting masculine status fails, both because he is allied with, yet outmanned by, the chief priests and because these efforts negate his divine service as a disciple. Judas's tale serves as a caution against rejecting or dismissing the values of discipleship that Jesus demands and problematizes or troubles the arenas of ancient masculinity as antithetical to discipleship and a source of despair.

The character of Judas combines a relatively small amount of material with a very significant role.[2] This combination means that scholarship is interested in Judas, but it is often interdisciplinary and multifaceted. For example, much of the work on Judas combines reception history with theological or spiritual questions: his guilt or innocence, his potential lack of agency in carrying out the divine plan, and the question of his damnation.[3] Recent work often seeks to question earlier assumptions about Judas's character and fate, either by suggesting alternative explanations for his actions, or by separating the oldest narratives about Judas from the increasingly judgmental interpretation throughout history.[4]

While full-length studies are somewhat limited, Judas is commonly addressed in an expanded discussion in a commentary, incorporating some or all of the elements described above.⁵ Judas is also a popular figure for studies using comparison and contrast. For example, in his argument about Peter as apostate, Robert Gundry links Judas with Peter in their apostasy.⁶ Another variation on the theme above is a composite sketch of Judas's character across the four Gospels, noting the considerable differences in his portrayal and positing a developmental shift in perception of Judas's character.⁷

An example of a scholar who combines several of these approaches is William Klassen. Klassen's work is important for this project because of his attention to the use and translation of παραδίδωμι, but his larger argument focuses on the theological question of Judas's guilt or innocence.⁸ Admittedly, it is difficult to separate theological and spiritual issues from the Gospel's portrayal of Judas, in part because his limited portrayal is so intimately tied to the arrest and death of Jesus. Care is taken in this study to do so, but the challenge is noted.

While some scholarship has no doubt included discussion on the power and importance of Judas's actions as they relate to Jesus, this study is unique in its focus on Judas's portrayal in Matthew and its foregrounding of those power issues in a discussion of ancient masculinity. I proceed to analyze Judas's character through the three aspects of masculinity used in this study—control over self and over others, wealth, and divine service—to argue that dominating control over self and over others, not wealth and divine service, dominates the construction of Judas's masculinity, the assertion of which is doomed to failure.

DOMINATING CONTROL OVER SELF AND OVER OTHERS

Judas is first mentioned in 10:1–4, in the list of disciples. Of the twelve, he is mentioned last. In the previous chapter, I observed that Peter was notable for his position in the list as "first," especially since the term is used (10:2). That being the case, presumably Judas's position may signal something with respect to his power and status. An obvious first conclusion is that his position signifies a lack of status. At the head of the list, Peter is dominant; Judas, by contrast, is not.

However, Judas's position at the end also makes him more memorable than those in the middle, suggesting that his placement may argue for different significance, or at least dominance of a different kind. Davies and Allison, for example, associate the placement of Judas and Peter with their relative honor. "Just as Judas, the last on the last, is the most dishonored apostle, so it is Peter, the first, the most honored."⁹ They also note that Judas is the only one to have his "future role" as the one to hand Jesus over noted early on.¹⁰ Judas is not alone in having a descriptor; in addition to Peter being described as "first," some of the disciples have further modifiers or nicknames.[11] But only Judas is singled out for his role, which is to hand over Jesus to the chief priests and elders.

The nature of this behavior warrants some discussion. The phrase accompanying his name (ὁ καὶ παραδοὺς αὐτόν) is usually translated "betray." Certainly, this translation associates Judas with something negative. In his literary analysis of Matthew, Edwards notes, "Since there is no incident about Judas up to this point in the story which is identifiable, and no other indication of what the information might mean, the text-connoted reader has a 'gap' and is led to anticipate a negative tendency from this disciple."[12]

However, the verb does not always have this negative connotation. In other parts of the Gospel παραδίδωμι is translated as "hand over" or even "entrusted" (11:27, 25:14, 20, 22). In the first reference, Jesus says that all things have been handed over to him by the father, while the other three come from the parable of the talents when the master hands over talents to his slaves; none is about betrayal. William Klassen strongly argues that "betrayal" is not a correct translation, advocating instead for "hand over."[13] He cites the variety of usage in ancient literature that usually, but not always, has to do with transferring power over something or someone from one entity to another.[14] By choosing the more neutral "hand over," he understands Judas's actions to be ambiguous, or even positive.[15]

It is not my intent to exonerate Judas's actions. But the sense of power or control connoted by the translation "hand over" is significant for this present discussion. The person doing the "handing over" has control over the person or thing being handed over, whether money, property, or human beings; as Klassen argues, "to hand something over, you must have it in your power."[16] The Gospel emphasizes this behavior by associating it with Judas from his introduction. If Judas is the one who hands Jesus over, then he is associated with domination and control, heightening his profile.

While the term may have a variety of possible meanings, in the context of Jesus and the disciples, it's clear that παραδίδωμι can have an ominous tone in terms of being subjected to control by others. In chapter 10:19 and 21, just a few verses after the disciples are introduced, it is used by Jesus to explain the perils of discipleship, which include being subject to the control of others in arrest, beatings, and death.[17] When Jesus speaks in 17:22–23 and 20:17–19 of his own fate of being subject to the control of others, he uses this same term, again accompanied by language of beatings and death. And, in 26:45, Jesus uses this word to wake the sleeping disciples to the reality of the crowd arriving with Judas.[18] The latter will exercise control over him in arresting him.

In the context of commitments of mentorship or community exhibited by Jesus and his disciples, handing someone or something over may constitute a betrayal of those commitments. Certainly, Judas's decision to hand Jesus over breaks with behavior expected of a disciple. But the evidence suggests that to limit the translation *only* to betray misses the expanded semantic field, including the aspect of dominating control that is important for the characterization of Judas. In this study, therefore, I primarily use "hand over" both to acknowledge the broader definition and to emphasize Judas's dominating control over Jesus which I foreground in this section. In the subsequent section on divine service, I foreground the concept of "betrayal" as a way of framing Judas's dominating control over Jesus as failed discipleship. The two translations "hand over" and "betray" are clearly linked but the different translations allow one of the dimensions to come to the fore in each section's discussion.

In terms of 10:4, the position of this descriptor at the very end of the list of the disciples is significant. It signals that something will happen to Jesus at the hands of Judas. While Judas is not dominant in the way that Peter is dominant, his character is defined in terms of an assertion of dominance over Jesus that effects Jesus's death. From the beginning, he is a threat to Jesus, something that is emphasized and made more memorable by his final position in the list of disciples.

Judas's introduction in chapter 10, then, introduces a fundamental tension into his character. His placement at the end of the list, and the description of his role, simultaneously acknowledge his attempt to control others, notably Jesus, and diminish his status within the group of disciples. The tension arises from the juxtaposition of Judas as both a disciple ("one of the Twelve") and the one who hands Jesus over. As a disciple, he is to be subjected to the control of his master. But the introduction makes clear that Judas's identity is not solely in following Jesus as a disciple, but in exertion of dominance. He initially follows Jesus but is not ultimately subject to his control.

This tension, and the importance it assigns to Judas, resurfaces in chapter 26. However, in the meantime, Judas essentially disappears from the narrative as an individual figure. From 10:5–26:14, Judas operates as "one of the Twelve," a silent, invisible, member of the group who is subject to Jesus's control. For these chapters, the emphasis is on the "disciple" aspect of Judas's character rather than the "handing over."[19] In terms of control over self and over others, his lack of distinction as a disciple emphasizes Judas's unimportance, rather than any significance.

For example, as argued in chapter 4, discipleship in Matthew is about losing control over one's own life and following Jesus instead. Followers of Jesus do not rely on their own financial resources, depending on others to provide for them (10:9–10; 19:16–27). They leave their occupations behind and make following Jesus their primary vocation (4:18–20). In response, they can expect hardship and persecution in this life (10:16–23; 16:24–25) with the hope of reward to come in the next (19:27–30).

It is true that the followers of Jesus retain certain kinds of power over others, including giving or withholding the peace of God (10:11–14) and forgiving sins (18:21–35). Luz says that the followers of Jesus "share in his own authority."[20] But this behavior is regulated and controlled, and the status of the master over the disciples is emphasized (10:24–25). Ultimately, discipleship is about losing control, not gaining it.

This is more the case for Judas than it was for Peter, as Judas displays none of the dominant behavior that Peter does with respect to the other disciples. Judas participates in the group recognition of Jesus (14:33) but does not receive his own commissioning as Peter does in 16:13–20. While Judas's voice is presumed to be part of the disciples' group responses, he does not speak individually prior to chapter 26. He is not part of the inner circle who attends the Transfiguration in 17:1–7. In Matthew, there is nothing—positive or negative—to set Judas apart between 10:5 and 26:14. When the focus is on Jesus's ministry, Judas remains in the background.

Even the arena in which Judas does exert dominance—handing Jesus over—is downplayed in these intervening chapters. When Jesus refers to his own arrest in multiple predictions, it is in the passive voice (17:22–23; 20:17–19), and once he omits being handed over altogether, focusing instead on the suffering and death (16:21). Further, when agents are mentioned, they are not Judas. In 16:21, Jesus names the elders, chief priests, and scribes; in 20:18 it is the chief priests and scribes, and then the Gentiles are added to this group in verse 19. In 17:22, he uses the term "human hands" (εἰς χεῖας ἀνθρώπων). In each instance, Judas is not mentioned. So, although the association of Judas as the one who hands Jesus over is introduced early in the Gospel, it is not consistently emphasized.

I return to Judas's lack of distinction as a disciple in the next section on divine service. In terms of control over self and over others, he shows no dominant behavior for much of the narrative, and certainly no hegemonic masculinity. This lack of prominence or dominance means that Judas is not masculine in the way that Peter is. In some ways, this mitigates a claim to Judas's masculinity defined in terms of consistent, thematic, hegemonic behavior. In others, however, it focuses all of the attention on Judas's behavior at the end of the narrative, where he hands Jesus over. With no other data available, Judas's masculinity becomes primarily, if not exclusively, defined in terms of this act of control and dominance.

Judas's dominant control becomes the focus when he bursts on the scene in 26:14. It is his action that turns the narrative from ministry to the predicted suffering and death. Following the anointing of Jesus at Bethany, Judas goes to the chief priests.[21] He is identified in verse 14 as "one of the twelve," (εἷς τῶν δώδεκα), a reminder of his status as a disciple. This intensifies his offer to hand Jesus over, of course, as he emerges from the closest followers of Jesus.

From the perspective of control over self and over others, however, this is important because it signals Judas's separation from the group. He becomes an individual who is marked by attempts to control another.

The theme of Judas's agency continues throughout this short scene. Klassen describes Judas as "outgoing, decisive, and able to take the initiative."[22] Luz notes that "Judas is almost the sole actor" in this exchange, and that "the chief priests merely react to his suggestion."[23] He initiates and directs the conversation, attempting to assert control over Jesus.[24] Luz also points out that the chief priests and elders had decided to wait to arrest Jesus until there would be fewer people (26:3–5); it is Judas's arrival that decreases the risk of a riot and prompts them to act sooner.[25]

Judas's agency is underscored further by his request for a reward. Rather than simply offering up Jesus's location, he secures something for himself.[26] And, in an indication of Judas's relative power, the chief priests pay him up front, rather than upon delivery. They have more power and status than he does, but he has something they do not have—access to Jesus—and they are willing to pay him for it. The little scene closes where it opens, with Judas's agency, as he focuses his attention on finding an opportunity to hand over Jesus. Beginning in 26:16, Jesus's future is in Judas's hands.

This scene is the first in which Judas speaks as an individual. As noted in other chapters in this study, the use of voice and public speech are markers of ancient masculinity. Unlike Joseph, Judas speaks, brokering a deal to hand over another human being. Unlike John the Baptist, Judas does not use his voice to challenge corrupt powers but to report to them. Unlike Peter, Judas does not use his voice to confess Jesus's identity or to ask questions about discipleship. He does not give a lengthy speech, rather he asks only a single question. But Judas uses his voice here to gain power over another man and to secure a benefit for himself. Judas's voice asserts power over others and for himself.

In this exchange, Judas uses the tools of hegemonic masculinity—public speech and control over others—to increase his power and status. He takes initiative, separating himself from a group. He visits powerful men who have control over other people's bodies, and who want control over the one he follows. He brings valuable information that they want, and negotiates a reward for providing it to them. He offers to turn over another person to the authorities, limiting Jesus's control over himself. The result is increased masculine status for Judas, at least for the moment.

The next scene involving Judas is the Last Supper in 26:20–25. After the preparations are made, Jesus eats with "the twelve" (v. 20). The phrase is a repetition from verse 14, and is a reminder that Judas is present. After a scene when Judas sets himself apart, the use of the phrase recalls his earlier position as one of the group. Rather than reintegrating him, however, the phrase focuses on his secretive, individual behavior and heightens the tension in the scene. The language is as it was in 26:14, but the situation and relationships are significantly altered.

Jesus begins to talk of being handed over, identifying the one who will dominate him as one of the Twelve (v. 21). His speech, alluding to knowledge he has that others do not, gives him the power in the conversation, even as he speaks of his own loss of power through being handed over. Others are left to question Jesus about the identity of the one who will hand him over (v. 22). The agency of Jesus's public speech, and the omission of Judas's name in Jesus's reference, assert Jesus's status and gut Judas's power, recalling the earlier predictions when Judas was not mentioned by Jesus (16:21, 17:22, 20:17–19).

In response to their questions, Jesus cryptically identifies the one who will hand him over as the one who dips his hand into the bowl with Jesus (v. 23). Judas's name is still not spoken. Although his intentions have already been made clear by the narrative, the lack of naming again diminishes Judas. The image of eating together with the one who will hand him over conveys intimacy and deepens the rupture. As Carter says, Judas is "one whom Jesus called, commissioned, accompanied, and instructed;" the reality of this prior relationship "underlines the tragedy of the events."[27]

Somewhat abruptly, Jesus issues a powerful judgment of the one who will hand him over. His "woe" statement intimates that even though it is Jesus who is handed over, it is the one who hands Jesus over who is worse off (v. 24). The idea that Jesus knows of the identity of the person beforehand, and yet allows himself to be dominated, confuses the sense of power in the scene. If Jesus has both the foreknowledge of Judas's act, and the power to speak or issue this statement of judgment, this questions Judas's agency and limits his efforts at dominance. Judas's assertions of masculine power do not go unchallenged, even if Jesus does not actively confront him. The tension created here continues throughout the next few chapters and is unresolved.

Finally, in verse 25, Judas speaks, asking the same question the others ask ("Surely not I?") and using the address "Rabbi" instead of "Lord," which all the disciples used. This is the same address Judas will use when he hands Jesus over in 26:49. While "Rabbi" on its own is a sign of respect, the Matthean context suggests that it is meant to minimize Jesus's authority. In chapter 23, Jesus instructs his followers not to use the title "rabbi" (23:8), and says that it is the one preferred by those scribes and Pharisees that Jesus criticizes (23:7).[28] This is not a neutral word. In addition, it is not as strong as "Lord," which the disciples have come to use for Jesus.

In addition to disobeying and diminishing Jesus, Judas's question itself is disingenuous. As Carter observes, Judas uses the same μήτι construction in verse 25 that the disciples used in verse 22, a construction that anticipates a negative response.²⁹ But both men know that Judas will hand Jesus over. Like Judas's previous question in 26:14, this question subtly asserts power. After Jesus's demonstration of power in speech and judgment, Judas responds by disobeying and disrespecting Jesus with the use of "rabbi" and asking what Davies and Allison call a "hypocritical" question.³⁰

The discussion ends without a confrontation. Jesus responds indirectly to Judas's disingenuous question, turning it back on him. The cryptic response deescalates the situation as Jesus shifts his focus to the meal itself. Davies and Allison call Jesus's response "a qualified affirmation which reveals Jesus's foreknowledge as well as Judas's responsibility."³¹ Jesus does not rise to the challenge to defend himself or identify Judas, but neither does he cede power. The confrontation is still to come, as is the final judgment on Judas's control over others.

This encounter between Jesus and Judas heightens the tension in the narrative. With the use of public speech, including naming, both men assert power, but there is no open conflict. The power to dominate the other, either through prophetic "woe" or by betrayal, is claimed but the consequences delayed. The scene is marked by Jesus's power, stated but not fully realized, and Judas's response, guarded but challenging, all occurring in the shadow of the looming threat of Jesus being handed over.

Judas's exit from the gathering is not narrated in Matthew. He moves secretively, but freely. His next appearance takes place after the sharing of the meal, the prediction of Peter's denial, and the prayers in Gethsemane. In 26:46, the scene shifts when Jesus tells the disciples that the moment has arrived; the one who will hand him over approaches. Significantly, Jesus makes this claim while the conversation is still about the disciples' falling asleep, and with no indication that anyone else recognizes what's happening. Judas's actions continue to be a surprise to most, but not to Jesus.

Davies and Allison point out that Jesus's response in 26:46 to Judas's arrival is not to retreat, but to go out and meet him.³² In terms of control over self, Jesus here shows discipline even as he opens himself up to weakness. Luz here goes so far as to say that "Jesus has everything under control."³³ While such a claim of control may be a stretch, I would argue that Jesus is definitely demonstrating special knowledge of what is transpiring, and still exhibiting agency, even as events transpire that limit his physical power.

In verse 47, Judas arrives with an armed mob. As with his visit to the chief priests, Judas's agency and independence are emphasized in his scene.³⁴ Further, his ability to raise a large crowd to come with him adds strongly to the perception of Judas's dominating control and alludes to his alliance with the chief priests and elders. With this show of force, arrest and bodily harm are now a very real threat for Jesus. Judas's next action closes the remaining gap, identifying Jesus to the mob.³⁵ According to a prearranged signal, in verse 49 he kisses Jesus and speaks, calling him "Rabbi." Both actions express aspects of Judas's masculine control over Jesus.

Judas's signal involves bodily contact; by touching Jesus, Judas makes him vulnerable to arrest. In addition, the kiss redefines a symbol of familiarity, respect, and solidarity.[36] Davies and Allison note that, with his kiss, "Judas brings not affection but violence."[37] In addition, Judas uses his voice both to identify Jesus and again to call him "Rabbi," repeating his earlier diminishment of Jesus's authority. Both the physical violation and the use of public speech are examples of masculinity expressed through control. This is Judas's strongest demonstration of masculine status, in terms of bodily control and domination. What began as a conversation with the chief priests culminates in this exchange where Judas emasculates Jesus, making his body vulnerable to arrest and attack.

Interestingly, however, Jesus's response does not change. When Judas greets him, Jesus again responds somewhat cryptically. First, he responds to Judas's ironic address with one of his own (ἑταῖρε).[38] Then, he tells him to do what he came to do (v. 50).[39] The indirect phrase seems intentionally unclear; by giving Judas "permission" to continue, it retains some of Jesus's power even as he is handed over by Judas. Then, when one of Jesus's friends moves to fight the mob, Jesus stops him with his words. He also chastises the crowd for having come out with violence, and asserts that what happens fulfills the prophets (vv. 55–56).

Jesus's masculinity is not the topic of this study, but his actions here are important because they affect Judas's display.[40] Judas utilizes behaviors of hegemonic masculinity to assert control over Jesus's body, including public speech and physical touch expressed as dominance. But Jesus's response indicates that Judas's actions are not as powerful as they might first appear. Jesus does not resist, commands others to stop resisting, and explains the events as fulfilment of biblical prophecy. On the one hand, a lack of resistance on Jesus's part might be interpreted as lack of masculinity; here, as in the supper scene, he does not rise to the challenge of defending his masculine status. On the other hand, Jesus's actions ultimately detract from Judas's expressions of power. He actively rejects the physical response of his followers, and characterizes the events not as an interruption or derailment of his mission, but its fulfilment in accord with his previous threefold prediction.[41]

Judas's actions make sense in the language of ancient masculinity. Utilizing physical dominance and control, he leads the group that takes Jesus into custody. Jesus's actions do not make the same kind of sense; he does not meet "like with like" to clearly establish dominance in a physical sense. But, even as his physical independence is lost, his voice maintains authority over his disciples and questions the real power behind his arrest. All of this combines to limit Judas's expression of masculine dominance, even at its height.[42]

So far, I have focused primarily on Judas's control over others, and noted briefly moments of agency that indicate a desire to control himself and his influence. For Judas, these issues are intertwined. Going to the authorities to offer to betray Jesus involves setting himself apart, taking control of his own future. The same is true for his request for a monetary reward. And, significantly, both of these actions distance Judas from the identity of a disciple. Rather than taking initiative, disciples follow Jesus's lead, subsuming their interests and desires to his (16:24–25). Judas separates himself from this group and lifestyle, pursuing his own independent interests. Also, following Jesus requires giving up financial resources (4:19–22; 10:8–10); acquiring them increases Judas's power and ability to provide for himself and distances himself from the life of a disciple.

Another example of this connection between self-control and control over others is present in Jesus's prediction in 26:20–25 that one of the disciples will hand him over. Although the tension in the scene is high (as the identity of the one who hands Jesus over is at issue), Judas appears to maintain equanimity. He does not confess, does not flee, does not deny or contest the answer, and does not strike out in anger. Both Judas and Jesus maintain self-mastery over their emotions in this scene. Also, because Judas is not identified by either himself or Jesus, he leaves the meal when he chooses, unnoticed by the narrative, maintaining control over his own body and actions.

This tension between dominating control over self and over others reaches its climax in Judas's final appearance in 27:3–10. In verse 3, Judas realizes that Jesus is condemned. The timing of this realization is curious, as it is before Jesus has been sentenced to death by Pilate. Some scholars see proof here that Judas did not intend for Jesus to die, or did not expect this particular outcome. Gubar, for instance, says that this verse "suggests that Judas may have had no intention whatsoever of bringing about Jesus's death," and therefore is surprised when he is handed over to the Romans.[43] Klassen says the implication of Judas's realization "is clear: This is not what he had intended."[44]

While possible, I do not find this line of psychologizing particularly helpful. What is important for this study is the association of Pilate's involvement with bodily harm for Jesus. Whatever Judas's intent, he recognizes that the outcome of Jesus "being handed over" (παρέδωκαν, 27:2) to Pilate, the Roman governor, means death.[45] The inclusion of Roman power in the mix introduces the idea of crucifixion, and the "elite's alliance" makes Jesus's death "inevitable."[46] This is important for this study because it directly links Roman power with Judas's control over others. The use of the παραδίδωμι in 27:2 links the action of the chief priests and elders with Judas's action in 26:45, putting Judas in the same company as the chief priests and elders.[47] The masculine attempt to control others—exhibited by Judas, Pilate, and the chief priests and elders—will result in Jesus's death.

I return to the issue of Judas's potential regret in the section on divine service. At present, I recognize that, beginning in 27:3, Judas has changed his mind about handing Jesus over. True to form, his response is to take the initiative again, returning to the chief priests and the elders. He tells them in verse 4 that he has sinned by using his power to take control over Jesus's body and hand it over to the authorities and attempts to give the money back. Judas is "completely rebuffed by the Jewish leaders," who "answer coldly."[48] It is noteworthy that Judas's actions here (speaking publicly to the authorities) continue in the vein of conventional masculinity highlighted previously, but his words now speak against the physical violation of Jesus's body. This time, he is rejected and dismissed. In verse 5, he throws the money into the temple, leaves, and hangs himself.

The relaying of these three actions in one verse (throwing the money down, leaving, and hanging himself) underscores their relationship with one another, and Judas's decisive and quick action. Here again, Judas shows agency and acts independently. But everything has changed. He is no longer in charge of what happens to other peoples' bodies. He is no longer negotiating a benefit for himself. Instead, he uses his power to give away his power. He first does this by throwing away the money, a symbol of masculinity and power, and the result of his engaging in negotiations to gain more control for himself. He tries to return it to the authorities, but they deny him this means of rejecting his earlier action. In response, he simply throws it away.

This act achieves several things. First, it signals Judas giving away this means of control.[49] If acquiring money conveys power, then this action suggests a rejection of it. He no longer has access to or interest in the potential power that particular money could provide. Second, it troubles the relationship between wealth and control over self and over others. Judas gained this wealth by asserting control over Jesus. Recognizing Jesus's innocence, he now speaks against the latter and returns the former, perhaps critiquing both as means of power. Further, if the lure of money had exerted power over Judas, discarding it liberates Judas from that power.

Similarly, Judas's suicide contains both elements of taking and ceding power over himself. Interpretations of Judas's death are varied and numerous, and often include discussions of sin and punishment. I focus more on those themes in the discussion on divine service, and here engage issues of power and control. In some ways, Judas's suicide continues the theme of him taking initiative to achieve a particular outcome. But, in this action, he gives up control over his own body and life. His suicide emasculates him—at least in part.

Judas's suicide by hanging clearly diminishes his masculinity in several respects. His death ends his agency in the narrative, and he has no further control over others or even over himself. In addition, Judas's death leaves his body vulnerable; its fate rests in the hands of the chief priests and elders, who do not value him. The one who wanted to control Jesus's body is now controlled by the ones who handed Jesus over. Judas's death by his own hand eliminates his ability to demonstrate masculine power by control over self and over others.

With this in mind, however, there are complexities to consider. While later interpretations have often assumed that suicide is negative or emasculating, it was not necessarily the case in the ancient world.[50] Sometimes neutral, suicides could also be construed as a form of "noble death."[51] For example, Conway mentions Suetonius's account of the suicide of Otho as brave and noble.[52] Luz mentions both Samson (Judges 16:26–31) and the final martyr in 4 Maccabees (4 Maccabees 12:19).[53] Reed includes the biblical example of Saul and his armor-bearer (1 Samuel 31:4–5; 1 Chronicles 10:4–5), as well as Seneca's rhetoric where he "singles out hanging as an appropriate and noble way to die."[54]

Conway's example of Otho is particularly important because his suicide was said to restore the bravery, and thus masculinity, that he lacked in life.[55] For Conway, noble death is a very powerful means of establishing masculinity in the ancient world.[56] Further, she emphasizes willingness as a key component in this kind of death, mitigating any feminization that might take place from the loss of power. "Making the death an act of one's will rather than a submission to the power of others turns it into a masculine rather than feminine event."[57]

This connection between suicide, noble death, and masculinity is important for viewing Judas's suicide, opening up the possibility that his self-inflicted death does not solely or completely diminish his masculinity. At the same time, the concept of noble death also includes a sense of vicarious death, or dying for others.[58] Does Judas's death qualify? Luz does not think so, claiming that "Judas is neither a righteous man who dies for a good cause nor someone in a hopeless situation who must resort to suicide to preserve his honor."[59] Judas's suicide is not a clear case of noble death such as a soldier "falling on his sword" or Jesus dying "for others." And yet, it is not necessarily wholly emasculating.

The means of Judas's death is also ambiguous when it comes to power. Luz discusses the mixed opinions about hanging in the ancient world, noting that for some, suicide was shameful or disreputable.[60] However, although it was not the most honorable way to die, suicide by hanging "was common in antiquity, especially among members of the lower classes."[61] For members of the lower classes, like Judas, hanging may have been simply a readily available option. In this case, hanging may point to Judas's relative lack of power and status, which would highlight his compromised masculinity as a non-elite man.

If hanging itself is not unequivocally shameful, there are still elements of shame in the narrative. For example, making connections with other ancient literature as well as contemporary cross-cultural perspectives, David Reed argues that Judas's suicide shares elements with other suicides that are meant to place blame or shame on others.[62] Reed draws on a number of biblical examples including Samson, and discusses the Gainj women of Papa New Guinea. According to Reed, Gainj women sometimes take revenge on their abusive husbands through public suicide. Not only are the men shamed because their wives' suicide indicates their abusive behavior, they are shamed because the suicides mean the men "could not control" their wives.[63]

Reed suggests that Judas's hanging places shame and blame on the authorities who not only handed Jesus over to Pilate but also refused to acknowledge Judas's confession of handing over an innocent man. If this is the case, then Judas's suicide is an act of defiance, shaming those who have exerted control over both Jesus and Judas. It is a means of gaining some honor by getting rid of their control over him. This comparison places Judas in the company of women, emasculating him and exposing his lack of masculine power. But his act also emasculates the chief priests and elders, exposing their shame and lack of control over him. This is an interesting acknowledgment, and a potential rejection of imperial masculine power that dominates others, a power that Judas's act exposes as sinful.

A final issue to consider is the idea that Judas's death is physical punishment or penalty for his sin.[64] I return to the issue of repentance in the section on divine service, but here I want to emphasize the physical nature of punishment and the connection to masculinity. If one accepts this interpretation of Judas's death, then the physical punishment inflicted on him, the violation of his body, connects Judas's death to a larger system of hegemonic masculinity that is divinely sanctioned. Part of the tragedy of Judas's death may be his participation in a system that values physical control over another, which ends up in his own physical domination and death. Matthew's Gospel considers Judas's physical punishment to be appropriate for his crime of handing Jesus over. But, viewing the system from a distance, the whole enterprise of handing people over seems to lead nowhere but death.

In some ways, Judas's suicide by hanging is simply frustrating and unsatistfying in its ambiguity and ambivalance. Given that Judas exerted such agency earlier in the narrative, he is capable of negotiation and action. A different choice to try and save Jesus might have resulted in a more noble death, fighting to release Jesus. Instead, Judas chooses this more ambiguous means of death that signals a loss of control, even as it potentially includes resistance. From the perspective of masculinity, Judas's death encompasses a number of complex issues about power and control, leaving unanswered questions about its significance. One thing is for certain, however. After 27:5, Judas is no longer able or trying to control his or other people's bodies.

This lack of control over himself and over others is observed in one additional scene. In 28:16, the Gospel is careful to note that there were eleven disciples who went to Galilee. After repeated references to "the twelve" in the Gospel, some in the context of Judas's actions, the phrase is important as it intentionally excludes him. With one brief reference, it reminds the reader of Judas's one-time existence as a disciple, his handing over Jesus, and his death. From here on out, his story is in the hands of others.

To summarize this section, from the perspective of control over self and over others, Judas initially expresses very conventional masculine behavior. After a period of invisibility, he emerges as an agent, affecting the course of the narrative, negotiating power for himself in the form of money, and physically violating Jesus's body in handing him over to the authorities. In addition, he demonstrates self-mastery as well as freedom of movement. This behavior resonates with ancient understandings of masculine behavior expressed as bodily control.

At the same time, this behavior is challenged by Jesus, in subtle and indirect ways. Jesus shows that he knows Judas's plan. Given multiple opportunities, he does not confront or attempt to dissuade Judas, asserting some power of his own and perhaps challenging the assumptions that conventional power is the only kind of power. And, in the end, Judas loses all this conventional masculine power. He regrets his decision, but his attempt to change the situation is rejected. He throws away the money he had acquired, a symbol of power. He uses his last bit of power over himself to end his own life, violating his own body and giving up control over it and over the way that his actions are interpreted. He performs no redeeming act, no attempted rescue.

Even so, the fact that he chooses his own death shares similarities with noble death, an aspect of masculinity, and his act of suicide may shame the very chief priests who rejected him. This act of suicide may point to the futility of the kind of masculine power that Judas formerly embraced, the kind that exerts control over the bodies of others. Although his suicide surely signals a defeat for Judas, it may also signal a defeat or a criticism of the kind of masculine power he initially displays.

The story of Judas is an example of a non-elite male utilizing conventional masculine tactics of dominating control over self and over others. Although he has some initial success, he later changes his mind about his actions and is unable to undo them. This points not only to the limits of Judas's masculine power but also possibly to a critique of bodily control itself. The narrative exposes the reality that assertions of masculinity in terms of dominant control over others risk destruction by opponents or rivals. Perhaps Judas's destruction is an example of this phenomenon. Or, less nihilistically, perhaps his suicide is a consequence of the dominant control he sought earlier to have over himself and over others when it spirals out of his control.

WEALTH

For much of the Gospel, Judas is not a prominent figure and wealth is not a prominent element in his story; it surfaces in chapter 26 as Judas contemplates handing Jesus over to the religious leaders. Prior to this time, however, the Gospel does consider wealth as a topic, and these ideas set the stage for Judas in chapter 26. For example, when Jesus calls the first disciples in chapter 4, they leave at least some of their livelihood to follow (4:20; 8:8–14). Although his call is not narrated, Judas presumably is subjected to the same expectation. This is made explicit in chapter 10 when "the twelve" (including Judas) are sent out by Jesus. He commands them not to bring money with them and not to expect monetary reward (10:8–10). Although they can expect to be fed and receive hospitality (10:10–11), disciples do not deal in currency as others do.

In another example, after the rich young man visits Jesus in 19:16–22, Jesus tells the disciples that it is difficult for the wealthy to enter the empire of heaven. Peter responds by saying, "we have left everything" in order to follow Jesus (ἰδοὺ ἡμεῖς ἀφήκαμεν πάντα). The use of the first person plural presumably includes all of the disciples, who are the audience for Jesus's speech in 10:23. By implication, Judas is included in this group, has done what is expected, and has left financial resources behind.[65]

In a final example, the story just prior to Judas's visit to the chief priests is the anointing at Bethany (26:6–13).[66] When the unnamed woman uses costly ointment to anoint Jesus, the disciples criticize her, saying that the money used to purchase the anointing ointment should have been given to the poor (26:8–9). Jesus responds to their accusation by praising the woman for anointing his body for burial (26:10–13). Although the disciples' claim about money is challenged by Jesus, the interaction upholds the idea that using wealth for power is not a goal for disciples. It can feed the poor, or anoint Jesus, but the goal is not to amass wealth or use it for power over others as Judas does.

The anointing story is immediately followed by Judas's visit to the chief priests to inquire about handing Jesus over (26:14–16). Here both Judas and wealth come into focus. The first words out of his mouth are, "What will you give me?" (τί θέλετέ μοι δοῦναι). If there is any doubt about the nature of Judas's request, the next statement clarifies that the chief priests paid him money. As Luz observes, "Judas's question in direct speech about payment gives added emphasis to the motif of money."[67]

There is no direct connection between the two stories,[68] but the juxtaposition of the two draws attention to Judas's interest in financial gain.[69] Jesus's "contempt for concern about money" in the anointing scene is followed directly by Judas's request for payment.[70] Judas's attitude provides a stark contrast not just with Jesus, but also with "the woman's costly act of service."[71] This gendered contrast puts Judas in a negative light, but it also interrupts automatic associations between masculinity and virtue that were ubiquitous in the ancient world. In one scene, an unnamed woman's expensive display is critiqued by the disciples but defended by Jesus. In the very next scene, a male disciple negotiates a monetary reward for handing Jesus over.

When viewed through the larger lens of wealth in the Gospel noted above, this association of Judas with wealth conveys a few additional things. First, asking about money is not associated with discipleship. Until this time, Judas has been an invisible, silent disciple, indistinguishable from the others except for the initial descriptor of the one who will hand Jesus over. His first words in the Gospel are to ask outright for money in exchange for handing over Jesus.[72] With this request, Judas breaks with the expectations of discipleship that have permeated the Gospel. Not only is Judas willing to hand Jesus over to the chief priests, he will do so expecting and requesting monetary gain. "Judas—in complete antithesis to everything Jesus has taught—wants money."[73]

Second, it shows that Judas understands and operates in the realm of conventional masculinity. He associates money with power over others and is willing to trade one for the other, to his benefit. This association is critiqued by the Gospel. Because the money is linked with handing Jesus over, both are marked as counter to God's purposes. By taking the money and handing Jesus over, Judas has "sold out," and aligned himself with those who wish to kill God's agent, Jesus. It is not clear whether Judas's desire for money drives his offer, or whether it is a nice side benefit of his primary desire to hand Jesus over, but the association between the two marks both the financial reward and handing Jesus over as counter to God's purposes.

Judas does not specify how much he wants from the chief priests. He simply asks what they will give him. The amount that Judas is paid—thirty pieces of silver—is interesting, both in terms of amount and symbolism. Although the exact value cannot be determined, interpreters emphasize that it is a relatively small amount.[74] The meaning of this is unclear, and the Gospel "leaves much unexplained" about this negotiation.[75] It is likely that an ironic sense of "value" is intended, emphasizing that Jesus is undervalued by the world.[76] And, as Luz further argues, Matthew's use of an amount used elsewhere in biblical texts is meant to convey that all is proceeding according to God's will.[77]

What does this mean for Judas? If the price is low, then perhaps Judas is desperate, or not a good negotiator.[78] Or perhaps the lower price amplifies Judas's scandalous deal. Not only is he willing to sell Jesus out, he does so for a shamefully low amount.[79] On the other hand, Gubar notes that direct parallels with Exodus 21:32 and Zechariah 11:12–13 "seem to identify Judas with righteous men defrauded of their goods and services, not with avarice."[80] Klassen, too, suggests that the low price might caution against a claim about Judas's "greed," although he acknowledges that "when greed is involved, amounts are not necessarily determinative."[81]

While the amount is generally considered to be low, it is imprecise and somewhat symbolic, resisting easy conclusions or associations. What the scene does say about Judas is that he requested payment for his actions. In terms of Judas's masculinity, this shows not only his initiative but his priority. He got what he wanted, wealth, playing by the rules of conventional masculinity, not the alternative of divine service.

The concept of wealth resurfaces in 27:3–10 when Judas returns to the chief priests and elders. This time, he wants to return the money, but they reject his offer. In verse 5, he responds by throwing the money into the temple (εἰς τὸν ναὸν) and departing in order to commit suicide. Judas's desire to return the money suggests that it is a very important symbol. He has changed his mind about his decision to hand over Jesus, and since the money is the symbol of this action, he wants to be rid of it.[82]

For some commentators, Judas's attempt to return the money is less about Judas and more about others. For Carter, the "callous indifference" of the chief priests and elders "bears witness to their corruption."[83] Davies and Allison claim that in this section (27:3–10) the focus is more on the money than it is on "the fate of Judas."[84] The idea here that Judas is "left to himself" by both the chief priests and elders, as well as by the narrative, emphasizes Judas's relative unimportance.[85] While the money originally symbolized Judas's power, now it signals his lack of power. Where before he was able to get the money he wanted, now he cannot return the money he does not want. Where before he was creating options for himself by gaining wealth, how he is facing limited ones. He cannot return the money, and cannot change Jesus's fate, so he simply throws it away.

Here the overall attitude of the Gospel toward wealth is again in view, namely an understanding of wealth as an obstacle to God's purposes. Like the rich young ruler in chapter 19, this scene involving Judas demonstrates how money can thwart discipleship, and how it can easily become associated with enemies of God. Judas's confession of sin by betraying "innocent blood" (αἷμα ἀθῷον) recalls Deuteronomy 27:25, which curses those who take bribes that cause the death of the innocent.[86] Judas has taken payment for handing over God's agent, Jesus, who now faces death with Pilate.

The chief priests and elders do not argue with Judas's assessment that he has sinned by taking money and handing Jesus over. Instead they dismiss Judas and his claim, thereby making it impossible for Judas to return the money. The meaning of their lack of argument is not clear. Maybe it means that they know that Judas is right. On the other hand, perhaps they disagree with Judas, but they don't care what he thinks, having already decided that Jesus is dangerous. Whatever the case, Judas's claim stands; he connects the money he received with his sin in handing Jesus over to them. This further associates the money itself with sin and separation from God's purposes.

The subsequent discussion in 27:6–10 emphasizes this association, as the chief priests discuss what is appropriate to do with the money Judas has left behind. They call it τιμὴ αἵματός, which is often translated as "blood money."[87] Whose blood is intended here? The statement by the chief priests comes just after the narrative relates Judas's death in verse 5. However, it is Jesus's blood that Judas refers to in verse 4. Luz notes that the same phrase is used in *Testament of Zebulon* as the price for which Joseph was sold.[88] Since Judas was not sold, this would suggest that the phrase is connected not with his blood, but with Jesus's blood.[89] In this case, the chief priests acknowledge Judas's claim of his guilt and Jesus's innocence. In either case, it is inappropriate now for it to be associated with the temple, which is holy. But if "blood money" refers to Jesus, then the money is directly associated with bribery and murder.

The choices of chief priests are restricted, but they find a suitable use for the money with the purchase of the potter's field (27:7–8). The allusions are not completely clear here, but include Zechariah and Jeremiah, focusing on God's judgment of unfaithful people and their rejection of a shepherd.[90] The point in the context of this discussion is that money here is associated with disobedience and separation from God. In terms of masculinity, wealth is associated with virtue and power, which usually go together. Here, this means of establishing masculine status is disrupted as wealth and evil are now coupled. Judas's attempts at claiming masculinity through gaining wealth are corrupted, as they have caused Jesus's arrest and labeled Judas an enemy of God. The tight connection between masculinity and virtue is broken, as Judas's attempts to deal in bodily control and wealth, both conventional masculine behaviors, result in money contaminated by the demise of God's agent, Jesus.

This scene illustrates the power, limits, and potential for corruption of money. As a tool of masculinity, these three aspects are critically important. In going to the chief priests initially, Judas exerts power over Jesus by betraying him, and gains further power by receiving payment. Here, changing his mind about his show of force, and realizing he has no further power with the chief priests, Judas gives up the remaining power he has by throwing away the money.

In addition to Judas seeking power through money, it is possible to speak of the money having had power over him. Judas's desire for money was strong enough to cause him to relinquish the commitments he had made as a disciple to follow Jesus and to forego wealth, and instead to receive monetary reward for handing Jesus over. Although there may be multiple reasons for doing so, the power of money is one of the forces driving Judas. His decision, then, to throw it away suggests some abandoning of or distancing from the power of money. Perhaps it signals a larger rejection of the kind of power that money demands and provides, or a recognition of the inability of money to help either Judas or Jesus in this situation.

Beyond this, Judas's rejection of the money puts the value of the money itself into question. If Judas doesn't want it, and neither do the chief priests and elders, then it has lost its value and power. The deliberation among the chief priests and elders in vv. 7–10 is an interesting moment. The power of the thirty pieces of silver is curbed by its association with the arrest and death of an innocent man, so they have to use it in a limited way. This reveals that the power of money is negotiable, contextual, and unstable, much like masculinity itself.

Reviewing this section, several observations are important. When taken in the context of the wider Matthean rhetoric about wealth, Judas's actions concerning wealth are highly critiqued. Not only does he go against the expectations of discipleship in requesting money, he does so as payment for betraying Jesus. The coupling of these two things further labels wealth as antithetical to discipleship in Matthew, with Judas as the prime example. His decision to throw away the money can be read in multiple ways. Most convincing for me is that it is an attempt by Judas to separate himself from the deed, and to relinquish both the power he thought he was gaining and the power that wealth ultimately had over him.

From the standpoint of conventional masculinity, this is a loss of masculine status for Judas. But, it is also potentially a statement about freedom from the conventional power of wealth and a rejection of the games he played with the chief priests and elders. Embedded in the details of this story is a further critique, common in Matthew, of the lure of money and its association with power over others that is antithetical to the ways of discipleship. Wealth is associated with those who wield control, punishing the innocent. When Judas throws the money into the temple, it may be too late for him to reclaim his freedom or to save Jesus. But, from the standpoint of the Gospel's attitude toward wealth, it is the right thing to do.

DIVINE SERVICE

In this final section, I consider divine service—behaviors or characteristics that establish congruence or alignment with divine purposes—as an aspect of Judas's masculinity. This is particularly poignant for Judas, who is identified both as "one of the twelve," (26:14, 47) and as "the one who handed Jesus over" (10:4; 26:46; 27:3). Foregrounding divine services reveals that Judas is set apart from the group and identified as a failure. In this section, it is appropriate to speak of Judas's handing over or dominating control over Jesus as betrayal, an act of failed discipleship. While God is active in the midst of this failure to bring about the vindication and resurrection of Jesus, Judas is not seen in Matthew as an agent of God, but ironically as an enemy. His suicide is not necessarily a redemption, but it is a recognition of the terribleness of his actions, an appropriate self-punishment for betraying Jesus.[91] Judas's suicide is an appropriately ambiguous exit for one whose divine service as a disciple is a failure.

So far in this study, I have emphasized the aspect of dominant control present in the meaning of παραδιδωμι. However, in this section, I am interested in Judas's divine service expressed in discipleship. Handing over Jesus becomes an act where Judas betrays his commitment to discipleship. So while παραδιδωμι does not always connote betrayal, there is a dimension of Judas's exercise of dominating control over Jesus that is best denoted by language of betrayal. Therefore, in this section, I will use both "hand over" and "betray," the latter when it emphasizes Judas's failure in divine service.

As argued in the first section, Judas's introduction in 10:4 encapsulates his conflicting identities. He is last in the list of disciples, which both attempts to diminish his influence and acknowledges his importance. That importance lies not in his identity as a faithful follower of Jesus, but as the one who betrays him by handing him over. His inclusion in the group cannot be ignored; he is a disciple. But this act of Judas labels and identifies him from the very beginning not only as one who fails to live up to aspects of discipleship, but who actively sabotages the work of God in the world.

After this first reference, Judas fades into the group of disciples for the next 16 chapters. It's almost as if the Gospel wants to ignore him for anything except his distinctive identity. If there are positive stories of his works as a faithful follower, they are not included. Because of this silence, it is good to remember that Judas presumably was present for the sending of the disciples in chapter 10, as well as Jesus's many miracles and teachings. He witnesses all that the others do, and makes the confession of faith that the rest do in 14:33.

Scholars draw different conclusions about the meaning of Judas's discipleship in these chapters. Gubar, for example, emphasizes Judas's similarity to the other disciples, who, along with them, comprehends Jesus's identity and makes a personal commitment to being his follower.[92] Carey, on the other hand, downplays his identity as a disciple and his understanding of Jesus's role, especially in light of Peter's confession in chapter 16.[93]

None of this is emphasized by the Gospel, however. What makes Judas noteworthy is his identity as the one who hands Jesus over. Judas's arrival in chapter 26 immediately raises questions about his loyalty and his discipleship. He is introduced as "one of the twelve" in 26:14, emphasizing that group identity, but immediately takes the initiative to do something on his own. By itself, this may not guarantee his disloyalty, but it suggests he is no longer operating strictly as a follower of Jesus.[94]

If Judas's intent is momentarily foggy in verse 14, it is clear in verse 15. He offers to hand Jesus over to the chief priests and elders. With these words and potential actions, Judas proves he is not a disciple. His desire to assert himself and to have control over another means he compromises his role in divine service. Judas's desire to secure a reward for himself in the process further distances him from discipleship. "Judas's desire for monetary gain shows him to be no true follower of Jesus."[95]

Here again, the juxtaposition of Judas's visit to the chief priests and elders with the anointing story is relevant. Luz says that Judas's "behavior stands in contrast to the woman. . . . He is driven by greed, she by absolute devotion."[96] The woman is anointing Jesus for burial; it is Judas who sets Jesus's death in motion. The contrast between her devotion to Jesus and Judas's offer to the chief priests and elders clearly identifies him to be an enemy of Jesus willing to betray his commitment to follow him and aligns him with others who seek to take Jesus's life.

Earlier in the same chapter, at 26:3–5, the chief priests and elders had conspired to kill Jesus. This decision is the culmination of rising conflict during the preceding chapters. The Pharisees, accompanied at times by the scribes and Sadducees, try to entrap Jesus by questioning him until giving up in 22:46.[97] Prior to this, after Jesus drives out the moneychangers and performs healings in the temple in 21:12–14, the chief priests emerge with the scribes as critics and enemies in 21:15–16. They subsequently challenge Jesus's authority in 21:23–27, and Jesus tells parables questioning theirs in 21:28–32 and 33–44. In 21:45–46, the chief priests and the Pharisees are joined together in their opposition to Jesus, but refrain from arresting him because of his popularity.

By chapter 26, when the chief priests and elders gather to plan Jesus's arrest, the Gospel has clearly identified them as enemies of Jesus and made clear the threat they pose to his life (16:21; 20:18). So, when Judas goes to them, he aligns himself solidly with those opposed to Jesus. The process of aligning Judas with Jesus's enemies and separating him from the disciples continues in the next section. Davies and Allison highlight the contrast between Judas's question in 26:15 and the disciples' question in 26:17. Judas inquires about a reward for handing Jesus over, while "the others ask how they can serve him."[98]

The next scene, when Jesus gathers again with the disciples, further implicates Judas. Davies and Allison emphasize that while Jesus has previously spoken about being handed over, "only now does he indicate to the twelve that he will be handed over by one of them."[99] The phrase "the twelve" is used in verse 20, but Judas has clearly set himself apart in the previous scene. When Jesus predicts that one of them will betray him, the rest of the disciples answer in verse 22 as a group. Though he uses similar words, Judas's response is delayed until verse 25. Because of the story relayed in vv.14–16, Judas's question has a different tone from the others; while the rest of the disciples are heard as incredulous, Judas is heard is disingenuous. He has already received payment and is seeking for an opportunity to hand Jesus over; he is lying.[100]

While the larger group calls Jesus "Lord" (κύριε), Judas calls him "Rabbi" (ῥαββί). I previously described the power dynamics in this change. Here I argue that this title is associated with what Carter calls "false discipleship;" Judas uses the term that Jesus has instructed disciples not to use (23:7–8).[101] In terms of Judas's masculinity, while the use of the less respectful address may be interpreted as claiming some power or control, it definitively undercuts his divine service, further separating him from the discipleship that is supposed to define his relationship with Jesus, God's agent.

Judas's question sets up a response from Jesus, who cryptically responds, "You have said so" (σὺ εἶπας). Jesus neither confirms nor denies Judas's words, placing the blame and the responsibility back on Judas himself. Jesus has already spoken judgment in verse 24, when he pronounces "woe" on the one who will betray Jesus by handing him over, and says it would have been better for that one not to have been born. The inclusion of the "woe" recalls the woes Jesus places on his enemies in chapter 23, reiterating Judas's alignment with them. The tension in the scene arises not from the mysterious identity of the one who will hand over Jesus, but from the fact that Judas and the reader know what Judas has already done, and it appears that Jesus does, too. Jesus is choosing not to act; the focus is on what Judas has done and will do.[102]

Through these scenes, Judas has been progressively separated from the disciples and aligned with Jesus's enemies, the chief priests and elders.[103] They are not portrayed as sympathetic characters, but as negative forces conspiring to execute Jesus. Judas is their accomplice. God and Jesus know this will happen, and God does not let death at their hands keep Jesus dead. But that does not exonerate the negative forces themselves, with whom Judas has aligned. Judas's actions are his own, and Jesus's judgment of them is clear. Judas is not a divine servant in Matthew; he is an enemy of God who betrays his role as a disciple in handing over Jesus.[104]

Sometime after the meal (26:26–29) and the departure to the Mount of Olives (26:30), Judas leaves, completing the physical separation from the disciples. He returns in 26:47 to hand Jesus over, accompanied by a large, armed, crowd representing the chief priests and elders. Although Matthew still calls Judas "one of the twelve" in 26:47, the ironic effect is to highlight his violation of that identity, not his inclusion.[105] Here, Judas violates the expectations of divine service as a disciple by bringing danger to Jesus. Although Jesus dissuades it, one of those with him tries to defend Jesus from the mob with violence (26:51). Not only does Judas not defend Jesus, he is the reason for the threat.

Further evidence of Judas's betrayal of divine service in discipleship is the greeting Judas gives Jesus. The kiss itself is not remarkable, but a "gesture of welcome and respect."[106] Judas's use of it here is a grotesque reinterpretation where the intimacy between Jesus and his disciples is violated. The same is true for the spoken greeting, where Judas again uses the title "Rabbi." Jesus has been Judas's teacher, and Judas the student and disciple; now he rejects that discipleship. "Judas's use of 'rabbi' recalls verse 25 and here as there tells us he is no authentic disciple of Jesus."[107] Used ironically, the title now identifies Jesus to the mob, facilitating his arrest. Both the physical and spoken greetings violate Jesus's trust, using Judas's former identity as a disciple and divine servant to provide access to those who attack Jesus. It is a rejection of divine service, a decision to use the privileges of being a disciple of Jesus against him, to expose him to harm and danger.

In terms of masculinity, Judas's desire to assert his own agency and control others has led him to hand over Jesus, betraying the discipleship he once claimed. The tension between disciple and betrayer has momentarily resolved itself in favor of the latter. Judas's status as a divine servant or disciple is a casualty of his power grab, a byproduct of dealing in the conventional masculine world of power exerted by physical control and wealth. This has a complex effect on Judas's masculinity. While power and control may have enhanced his claim to masculine power, abandoning his divine service has detracted from it. This is particularly true in the eyes of the Gospel, which values discipleship so highly.

Judas's next appearance in 27:3 further complicates this dynamic between power and discipleship. After Jesus is bound and led away to Pilate, Judas recognizes that Jesus is "condemned" (κατεκρίθη) and returns to the chief priests to state Jesus's innocence and his own guilt (27:4). Judas's reaction here is curious, given his active pursuit of Jesus's arrest by the chief priests and elders and that fact that Jesus has not yet come before Pilate.[108] Earlier, focusing on power and control, I noted that the transfer of Jesus from the chief priests and elders to Pilate implies crucifixion as Jesus's fate. In terms of divine service, the significance is not immediately clear.

The verb used in 27:3 is μεταμέλομαι and not μετανοέω, the common word for repentance. Despite this, many scholars argue that Judas's remorse is genuine, or at least possible, given his confession of sin and return of the money.[109] Van Unnik argues that this verb, used also in 21:29 and 32 in the story of the two sons asked to work in the field, is best understood as "changing one's mind," with less emphasis on motive.[110] Although it is possible to see repentance here, it is probably safest to speak of regret or second thoughts, as Klassen does.[111]

Judas's change of mind here fits with the trajectory of the narrative. At first, he was introduced in chapter 10 as a disciple who would eventually hand over Jesus. In chapter 26, the tension between the two was heightened. By chapter 27, his choices have made him primarily "the one who hands Jesus over," who emerged from "the twelve." His role as disciple serves only to deepen the tragedy of his betrayal and rejection of divine service.

In terms of this project, the difference between remorse and regret is not substantial, since I am not focused on Judas's salvation or eternal fate. What matters here in terms of divine service and masculinity is Judas's acknowledgement that he has not acted as a disciple or divine servant, but instead handed over God's servant. Judas returns to the chief priests and elders to confess his sin, saying that he has handed over "innocent blood" (αἷμα ἀθῷον). As discussed in the previous section, the phrase "innocent blood" recalls Deuteronomy 27:25, which curses anyone who takes a bribe to shed innocent blood.[112] It also anticipates 27:24, when Pilate will claim his own innocence with respect to Jesus using the same expression, stating Jesus's innocence by implication.[113]

Judas confesses this specific sin to the chief priests and elders, declaring Jesus's innocence, but they rebuff him (27:4). In terms of divine service, their reaction is important because they do not argue with Judas. His assessment of his own sin and Jesus's innocence stands. While theological questions and implications might remain, in terms of the narrative, the assignment of guilt is clear. Judas's decision to hand Jesus over is prompting the death of an innocent man, God's agent Jesus.

The chief priests and elders are also important here because they neither exonerate nor punish Judas. As Carter points out, new testimony about Jesus's innocence does not lead to a new trial or further investigation, which could have saved Jesus and possibly restored Judas's role as divine servant.[114] Neither do they punish Judas, which according to Leviticus

24:17 would mean death.[115] Since Judas "cannot undo his evil deed,"[116] he is left to punish himself. He leaves behind the money he gained from handing Jesus over, and hangs himself.

This interpretation of Judas's death focuses not on eternal salvation, but on punishment for sin. Judas recognizes that he is guilty of a crime. When he is unable to resolve the situation with the chief priests and elders, he punishes himself. It is interesting to consider Judas's alternatives in this moment. His death seems to verify Jesus's assessment of him in 26:24. But might he have died in a different way? If he had attempted to rescue Jesus, securing his own death in the process, would that have been seen as noble or reinstating his divine service? What if he'd lived out a long life of regret and service to the poor?

As argued earlier, suicide itself is not an argument for further estrangement from God. On the contrary, suicide can be understood in noble terms, or at least not immediately shameful or ignoble.[117] If Judas had attempted to rescue Jesus and died in the process, perhaps his masculinity would have been enhanced in one way. But his guilt would have remained. The self-inflicted punishment related in 27:5 "executes the sentence" for Judas's crime, removing the curse proclaimed in Deuteronomy 27:25.[118]

I earlier considered the suicide from the standpoint of control, noting that Judas uses his predilection for bodily control finally to give up control of his own life and body. Here, I recognize that Judas's suicide resolves the tension between being a follower of Jesus, a divine servant, and also the one who hands Jesus over to the chief priests and elders, betraying his role as disciple. Judas prioritizes dominating control over discipleship. Although he is no longer a disciple, his act of suicide removes his guilt. It is possible then to speak of divine service, or at least alignment with divine expectations, in Judas's final act. In terms of masculinity, the effect is ambiguous. Judas's self-inflicted punishment does not necessarily detract from his masculinity expressed in divine service, but neither does it claim anything. Overall, Judas's suicide signals acknowledgment that handing Jesus over is a forfeiture of his discipleship.

Judas's absence in chapter 28 bears mention. "The twelve" (last assembled as a group in 26:20), are now "the eleven." Judas is no longer a disciple, and he is no longer remembered by name. At the beginning, he was both a disciple and one marked to hand Jesus over. In chapters 26–27, he was separated from the disciples and understood primarily through his dominating control of Jesus. By chapter 28, he is not mentioned at all, only recognizable in his absence.

CONCLUSION

The masculinity of Judas is defined primarily by his attempts at control over self and others. These attempts are initially successful, gaining him both control over Jesus and himself, as well as some measure of wealth. However, Judas's actions also betray his role as a disciple, compromising any sense of divine service. Despite achieving control over Jesus, Judas is ultimately defeated. While Jesus dies, God raises him. While Judas initially achieves power and some wealth, he dies by his own hand, carrying out self-punishment for handing over Jesus's innocent body. The price for Judas's power grab is his role as divine servant, which is not reinstated at the end of the narrative. In the final scene where the disciples are mentioned, he is recognizable only in his absence. He is purposefully omitted.

Inherent in the Judas story is a larger critique of the conventional aspects of masculinity. Judas's attempts to assert masculine status on the basis of wealth and control over self and over others lead him to hand Jesus over to his enemies. Not only does this compromise Judas's divine service and ultimately end his life, it points to the dangers of such behavior as antithetical to discipleship. For readers of the Gospel, Judas is a warning to be avoided. There is no defeating God's purposes, but alignment with God's enemies brings consequences. Judas's attempts to secure his own masculine power and status mark him as God's enemy, and his story ends in tragedy as he inflicts divine punishment upon himself for having betrayed his identity as a disciple.

This last observation reveals one other troubling possibility. If God is seen as an agent in this story, even the most powerful display of hegemonic masculinity, then maybe masculine control over self and over others is not ultimately undermined but proceeds exactly as it "should." God simply wins. Perhaps this is merely a warning to those who engage in these kinds of power games contrary to divine purpose that their efforts are ultimately futile. But, as in other examples in this study, such rhetoric continues to associate this problematic masculine behavior with God. Discipleship is described as giving up the kind of power associated with imperial masculinity. But if that kind of masculine power remains, and is reserved for God, then masculine dominance is not truly undermined in this Gospel, but perpetuated.

NOTES

1. As discussed in chapters 1 and 2, divine sanction for masculine authority was important in the ancient world. I use "divine service" in this project to describe a variety of behaviors and characteristics that establish congruence or alignment with divine purposes. For Judas, this is primarily expressed as discipleship.

2. As Raymond Brown observes, "The NT tells us relatively little about Judas; but . . . what it reports is highly dramatic." Raymond Brown, *The Death of the Messiah: From Gethsemane to the Grave: A Commentary on the Passion Narratives in the Four Gospels*, 2 vols (New York: Doubleday, 1994), 2:1394.

3. For representative work, see Susan Gubar, *Judas: A Biography* (New York: W. W. Norton & Company, 2009); Jean-Yves Leloup, *Judas and Jesus: Two Faces of a Single Revelation*, trans. Joseph Rowe (Rochester, VT: Inner Traditions, 2006); Marvin. W. Meyer, *Judas: The Definitive Collection of Gospels and Legends about the Infamous Apostle of Jesus* (New York: HarperOne, 2007); Kim Paffenroth, *Judas: Images of the Lost Disciple* (Louisville: Westminster John Knox Press, 2001); Peter Stanford, *Judas: The Most Hated Name in History* (Berkeley: Counterpoint Press, 2016).

4. For example, Gubar calls Judas "one of us" in Mark and Matthew, and "one of them" in Luke and John. "In the earlier Gospels," she says, "a self-condemned sinner can be forgiven, but in the later Gospels a wicked reprobate remains unforgiven." This process continues through the centuries as the Judas traditions develop and the negative judgment intensifies. Gubar, *Judas: A Biography*, 55.

5. Representative works include: Ian Boxall, *Discovering Matthew: Content, Interpretation, Reception* (Grand Rapids: Eerdmans, 2015), 158–61; Brown, *Death of the Messiah*, 2:1394–418; W. D. Davies and D. C. Allison, *A Critical and Exegetical Commentary on the Gospel According to Saint Matthew*, 3 vols., International Critical Commentary (Edinburgh: T&T Clark, 2004), 3:557–73; Craig S. Keener, *A Commentary on the Gospel of Matthew* (Grand Rapids: Eerdmans, 1999), 656–661; Ulrich Luz, *Matthew 21–28: A Commentary*, trans. James E. Crouch, ed. Helmut Koester, Hermeneia (Minneapolis: Fortress Press, 2005), 3:478–90; David L. Turner, *Matthew* (Grand Rapids: Baker, 2008), 621–22, 624–25, 648–51.

6. Robert H. Gundry, *Peter: False Disciple and Apostate according to Saint Matthew* (Grand Rapids: Eerdmans, 2015), 43–62. For other points of view on this comparison, see David E. Garland, *Reading Matthew: A Literary and Theological Commentary on the First Gospel* (New York: Crossroad, 1993), 254–55; Keener, *Matthew*, 656; and Turner, *Matthew*, 650.

7. Holly J. Carey, "Judas Iscariot: The Betrayer of Jesus;" in *Jesus Among Friends and Enemies*, ed. Chris Keith and Larry W. Hurtado (Grand Rapids: Baker Academic, 2011); Horacio E. Lona, *Judas Iskariot. Legende und Wahrheit: Judas in Den Evangelien Und Das Evangelium Des Judas* (Freiburg: Herder, 2007). Carey's work is combination of reception history with this kind of comparison across Gospels. Both studies also include depictions of Judas from *The Gospel of Judas*.

8. William Klassen, *Judas: Betrayer or Friend of Jesus?* (Minneapolis: Fortress Press, 1996).

9. Davies and Allison, *The Gospel According to Saint Matthew*, 2:154. I note that Davies and Allison are using Judas to make an argument about Peter, while I am doing the opposite. In this case, the assumption about Judas's lack of honor or status comes first.

10. Davies and Allison, *The Gospel According to Saint Matthew*, 2:156.

11. 10:2–4 includes some with modifiers and some without: "first, Simon, also known as Peter, and his brother Andrew; James son of Zebedee, and his brother John; Philip and Bartholomew; Thomas and Matthew the tax collector; James son of Alphaeus, and Thaddeus; Simon the Caanaean, and Judas Iscariot, the one who betrayed him."

12. Richard A. Edwards, *Matthew's Narrative Portrait of the Disciples: How the Text-Connoted Reader is Informed* (Harrisburg: Trinity Press International, 1997).

13. "This widespread variation in usage of the term underscores that we commit an error to translate παραδίδωμι as 'betray.' It is 'handed over.'" Klassen, *Judas: Betrayer or Friend*, 51.

14. Klassen, *Judas: Betrayer or Friend*, 47–58.

15. Klassen prefers the term "informant" for Judas, leaving open the possibility that his role was prearranged by Jesus and the outcome (Roman crucifixion) unintended. His overall argument is to exonerate Judas, or to understand his actions as in line with his discipleship. Klassen, *Judas: Betrayer or Friend*, 62–76.

16. Klassen, *Judas: Betrayer or Friend*, 44. Klassen questions the line of thinking that would assume that Judas could have power over Jesus in this way. I do not share his assumption that such a thing could not happen, but rather contend that this is *an attempt* by Judas to secure that kind of control.

17. 10:19 reads "When they hand you over (παραδῶσιν), do not worry about how you are to speak or what you are to say; for what you are to say will be given to you at that time." 10:21 reads, "Brother will betray/hand over (παραδώσει) brother to death, and a father his child, and children will rise against parents and have them put to death."

18. Raymond Brown advocates for the translation "hand over" even in this place where Judas is identified because it connects this event with others who hand Jesus over. Using "betray," he says, "blurs the parallelism to the agency of others expressed by this verb." Brown, *The Death of the Messiah*, 1:211–13.

19. I revisit other aspects of Judas's prior discipleship in the section on divine service. Here I focus on the parts related to control.

20. Ulrich Luz, *Matthew 8–20: A Commentary*, trans. James E. Crouch and Helmut Koester, Hemeneia (Minneapolis: Fortress Press, 2001), 2:67.

21. Unlike in John 12:4–6, there is no direct association between Judas and the anointing. Matthew places Mark's general, anonymous, criticism (Mark 14:4) in the mouths of the disciples (Matthew 26:8), but Judas is not singled out. (Luke's version in 7:36–50 does not follow the same order as the others.) Luz argues that "the section reaches back beyond the anointing to 26:1–5 and connects the two parts." Luz, *Matthew*, 3:344. Gundry sees a narrative connection between the two, where Judas's act is the unfolding of the prediction that Jesus makes in 26:12. Once Jesus is anointed for burial, then the final drama commences. Robert H. Gundry, *Matthew: A Commentary on His Handbook for a Mixed Church under Persecution*, 2nd ed. (Grand Rapids: Eerdmans, 1994), 522. Carter sees a potential contrast between "a woman's costly act of service" and a male disciple asking "the religious elite for money to betray Jesus," something I revisit in subsequent sections. Warren Carter, *Matthew and the Margins: A Sociopolitical and Religious Reading* (Maryknoll: Orbis, 2000), 503.

22. Klassen, *Judas: Betrayer or Friend of Jesus,* 103.

23. Luz, *Matthew* 3:344. Others observe Judas's agency, as well. Carter says that Judas "takes the initiative." Carter, *Matthew and the Margins,* 504. Davies and Allison emphasize that it is Judas who asks the initial question, and that the exchange of money is "the response to his overture." Davies and Allison, *The Gospel According to Matthew* 3:450.

24. Carter describes Judas's role here as "strange," because the chief priests really don't need him, just "a compliant crowd." By his initiative, Judas makes himself useful and powerful in a situation where he's not technically needed. Carter, *Matthew and the Margins,* 504.

25. Luz, *Matthew* 3:332. Interestingly, he goes on to observe that Jesus's "opponents not only act maliciously, they also do not even carry out their own plan." Luz, *Matthew* 3:332. On the one hand, this could be read to decrease Judas's power, as he "does their dirty work." On the other hand, Judas is the one who instigates and makes possible what they had decided to delay. Certainly, the power dynamics change the next time they meet, but that is unknown at this point in the narrative. I return to the negotiation of power with the authorities later in this section; here I focus on Judas's agency that sets things in motion.

26. I deal with other aspects of this negotiation, including the significance of the amount of the reward, in the next section.

27. Carter, *Matthew and the Margins,* 512.

28. See Warren Carter, *Matthew: Storyteller, Interpreter, Evangelist* (Peabody, MA: Hendrickson, 2004), 72. Asserting that Matthew "recasts" the use of the term, Carter notes that of the three uses of "rabbi" in Mark, Matthew omits one (see Mark 11:21 and Matthew 21:20), changes one to "Lord" (see Mark 9:5 and Matthew 17:4), and the third is the present scene in chapter 26.

29. Carter, *Matthew and the Margins,* 505.

30. Davies and Allison, *The Gospel According to Saint Matthew,* 3:464.

31. Davies and Allison, *The Gospel According to Saint Matthew,* 3:464.

32. Davies and Allison, *The Gospel According to Saint Matthew,* 3:501.

33. Luz, *Matthew,* 3:392.

34. "By describing a disciple who acts on his own, independent from other followers, this incident differs from other portrayals of the disciples in this narrative world." Edwards, *Matthew's Narrative Portrait of the Disciples,* 116.

35. Whether the arresting party could have identified Jesus without Judas is not stated. But Judas's action confirms Jesus's identity beyond a doubt.

36. For a discussion of the symbolism of kisses in biblical tradition, see Luz, *Matthew,* 3:415–16.

37. Davies and Allison, *The Gospel According to Saint Matthew,* 3:508.

38. Sometimes translated "friend," the word can also mean "colleague." It is surely ironic here. See Luz, *Matthew,* 3:418 and Carter, *Matthew and the Margins,* 513.

39. For a discussion of the range of meanings of this phrase, see Davies and Allison, *The Gospel According to Saint Matthew,* 3:509–10 and Luz, *Matthew,* 3:418–19.

40. Here I disagree with Paffenroth, who says that the betrayal scene "doesn't show us anything new about Judas but focuses squarely on Jesus." I think important

198   Chapter 5

aspects of Judas's character are revealed and emphasized in this scene. Paffenroth, *Judas: Images of the Lost Disciple,* 113.

41. Jesus's command to his disciples to stop resisting also protects them. If he were interested in self-preservation, the physical sacrifice of his followers would be expected. As it is, Jesus is self-giving, and does not want his followers to be harmed, even if he is going to be arrested.

42. The final line in v. 56 says that all the disciples (οἱ μαθηταὶ πάντες) deserted him and fled. It does not say whether Judas is still counted among the disciples. If so, then his fleeing underscores this lack of power as he runs for cover. If not, the fact that he is not mentioned by name at the end of the scene means his brief moment is over and the attention turns to others in power.

43. Gubar, *Judas: A Biography,* 72. Edwards, too, thinks that Judas "did not expect that Jesus would be condemned." Edwards, *Matthew's Narrative Portrait of the Disciples,* 123.

44. Klassen, *Judas: Betrayer or Friend,* 161–62.

45. "It is not Judas who delivers Jesus to crucifixion; he has delivered Jesus to the chief priests and elders; they deliver him to Pilate." Audrey Conard, "The Fate of Judas: Matthew 27:3–10," *Toronto Journal of Theology* 7, no. 2 (Fall 1991), 165.

46. Carter, *Matthew and the Margins,* 522.

47. Davies and Allison observe here "a series of related actions—Jesus is delivered by Judas to the Jewish authorities; the Jewish authorities deliver Jesus to Pilate; Pilate delivers Jesus to be crucified." Davies and Allison, *The Gospel According to Saint Matthew,* 3:555. Conard asserts that Jesus's "woe" in 26:24 is ambiguous enough to include those who hand Jesus over to Pilate, as well. When Judas commits suicide, he absolves himself of guilt, leaving just the chief priests. I return to this in the section on divine service. Conard, "Fate of Judas," 165.

48. Luz, *Matthew,* 3:471.

49. In the next section, I expand the discussion of wealth to other aspects. Here I'm focused on wealth as an expression of power over self and over others.

50. For a discussion of these traditional interpretations and evidence from ancient literature see Luz *Matthew,* 3:471–73 and David A. Reed, "Saving Judas: A Social-Scientific Approach to Judas's Suicide in Matthew 27:3–10," *Biblical Theology Bulletin* 35, no. 2 (May 2005), 51–59.

51. Colleen M. Conway, *Behold the Man: Jesus and Greco-Roman Masculinity* (Oxford: Oxford University Press, 2008), 70–72.

52. Conway, *Behold the Man,* 29.

53. Luz, *Matthew,* 3:472.

54. Reed, "Saving Judas," 52–53. Reed quotes Suetonius identifying suicide as a means out of the despair of servitude, saying, "See you that tree, stunted, blighted, and barren? Yet from its branches hangs liberty." Reed, "Saving Judas," 52.

55. Conway, *Behold the Man,* 29.

56. Conway, *Behold the Man,* 71.

57. Conway, *Behold the Man,* 73.

58. Conway emphasizes this aspect when talking about Jesus's death as a noble death. Conway, *Behold the Man,* 73.

59. Luz, *Matthew*, 3:473.

60. Luz, *Matthew*, 3:472.

61. Luz, *Matthew*, 3:472. Luz draws on the work of Hooff and Grisé, noting that despite some negative views of hanging, it was the "second most common form of suicide documented in the sources." Luz, *Matthew*, 472–73, note 60. Anton J.L. van Hooff, *From Autothanasia to Suicide: Self-killing in Classical Antiquity* (London: Routledge, 1990), 235; Yolande Grisé, *Le suicide dans la Rome antique*, Collection d'etudes Anciennes (Montreal: Bellarmin, 1982), 107–9.

62. Reed, "Saving Judas."

63. Reed, "Saving Judas," 56.

64. See Carter, *Matthew and the Margins*, 522–23; Luz, *Matthew*, 3:473.

65. Jesus does promise rewards for those who follow him in 19:29, but they are for the next life, not for this one.

66. Unlike in John, no comment about Judas and theft is made in Matthew (John 12:4–6).

67. Luz, *Matthew*, 3:344.

68. Some scholars do see a potential connection here, even without the explicit reference to Judas in Matthew, but reaching that conclusion requires a substantial bit of psychologizing that is not part of the methodology of this project. For an example, see Gubar, *Judas: A Biography*, 68–70.

69. This thematic juxtaposition is unique to Matthew. In Mark, there is a similar juxtaposition of stories, but Judas does not ask for money. Rather, the chief priests receive gladly his offer of betrayal and promise him money (Mark 14:10–11). In Luke, the story of anointing has a different emphasis on forgiveness (Luke 7:36–50). This is separated from the account of Judas going to the chief priests in 22:1–6. As in Mark, Judas does not ask for money in Luke, but is promised a monetary reward in v. 5. Likewise, in John there is no juxtaposition, although Judas is established as a thief in the anointing story in chapter 12. A visit from Judas to the chief priests is not narrated in John.

70. Davies and Allison, *Matthew*, 3:451.

71. Carter, *Matthew and the Margins*, 503; Davies and Allison, *The Gospel According to Saint Matthew*, 3:450; Luz, *Matthew*, 3:346.

72. As Edwards says, the lack of any previous "rationale or indication of discussion" means that "given the payment, greed is implied as the motivation for the betrayal." Edwards, *Matthew's Narrative Portrait of the Disciples*, 104.

73. Davies and Allison, *The Gospel According to Saint Matthew*, 3:452.

74. Commentators suggest that it could be as little as the amount a day laborer could earn in a month (see Zechariah 11:8–14) or the value of a slave (see Exodus 21:32). In any case, "the amount would have seemed low to most readers." Luz, *Matthew*, 3:345. See also Carter, *Matthew and the Margins*, 504; Davies and Allison, *Matthew*, 3:452–53.

75. Davies and Allison, *The Gospel According to Saint Matthew*, 3:452.

76. Carter, *Matthew and the Margins*, 504; Davies and Allison, *The Gospel According to Saint Matthew*, 3:452; Luz, *Matthew* 3:345.

77. Luz, *Matthew*, 3:345.

78. Paffenroth says that "Judas has sold his master as one would a slave, and at the same time, he has ironically sold himself far too cheaply by accepting such a shameful sum for his services." Paffenroth, *Judas: Images of the Lost Disciple*, 112.

79. While not making this specific argument, Luz discusses these interrelated ideas. Luz, *Matthew*, 3:345.

80. Gubar, *Judas: A Biography*, 69.

81. Klassen, *Judas: Betrayer or Friend of Jesus*, 99. Paffenroth also claims that the money can't be the motive "because the amount is too small." Paffenroth, *Judas: Images of the Lost Disciple*, 112.

82. I return to Judas's potential regret or repentance in the next section. Here I focus on the money, which for Unnik, is the point of Judas's actions. "The idea of regret is not stressed," but instead changing his mind leads to the "real action" of returning the money. Willem Cornelis van Unnik, "The Death of Judas in St. Matthew's Gospel," *Anglican Theological Review*, Supplement Series (3 March 1974), 48

83. Carter, *Matthew and the Margins*, 522.

84. Davies and Allison, *The Gospel According to Saint Matthew*, 3:557.

85. Luz, *Matthew*, 3:471.

86. In addition to this reference Carter notes 2 Kings: 21:16; 21:1–4; Jeremiah 7:5–7, 1 Maccabees 1:37; 2 Maccabees 1:7–8. Luz notes the phrase is used about 19 times in the Septuagint. Luz, *Matthew*, 3:470. I return to the question of Jesus's innocence and Judas's guilt in the section on divine service. Here I am focused on the meaning of the money itself.

87. Carter uses "the price for blood." Carter, *Matthew and the Margins*, 523.

88. Luz, *Matthew*, 3:473, note 68.

89. Brown also assumes that it is Jesus's blood that is indicated, saying that Judas "entangles" the chief priests and elders with the money not with his suicide but when he throws it into the temple. The assumption, then, is that the money is associated with Jesus's death, not Judas's. Brown, *Death of the Messiah*, 1:644.

90. For discussion on these references, see Brown, *Death of the Messiah*, 1:650–51; Luz, *Matthew*, 3:474–75. As Carter summarizes, while the allusions have been understood multiple ways, the most helpful way is "the recognition that while the *words* mostly come from Zechariah, they (along with the preceding verses) reflect the content of Jeremiah 18–19 and 32:6–15." Carter, *Matthew and the Margins*, 523. (emphasis original)

91. As stated in the first section, I am not interested here in theological questions about Judas's eternal fate, or in his emotional or psychological state in terms of repentance. I evaluate Judas's divine service expressed in discipleship based on the criteria for discipleship set forth by the narrative, and the Gospel's understanding of Judas's action with respect to God's agent, Jesus.

92. Gubar, *Judas: A Biography*, 66.

93. Carey, "Judas Iscariot: Betrayer of Jesus," 260.

94. As I discussed in chapter 4, Peter, too, goes awry as a disciple when he takes the initiative, arguing with Jesus about Jesus's death in chapter 16, and making the suggestion about the booths at the Transfiguration in chapter 17.

95. Davies and Allison, *The Gospel According to Saint Matthew*, 3:453.

96. Luz, *Matthew*, 3:346

97. In 12:1–8, Jesus and his followers pick grain on the Sabbath, and later that same day Jesus heals the man with the withered hand in the synagogue (12:9–13). As a result, the Pharisees begin to conspire against him (12:14). The Pharisees, accompanied at times by the scribes or Sadducees, begin to question Jesus and this continues throughout the Gospel (12:38–42; 15:1–9; 16:1–4; 19:3–9; 22:15–46). Following 22:46 when "no one dared to ask him any more questions," Jesus pronounces the "woes" of chapter 23 on the scribes and Pharisees.

98. Davies and Allison, *The Gospel According to Saint Matthew*, 3:457.

99. Davies and Allison, *The Gospel According to Saint Matthew*, 3:461.

100. Carter, *Matthew and the Margins*, 505.

101. Carter, *Matthew: Storyteller, Interpreter, Evangelist*, 72.

102. From a theological perspective, the role of Judas as both disciple and enemy of God is problematic and leads to the suggestion that Judas was in an impossible situation, or that his role was ordained by God. It is important to say that the Gospel itself makes no such claims. It is true that Judas plays an important part in the plan. And it is also true that Jesus does not resist the arrest because it is part of the divine plan. But this does not mean that Judas is somehow understood as an agent of God.

103. It is interesting to me that people are inclined to portray Judas sympathetically, but not the chief priests and elders. If Judas is caught up in a theological game, and unknowingly doing what God wants, so are they. The difference may lie in Judas's identity as a disciple, and the discomfort in the idea of a true betrayer, as well as in the propensity toward anti-Judaism that would blame the chief priests and elders but find a disciple of Jesus at least partially sympathetic.

104. Unlike John, Matthew does not call Judas an agent of the devil (John 13:27). But Judas is actively working against God's agent and aligned with Jesus's enemies.

105. Davies and Allison say the reference "adds pathos" and recalls Jesus's prediction in 26:20–21. Davies and Allison, *The Gospel According to Saint Matthew*, 3:508. See also Luz, *Matthew*, 3:412.

106. Carter, *Matthew and the Margins*, 513.

107. Davies and Allison, *The Gospel According to Saint Matthew*, 3:506.

108. As pointed out in the first section, some scholars do not think that Judas intended for Jesus to die. I think this is unlikely, given Judas's active pursuit of handing Jesus over to the chief priests. But it is impossible to know for sure. See Gubar, *Judas: A Biography*, 72; Edwards, *Matthew's Narrative Portrait of the Disciples*, 123; Klassen, *Judas: Friend or Betrayer of Jesus*, 161–62.

109. Luz, *Matthew*, 3:471; Davies and Allison, *The Gospel According to Saint Matthew*, 3:561–64; Carter, *Matthew and the Margins*, 522; Gundry, *Peter: False Disciple and Apostate*, 58–59; Gubar, *Judas: A Biography*, 66. Paffenroth, *Judas: Images of the Lost Disciple*, 115.

110. Unnik, "The Death of Judas in Saint Matthew's Gospel," 47–48.

111. Klassen, *Judas: Friend or Betrayer of Jesus*, 162. The question of remorse or repentance is usually caught up together with the theological issue of Judas's salvation, which is not in view in this project. For example, although Gundry considers Judas's remorse to be sincere, he considers his confession to be "nonsalvific" because

of the use of the verb μεταμέλομαι. Gundry, *Peter: False Disciple and Apostate,* 58–59. I am not focused on Judas's eternal fate, but on the way the narrative portrays his divine service through discipleship.

112. Luz notes that this phrase is used "about 19 times" in the Septuagint. Luz, *Matthew,* 3:470, note 33. Carter highlights its use in 2 Kings 21:16; 24:1–4; Jeremiah 7:5–7; 1 Maccabees 1:37; 2 Maccabees 1:7–8, as well as the presence of blood of the innocent in Jeremiah 19:4, which includes the purchase of a potter's field. Carter, *Matthew and the Margins,* 522–23.

113. Davies and Allison also note here the difference between Judas, who acknowledges his guilt, and Pilate who denies his. *The Gospel According to Saint Matthew,* 3:563–64. For another take on this comparison, see Brown, *Death of the Messiah,* 1:659–60. See also Luz, *Matthew,* 3:471. In 27:19, the NRSV translates the words of Pilate's wife also to declare Jesus's innocence, although the phrase is different in Greek (τω δικαίω ἐκείνω).

114. Carter, *Matthew and the Margins,* 522.

115. See Carter, *Matthew and the Margins,* 522.

116. Luz, *Matthew,* 3:471.

117. Attitudes among scholars about suicide in the ancient world vary. Reed sees little evidence of suicide as ignoble. Reed, "Saving Judas," 54. Gundry describes a spectrum from noble to ignoble. Gundry, *Peter: False Disciple and Apostate,* 59. Davies and Allison emphasize the positive connotations of suicide in Jewish tradition. Davies and Allison, *The Gospel of Saint Matthew,* 3:562–63. Keener includes a list of references to noble suicide in the ancient world, including Jewish texts. However, he maintains that Judas's death is "dishonorable." Keener, *Matthew,* 658–59. Luz's discussion includes the potential polyvalence of hanging, concluding that although other methods were preferable, hanging was common and that attitudes toward it were ambivalent. Luz, *Matthew,* 3:472–73. In their work on noble death, Droge and Tabor do not label Judas's suicide as a noble death, but they do emphasize that the text does not associate shame or divine disfavor with the suicide itself. Arthur J. Droge and James D. Tabor, *A Noble Death: Suicide and Martyrdom Among Christians and Jews in Antiquity* (San Francisco: Harper Collins, 1992), 113–14. For the purposes of this discussion, suicide is clearly a polyvalent symbol, so Judas's suicide is not restricted to a particular interpretation.

118. Unnik, "The Death of Judas in Saint Matthew's Gospel," 56–57; Daniel Patte, *The Gospel According to Matthew: A Structural Commentary on Matthew's Faith* (Philadelphia: Fortress Press, 1987), 376.

Conclusion

In this study, I have engaged characters in the Gospel of Matthew through the lens of masculinity in the ancient world. While studies in terms of characterization or qualities of discipleship in the Gospel have been undertaken, such a study in terms of masculinity has not been attempted previously. In addition, while masculinity in the ancient world has been a focus of study, the emphasis has been on elite expressions; this project applies aspects of these elite constructions to a variety of non-elite males in the Gospel. This project, then, constitutes a new contribution to discourse on the New Testament, and on Matthew's Gospel in particular, focused on gender and power expressed through masculinity in ancient non-elites.

I have focused on four non-elite males with significant relationships with Jesus—Joseph, John the Baptist, Peter, and Judas—and incorporated discussions along the way with contrasting figures King Herod and Herod Antipas. I have made use of three criteria of ancient masculinity: dominating control over self and over others, wealth, and divine service. These three criteria, important for constructing elite masculinity in the Roman world, are well-suited for Matthew's Gospel, which emerges from this imperial context. Using the same three criteria for each figure also has facilitated comparison and allowed for themes to emerge. Applying them to non-elite men, however, raises important questions about how appropriate or helpful they are for understanding non-elite masculinity.

For Joseph, his masculinity is primarily constructed in terms of divine service expressed in righteousness. His social status limits his expressions of control and his access to wealth, although the Gospel's redefinition of status along the lines of divine service benefits this son of David. But Joseph clearly demonstrates masculine status through obedient righteousness in service to God. This obedience is often manifested in dominating control over himself and over others, particularly Mary and the infant Jesus, allowing them to survive the dominating masculinity exerted by Herod. Even as his social status remains ambivalent, Joseph retains some patriarchal control in his role as divine servant.

King Herod provides a helpful foil as one whose masculinity is constructed in terms of control over others as the ruling provincial king. But he ignores the Gospel's central criterion of divine service, so his attempts to control others defy God and harm others. His attempts at dominating control are also compromised; he cannot control Joseph and Jesus. These failures, as well as his lack of obedience to God, emasculate what should be the most powerful male in the story. The characterizations of Joseph and King Herod provide a hint of a critique about masculine power expressed in wealth and dominant control, while reinscribing or reinterpreting those values when they conform to divine service.

John the Baptist's masculinity is more complex, combining an emphasis on divine service, a rejection of wealth, and a complex negotiation of dominating control over self and over others in a strong claim to an alternative form of masculinity. His role in divine service is clearly visible in his prophetic comparison with Elijah and his identity as forerunner of Jesus, yet he is plainly subordinate to Jesus and does not always demonstrate comprehension of Jesus's role. His asceticism means he does not wield wealth as a means of masculine power; instead, he challenges and rejects the virtue of wealth in line with the Gospel's broader message. In terms of self-control, John's asceticism mimics the ancient ideal, but he is unable to protect his body from physical violation. His control over others is demonstrated in his public, prophetic speech that challenges those in power. Although he loses his head and that voice, John's presence remains as Jesus lifts up his witness in the Gospel.

The contrast with Herod Antipas, whose control over John is both emphasized and mitigated, illustrates John's alternative construction. While John demonstrates ascetic self-control, the narrative highlights Herod's excess in emotions and in wealth, making John more of a man than Herod. While Herod physically defeats John, John's death is defined by the narrative in terms of divine service, which is the Gospel's priority. So John's death serves as a judgment on Herod's domination over others rather than of John's masculinity. While John is a divine servant, Herod is a threat to God's servants.

Peter's masculinity is constructed with a combination of dominance and ambivalence present in each of the three categories. Peter is the "first" disciple and the one who denies Jesus, the one who both walks on water and sinks, and the one who confesses Jesus's identity and is rebuked for disagreeing with him because he does not understand. His instincts toward self-preservation and away from Jesus's suffering and death, while conforming to masculine standards of dominating control over self and over others, compromise his divine service expressed in discipleship. Peter's negotiation of power as a leader among the followers and yet one submissive to Jesus exposes a fundamental tension between discipleship and conventional dominating masculinity that is problematic and unresolved.

Another form of this tension is present in the characterization of Judas, who is both "one of the Twelve" and the one who hands Jesus over to the authorities for crucifixion. The tension in Judas's character is resolved when his control over others—notably Jesus—leads to his failure as a disciple (betrayal). Judas's masculinity, then, is primarily defined in terms of dominating control over self and over others (symbolized partly by acquiring wealth), but his expressions of dominating control compromise his divine service and render him a betrayer. Judas's story ultimately ends in his suicide, a polyvalent symbol that combines agency with loss of control within the context of punishment for betraying divine service. Like Peter, Judas's characterization reveals the problematic aspects of masculine power for those who seek to follow Jesus.

This analysis produces some interesting observations concerning non-elite masculinity. Central is the Gospel's privileging of divine service, which results in a different attitude toward wealth and dominating control than in the wider Roman imperial culture. Because of the social location of the major figures as followers and subordinates to Jesus, conventional masculinity comprising domination is not easily expressed. Each figure is limited in his ability to control others in the way that hegemonic masculinity demands. Each also lacks access to the kind of wealth necessary to assert status and establish dominance. But divine service remains both accessible and essential as a means of establishing masculine status. The expressions of masculinity in this Gospel, then, involve different measures of negotiation, resistance, reinterpretation, and mimicry, all of which revolve around divine service as the definitive element.

For example, wealth is critiqued throughout the Gospel as an obstacle to discipleship. Judas's desire for monetary reward is highlighted, John criticizes the wealthy, and the disciples are instructed to bring no money with them on their journeys. The figures in the Gospel who do have higher status, King Herod and Herod Antipas, are not praised for their wealth and correlating dominance, but critiqued for lack of self-control and disobedience to God. At this point, the Gospel makes the strongest departure from the masculinity of the ancient world, constructing status in alternative ways and vocally criticizing wealth.

At the same time, status is still highly valued in the Gospel, but is reinterpreted along the lines of divine service and obedience to God. Joseph's status is elevated because of his connection to David and his righteous obedience to God in the context of danger and dislocation. While John the Baptist rejects wealth, he receives high status from Jesus as one who speaks for God and witnesses to Jesus. The authority of the disciples over forgiveness is described in monetary terms, and their status over others is endorsed by the Gospel. This suggests that these versions of masculinity retain an emphasis on status and reassign its measure to elements more readily available to non-elites.

The reinterpretation of masculinity along the lines of divine service is also present in dominating control over self and over others. Certain forms of control that are sanctioned by God are highly valued, such as John's asceticism, Peter's dominance over the other disciples, and Joseph's control over Mary and the infant Jesus which defies King Herod's control. Other forms of control, especially those employing destructive violence, such as Judas's asserted control over Jesus, and the attempts of King Herod and Herod Antipas to control Jesus and John, are critiqued. Defining or identifying dominating control as an aspect of divine service is important for the Gospel's approval of such behavior. The ends justify the means.

It is not new to say that the Gospel of Matthew privileges and prioritizes divine service, expressed both as discipleship and as obedience. What is interesting in this study is how that emphasis plays out in constructions of masculinity. While some forms of masculine behavior are rejected (Judas's asserting dominance over Jesus and gaining wealth, Peter challenging Jesus, Herod's control over John's body), other forms are endorsed (John challenging the authorities, Joseph exerting control over Mary and the infant Jesus, disciples receiving authority over others' forgiveness). Obedience to God becomes the standard by which that behavior is judged. The power of God in the Gospel, which in many cases is described in hegemonic terms, changes the criteria by which masculine behavior is evaluated, but, significantly, leaves the system of dominating masculine power and control intact. God exhibits and sanctions hegemonic masculinity performed by *his* agents for *his* purposes.

Another important observation from this project is the way that the three elements of masculinity—control over self and over others, divine service, and wealth—are often interrelated. For example, wealth can be a means of control over others, but its use, and thereby its approval, are subject to divine service. Judas's desire for monetary reward is judged negatively, because it leads to the destruction of Jesus. But Peter and the disciples are promised thrones, resources, and power over others in the future eschatological age as a reward for obedience to God in this life. In an ideal situation, it is clear how these facets of masculinity can work together to strengthen a claim toward hegemony. However, in the case of non-elites in Matthew's Gospel, the result is a complicated mix of conflicting and problematic combinations.

Highlighting the masculinities of four figures in the Gospel of Matthew demonstrates something of the variety of the combinations of non-elite masculinities and their various negotiations with the ideal. Joseph's marginalized masculinity, defined in terms of obedience, nevertheless retains the patriarchal dividend, comprising control over those in his family. John's alternative masculinity emphasizes divine service as the lens through which wealth is critiqued, prophetic public speech against God's enemies is praised, self-control is valued, and the loss of control in death is redefined in terms of martyrdom. Peter's conventional demonstration of dominant masculinity is positive when it performs divine functions, but critiqued when it challenges Jesus; conflict arises from the friction between divine service and dominating control. Judas's masculinity mimics the ideal through assertive control over others and acquisition of wealth and is judged harshly by the Gospel as counter to divine purposes.

This diversity emphasizes that masculinity, like femininity, is socially constructed. Further, the Gospel's privileging of divine service as determinative for masculinity illustrates the subjectivity of social constructions; the standards for masculinity can vary according to values, contexts, or priorities. Showing alternate forms is a reminder that masculinity is subjective and unstable.

This study creates several potential areas for future investigation. The discussion of each of the four figures in this dissertation could be expanded to include other characteristics of masculinity that would complexify and deepen the analysis. Future projects could focus on other Matthean figures not in view in this dissertation, such as Pilate, Joseph of Arimathea, some of the named disciples (James, John), or those who comprise the alliance of Jerusalem-based leaders. Future studies could also apply concepts of masculinity across other sections of the Gospel; for example, considering the Sermon on the Mount or Jesus's parables through the lens of masculinity would be worthwhile. Similar approaches could also be applied to masculine figures in the other Gospels, yielding an opportunity not only for comparison of characters across the texts but also expanding the understanding of masculinity in individual Gospels.

Finally, the question of God's hegemony and the effect this has on early Christian concepts of masculinity is an important one that needs much consideration. On the one hand, God's agent Jesus emphasizes self-sacrifice, care for the poor, and communal care for one another. These values are counter to those held by hegemonic masculinity that emphasize competition, status, powerful wealth, and a focus only on the ideal. On the other hand, rather than critiquing power itself, the Gospel places ultimate power in the hands of the divine, who is imaged in terms of male power, as the father in the heavens whose will is to extend over the earth (6:10).

While such a move advocates for a change in the way humans relate to one another by valuing the lives of those without money or power, it also leaves room for those who claim to speak for hegemonic divinity to claim power for themselves over everyone else, both men and especially women. Wielding power in this way allows for a focus on status and control, as long as it purports to serve divine ends. This problematizes submission to the divine will, urging caution and consideration for the implications and potential casualties of obeying a God defined in terms of male hegemony. It is not irrelevant that two of the agents of divine hegemony—John and Jesus—end up dead.

Still, removing the "top spot" of masculinity from human access is a significant shift. As Eilberg-Schwartz observes, putting God and humans together in a hegemonic system exposes the instability of the system.[1] If ideal masculinity is unavailable to humans, then there is room for many other alternative forms that can reject wealth and power and emphasize collaboration, sacrifice, and advocacy for others. Ultimately, this does not result in the deconstruction of the concept of divine hegemonic masculinity. But perhaps it relativizes the construction and opens the door for a more realistic conversation about the social construction of masculinities and their merits and dangers. Bringing masculinity to the forefront hopefully exposes and de-centers some of its destructive power and envisions potentially constructive power instead, enabling further work that will critique and shape discourse on masculinity toward a more equitable and creative future.

NOTE

1. Howard Eilberg-Schwartz, *God's Phallus: And Other Problems for Men and Monotheism* (Boston: Beacon Press, 1994), 2.

Bibliography

Albright, W. F., and C. S. Mann. *Matthew.* Anchor Bible 26. Garden City, NY: Doubleday, 1971.
Alföldy, Géza. *The Social History of Rome.* Translated by David Braund and Frank Pollock. Baltimore, MD: The Johns Hopkins University Press, 1985.
Allison, Dale C., Jr. "Divorce, Celibacy, and Joseph (Matthew 1:18–25 and 19:1–12)." *Journal for the Study of the New Testament* 49 (Jan 1993): 3–10.
Anderson, Janice Capel. "Feminist Criticism: The Dancing Daughter." In *Mark & Method: New Approaches in Biblical Studies,* 2nd ed., edited by Janice Capel Anderson and Stephen D. Moore, 103–34. Minneapolis, MN: Fortress Press, 2008.
———. "Mark and Matthew in Feminist Perspective: Reading Matthew's Genealogy." In *Mark and Matthew II,* edited by Eve-Marie Becker and Anders Runesson, 271–88. Tübingen: Mohr Siebeck, 2013.
———. "Mary's Difference: Gender and Patriarchy in the Birth Narratives." *Journal of Religion* 67, no. 2 (Apr 1987): 183–202.
———. "Matthew: Gender and Reading." *Semeia* 28 (1983): 3–27.
———. *Matthew's Narrative Web: Over, and Over, and Over Again.* Sheffield: Sheffield Academic Press, 1994.
Anderson, Janice Capel, and Stephen D. Moore. "Matthew and Masculinity." In *New Testament Masculinities,* edited by Stephen D. Moore and Janice Capel Anderson, 67–91. Atlanta, GA: Society of Biblical Literature, 2003.
Asikainen, Susanna. *Jesus and Other Men: Ideal Masculinities in the Synoptic Gospels.* Leiden: Brill, 2018.
Augustus, Emperor of Rome, 63 BCE–14 CE. *Res Gestae Divi Augusti.* Translated by Frederick W. Shipley. Loeb Classical Library 152. Cambridge, MA: Harvard University Press, 1924.
Bauer, David R. *The Structure of Matthew's Gospel: A Study in Literary Design.* Sheffield: Sheffield Academic Press, 1988.
Beare, Francis Wright. *The Gospel According to Matthew.* Oxford: Basil Blackwell, 1981.
Beauvoir, Simone de. *The Second Sex.* Translated by Constance Borde and Sheila. Malovany-Chevallier. New York: Alfred A. Knopf, 2010.

Berkey, Robert F. "ΕΓΓΙΖΕΙΝ, ΦΘΑΝΕΙΝ, and Realized Eschatology." *Journal of Biblical Literature* 82, no. 2 (Jun 1963): 177–87.
Bennema, Cornelis. *A Theory of Character in New Testament Narrative*. Minneapolis, MN: Fortress Press, 2014.
Bhabha, Homi K. *The Location of Culture*. London: Routledge, 1994.
Boatwright, Mary Taliaferro. "Plancia Magna of Perge: Women's Roles and Status in Roman Asia Minor." In *Women's History and Ancient History*, edited by Sarah Pomeroy, 249–72. Chapel Hill: University of North Carolina Press, 1991.
Bockmuehl, Markus N. A. "Matthew 5:32, 19:9 in the Light of Pre-Rabbinic Halakhah." *New Testament Studies* 35, no. 2 (Apr 1989): 291–95.
Bockmuehl, M. *Simon Peter in Scripture and Memory: The New Testament Apostle in the Early Church*. Grand Rapids, MI: Baker Academic, 2012.
Booth, Wayne C. *The Rhetoric of Fiction*. Chicago: University of Chicago Press, 1961.
Bordo, Susan. *Unbearable Weight: Feminism, Western Culture, and the Body*. Berkeley: University of California Press, 1993.
Bosworth, Brian. "Augustus, the Res Gestae, and Hellenistic Theories of Apotheosis." *Journal of Roman Studies* 89 (1999): 1–18.
Boxall, Ian. *Discovering Matthew: Content, Interpretation, Reception*. Grand Rapids, MI: Eerdmans, 2015.
Branden, Robert Charles. *Satanic Conflict and the Plot of Matthew*. New York: Peter Land, 2006.
Brown, Jeannine K. *The Disciples in Narrative Perspective: The Portrayal and Function of the Matthean Disciples*. Atlanta, GA: Society of Biblical Literature, 2002.
Brown, Raymond. *Biblical Reflections on Crises Facing the Church*. New York: Paulist, 1975.
———. *The Birth of the Messiah: A Commentary on the Infancy Narratives in the Gospels of Matthew and Luke*. New York: Doubleday, 1993.
———. *The Death of the Messiah: From Gethsemane to the Grave: A Commentary on the Passion Narratives in the Four Gospels*. 2 vols. New York: Doubleday, 1994.
Brown, Raymond, Karl Donfried, and John Reumann, eds. *Peter in the New Testament: A Collaborative Assessment by Protestant and Roman Catholic Scholars*. Eugene, OR: Wipf and Stock, 2002.
Butler, Judith. *Gender Trouble: Feminism and the Subversion of Identity*. New York: Routledge, 2006.
Carey, Holly J. "Judas Iscariot: The Betrayer of Jesus." In *Jesus Among Friends and Enemies*. Edited by Chris Keith and Larry W. Hurtado. Grand Rapids, MI: Baker Academic, 2011.
Carter, Warren. "Are There Imperial texts in the Class? Intertextual Eagles and Matthean Eschatology as 'Lights Out' Time for Imperial Rome (Matthew 24:27–31)." *Journal of Biblical Literature* 122, no. 3 (2003): 467–87.
———. *John and Empire: Initial Explorations*. New York: T&T Clark, 2008.
———. "Kernels and Narrative Blocks: The Structure of Matthew's Gospel." *The Catholic Biblical Quarterly* 54, no. 3 (July 1992): 463–81.
———. *Matthew: Storyteller, Interpreter, Evangelist*. Peabody, MA: Hendrickson, 2004.

———. *Matthew and Empire: Initial Explorations.* Harrisburg: Trinity Press, International, 2001.
———. *Matthew and the Margins: A Sociopolitical and Religious Reading.* Maryknoll: Orbis, 2000.
———. "Matthew's Gospel, Rome's Empire, and the Parable of the Mustard Seed (Matthew 13:31–32)." In *Hermeneutik Der Gleichnisse Jesu: Methodische Neuansätze Zum Verstehen Urchristlicher Parabeltexte.* Edited by R. Zimmerman, 181–201. Tübingen: Mohr Siebeck, 2008.
———. "Narrative Readings, Contextualized Readers, and Matthew's Gospel." In *The Oxford Handbook of Biblical Narrative,* edited by Donna Nolan Fewell, 307–18. New York: Oxford University Press, 2016.
———. "Paying the Tax to Rome as Subversive Praxis: Matthew 17:24–27." *Journal for the Study of the New Testament* 22, no. 76 (Apr 2000): 3–31.
———. *Pontius Pilate: Portrait of a Roman Governor.* Collegeville, PA: Liturgical Press, 2003.
———. *The Roman Empire and the New Testament: An Essential Guide.* Nashville: Abingdon Press, 2006.
———. *What Does Revelation Reveal?: Unlocking the Mystery.* Nashville: Abingdon Press, 2011.
Cassidy, Richard J. *Four Times Peter: Portrayals of Peter in the Four Gospels and at Philippi.* Collegeville, PA: Liturgical Press, 2007.
Casson, Lionel. *Travel in the Ancient World.* Toronto: Hakkert, 1974.
Chatman, Seymour. *Story and Discourse: Narrative Structure in Fiction and Film.* New York: Cornell University Press, 1978.
Cobb, L. Stephanie. *Dying to be Men: Gender and Language in Early Christian Martyr Texts.* New York: Columbia University Press, 2008.
Conard, Audrey. "The Fate of Judas: Matthew 27:3–10." *Toronto Journal of Theology* 7, no. 2 (Fall 1991): 158–68.
Connell, R. W. *Gender and Power: Society, the Person and Sexual Politics.* Stanford: Stanford University Press, 1987.
———. *Masculinities*, 2nd ed. Berkeley: University of California Press, 2005.
Connell, R. W., and James W. Messerschmidt. "Hegemonic Masculinity: Rethinking the Concept." *Gender and Society* 19, no. 6 (Dec. 2005): 829–59.
Conway, Colleen M. *Behold the Man: Jesus and Greco-Roman Masculinity.* Oxford: Oxford University Press, 2008.
Corley, Kathleen. *Private Women, Public Meals: Social Conflict in the Synoptic Tradition.* Peabody, MA: Hendrickson, 1993.
Cotter, Wendy J. "Greco-Roman Apotheosis Traditions and the Resurrection Appearances in Matthew." In *The Gospel of Matthew in Current Study,* edited by David Aune, 127–53. Grand Rapids, MI: Eerdmans, 2001.
Crossan, John Dominic, and Jonathan L. Reed. *In Search of Paul: How Jesus's Apostle Opposed Rome's Empire with God's Kingdom.* San Francisco: Harper Collins, 2004.
Cullmann, Oscar. *Peter: Disciple, Apostle, Martyr.* Translated by Floyd V. Filson. Philadelphia: Westminster Press, 1953.

D'Angelo, Mary Rose. "*Abba* and 'Father': Imperial Theology and the Jesus Traditions." *Journal of Biblical Literature* 111, no. 4 (Winter 1992): 611–30

———. "Theology in Mark and Q: *Abba* and 'Father' in Context." *Harvard Theological Review* 85, no. 2 (Apr 1992): 149–74.

Daly, Mary. *Beyond God the Father: Toward a Philosophy of Women's Liberation*. Revised ed. Boston: Beacon Press, 1993.

———. *Gyn/Ecology: The Metaethics of Radical Feminism*. Boston: Beacon Press, 1990.

Danker, Frederick W., Walter Bauer, William F. Arndt, and F. Wilbur Gingrich. *Greek-English Lexicon of the New Testament and Other Early Christian Literature*, 3rd ed. Chicago: University of Chicago Press, 2000.

Davies, W. D., and D. C. Allison. *A Critical and Exegetical Commentary on the Gospel According to St. Matthew*. 3 vols. International Critical Commentary. Edinburgh: T&T Clark, 2004.

Demetriou, Demetrakis Z. "Connell's Concept of Hegemonic Masculinity: A Critique." *Theory & Society* 30, no. 3 (June 2001): 337–61.

Dench, Emma. "Austerity, Excess, and Failure in Hellenistic and Early Imperial Italy." In *Parchments of Gender: Deciphering the Body in Antiquity*, edited by Maria Wyke, 121–46. Oxford: Oxford University Press, 1998.

Deutsch, Celia. "Jesus as Wisdom: A Feminist Reading of Matthew's Wisdom Christology." In *A Feminist Companion to Matthew*, edited by Amy-Jill Levine and M. Blickenstaff, 88–113. Sheffield: Sheffield Academic Press, 2001.

———. *Lady Wisdom, Jesus, and the Sages: Metaphor and Social Context in Matthew's Gospel*. Valley Forge, PA: Trinity Press International, 1996.

Dionysius of Halicarnassus. *Roman Antiquities*. 7 volumes. Translated by Earnest Cary. Loeb Classical Library 319, 347, 357, 364, 372, 378, 388. Cambridge, MA: Harvard University Press, 1937–50.

Doane, Sébastien. "Masculinities of the Husbands in the Genealogy of Jesus (Matt. 1:2–16)" *Biblical Interpretation* 27, no. 1 (2019): 91–106.

Dodson, Derek S. *Reading Dreams: An Audience-Critical Approach to the Dreams in the Gospel of Matthew*. London: T&T Clark, 2009.

Doyle, Michael W. *Empires*. Ithaca, NY: Cornell University Press, 1986.

Droge, Arthur J., and James D. Tabor. *A Noble Death: Suicide and Martyrdom Among Christians and Jews in Antiquity*. San Francisco: Harper Collins, 1992.

Dube, Musa W. *Postcolonial Feminist Interpretation of the Bible*. St. Louis: Chalice Press, 2000.

Duling, Dennis C. "Empire: Theories, Methods, Models." In *The Gospel of Matthew in its Roman Imperial Context*, edited by John Riches and David C. Sim, 49–74. London: T&T Clark International, 2005.

Eck, Werner. *The Age of Augustus*, 2nd ed. Translated by Deborah Lucas Schneider. Malden, MA: Blackwell, 2007.

Edwards, Catharine. *The Politics of Immorality in Ancient Rome*. Cambridge: Cambridge University Press, 1993.

Edwards, Richard A. *Matthew's Narrative Portrait of the Disciples: How the Text-Connoted Reader Is Informed*. Harrisburg: Trinity Press International, 1997.

———. *Matthew's Story of Jesus*. Philadelphia: Fortress Press, 1985.
Eilberg-Schwartz, Howard. *God's Phallus: And Other Problems for Men and Monotheism*. Boston: Beacon Press, 1994.
Eisenstadt, S. N. *The Political Systems of Empires: The Rise and Fall of the Historical Bureaucratic Societies*. Glencoe: Free Press, 1963.
Elliott, Neil. *The Arrogance of Nations: Reading Romans in the Shadow of Empire*. Minneapolis, MN: Fortress Press, 2010.
Elliott, Scott S. *Reconfiguring Mark's Jesus: Narrative Criticism after Poststructuralism*. Sheffield: Sheffield Phoenix Press, 2011.
Engelhardt, Jillian. "Performing Power in the Public Court of Reputation: Capital Punishment, John the Baptist, and Julius Jones." *Review and Expositor* 119, 3–4 (2023): 303–14
Erickson, Richard J. "Joseph and the Birth of Isaac in Matthew 1." *Bulletin for Biblical Research* 10, no. 1 (2000): 35–51.
Evans, Craig A. *Matthew*. New York: Cambridge University Press, 2012.
Fausto-Sterling, Anne. *Sexing the Body: Gender Politics and the Construction of Sexuality*. New York: Basic Books, 2000.
Fears, J. Rufus. "The Cult of Jupiter and Roman Imperial Ideology." In *Principat 17/1; Heidentum: Roemische Goetterkulte, Orientalische Kulte in Der Roemischen Welt*, 3–141. Berlin: Walter de Gruyter, 1981.
———. "Nero as the Vicegerent of the Gods in Seneca's de Clementia." *Hermes* 103, no. 4 (1975): 486–96.
Fitzmyer, Joseph. *Saint Joseph in Matthew's Gospel*. Philadelphia: Saint Joseph's University Press, 1997.
Flessen, Bonnie J. *An Exemplary Man: Cornelius and Characterization in Acts 10*. Eugene, OR: Pickwick, 2011.
Foucault, Michel. *The History of Sexuality, Volume 1: An Introduction*. New York: Pantheon Books, 1978.
Friedan, Betty. *The Feminine Mystique*. New York: Norton & Co., 1963.
Friesen, Steven J. "Poverty in Pauline Studies: Beyond the So-Called New Consensus." *Journal for the Study of the New Testament* 26, no. 3 (Mar 2004): 323–61.
Galinsky, Karl. *Augustan Culture: An Interpretive Introduction*. Princeton, NJ: Princeton University Press, 1996.
Garland, David E. *Reading Matthew: A Literary and Theological Commentary on the First Gospel*. New York: Crossroad, 1993.
Glancy, Jennifer. "Slaves and Slavery in Matthean Parables." *Journal of Biblical Literature* 119, no. 1 (Spring 2000): 67–90.
———. "Unveiling Masculinity: The Construction of Gender in Mark 6:17–29." *Biblical Interpretation* 2, no. 1 (Mar 1994): 34–50.
Gleason, Maud. "Elite Male Identity in the Roman Empire." In *Life, Death, and Entertainment in the Roman Empire*, edited by D. S. Potter and D. J. Mattingly, 67–84. Ann Arbor: University of Michigan Press, 1999.
———. *Making Men: Sophists and Self-Presentation in Ancient Rome*. Princeton, NJ: Princeton University Press, 1995.

Goffman, Erving. *Stigma: Notes on the Management of Spoiled Identity.* New York: Simon & Schuster, Inc., 1963.
Grisé, Yolande. *Le suicide dans la Rome antique.* Collection d'etudes Anciennes. Montreal: Bellarmin, 1982.
Gubar, Susan. *Judas: A Biography.* New York: W. W. Norton & Company, 2009.
Guest, Deryn. *Beyond Feminist Biblical Studies.* Sheffield: Sheffield Phoenix Press, 2012.
Gunderson, Erik. *Staging Masculinity: The Rhetoric of Performance in the Roman World.* Ann Arbor: University of Michigan Press, 2000.
Gundry, Robert H. *Matthew: A Commentary on His Handbook for a Mixed Church under Persecution,* 2nd ed. Grand Rapids, MI: Eerdmans, 1994.
———. *Peter: False Disciple and Apostate According to Saint Matthew.* Grand Rapids, MI: Eerdmans, 2015.
Hanson, K. C. "Galilean Fishing Economy and the Jesus Tradition." *Biblical Theological Bulletin* 27, no. 3 (Fall 1997): 99–111.
Hanson, K. C., and Douglas E. Oakman. *Palestine in the Time of Jesus: Social Structures and Social Conflicts,* 2nd ed. Minneapolis, MN: Fortress Press, 2008.
Hardwick, Lorna. "Concepts of Peace." In *Experiencing Rome: Culture, Identity, and Power in the Roman Empire,* 3rd ed., edited by Janet Huskinson, 335–69. New York: Routledge, 2009.
Harvey, W. J. *Character and the Novel.* Ithaca, NY: Cornell University Press, 1965.
Helyer, Larry R. *The Life and Witness of Peter.* Downers Grove, IL: InterVarsity Press, 2012.
Hengel, Martin. *Saint Peter: The Underestimated Apostle.* Translated by T. Trapp. Grand Rapids, MI: Eerdmans, 2010.
Hezser, Catherine. *Jewish Travel in Antiquity.* Tübingen: Mohr Siebeck, 2011.
Hochman, Baruch. *Character in Literature.* Ithaca: Cornell University Press, 1985.
Hooff, Anton J. L. van. *From Autothanasia to Suicide: Self-Killing in Classical Antiquity.* London: Routledge, 1990.
hooks, bell. *Talking Back: Thinking Feminist, Thinking Black.* Boston: South End Press, 1989.
Hope, Valerie. "The City of Rome: Capital and Symbol." In *Experiencing Rome: Culture, Identity, and Power in the Roman Empire,* 3rd ed., edited by Janet Huskinson, 63–93. New York: Routledge, 2009.
———. "Status and Identity in the Roman World." In *Experiencing Rome: Culture, Identity, and Power in the Roman Empire,* 3rd ed., edited by Janet Huskinson, 125–52. New York: Routledge, 2009.
Horsley, Richard A. "The Apostle Paul and Empire." In *In the Shadow of Empire: Reclaiming the Bible as a History of Faithful Resistance,* edited by Richard A. Horsley, 97–116. Louisville, KY: Westminster John Knox Press, 2008.
———. *The Liberation of Christmas: The Infancy Narratives in Social Context.* New York: Crossroad, 1989.
Hunt, Steven A., D. Francois Tolmie, and Ruben Zimmermann, eds. *Character Studies in the Fourth Gospel.* Tübingen: Mohr Siebeck, 2013.

Irigaray, Luce. *The Irigaray Reader.* Edited by Margaret Whitford. Cambridge: Basil Blackwell, 1991.
Josephus. *Jewish Antiquities, Volume IV: Books 9–11.* Translated by Ralph Marcus. Loeb Classical Library 326. Cambridge, MA: Harvard University Press, 1937.
———. *Jewish Antiquities, Volume VI: Books 14–15.* Translated by Ralph Marcus, Allen Wikgren. Loeb Classical Library 489. Cambridge, MA: Harvard University Press, 1943.
———. *Jewish Antiquities, Volume VII: Books 16–17.* Translated by Ralph Marcus, Allen Wikgren. Loeb Classical Library 410. Cambridge, MA: Harvard University Press, 1963.
———. *Jewish Antiquities, Volume VIII: Books 18–19.* Translated by Louis H. Feldman. Loeb Classical Library 433. Cambridge, MA: Harvard University Press, 1965.
———. *The Jewish War, Volume II: Books 3–4.* Translated by H. St. J. Thackeray. Loeb Classical Library 487. Cambridge, MA: Harvard University Press, 1927.
Juvenal. *Satires.* Edited and translated by Susanna Morton Braund. Loeb Classical Library 91. Cambridge, MA: Harvard University Press, 2004.
Kazmierski, Carl R. *John the Baptist: Prophet and Evangelist.* Collegeville, PA: Liturgical Press, 1996.
Kautsky, John. *The Politics of Aristocratic Empires.* Chapel Hill: University of North Carolina Press, 1982.
Keener, Craig S. *A Commentary on the Gospel of Matthew.* Grand Rapids, MI: Eerdmans, 1999.
Kelhoffer, James A. *The Diet of John the Baptist: "Locusts and Wild Honey" in Synoptic and Patristic Interpretation.* Tübingen: Mohr Siebeck, 2005.
King, Helen. *The One-Sex Body on Trial: The Classical and Early Modern Evidence.* Burlington: Ashgate Publishing, 2013.
Kingsbury, Jack Dean. "The Figure of Peter in Matthew's Gospel as a Theological Problem." *Journal of Biblical Literature* 98, no. 1 (Mar 1979): 67–83.
———. *Matthew as Story.* Philadelphia: Fortress Press, 1986.
Klassen, William. *Judas: Betrayer or Friend of Jesus?* Minneapolis, MN: Fortress Press, 1996.
Knapp, Robert. *Invisible Romans.* Cambridge, MA: Harvard University Press, 2011.
Kraeling, Carl H. *John the Baptist.* New York: Scriber's Sons, 1951.
Kraemer, Ross. "Implicating Herodias and Her Daughter in the Death of John the Baptizer: A (Christian) Theological Strategy?" *Journal of Biblical Literature* 125, no. 2 (Summer 2006): 321–49.
Kuefler, Matthew. *The Manly Eunuch: Masculinity, Gender Ambiguity, and Christian Ideology in Late Antiquity.* Chicago: University of Chicago Press, 2001.
Laqueur, Thomas. *Making Sex: Body and Gender from the Greeks to Freud.* Cambridge, MA: Harvard University Press, 1990.
Leloup, Jean-Yves. *Judas and Jesus: Two Faces of a Single Revelation.* Translated by Joseph Rowe. Rochester, VT: Inner Traditions, 2006.
Lenski, Gerhard. *Power and Privilege: A Theory of Social Stratification.* Chapel Hill: University of North Carolina Press, 1984.

Levine, Amy-Jill. "Discharging Responsibility: Matthean Jesus, Biblical Law, and Hemorrhaging Woman." In *A Feminist Companion to Matthew*, edited by Amy-Jill Levine and M. Blickenstaff, 379–97. Sheffield: Sheffield Academic Press, 2001.

———. "Herod the Great." In *The Anchor Bible Dictionary*, edited by David Noel Freedman, 3:161–69. New York: Doubleday, 1992.

Liew, Tat-siong Benny. "Re-Mark-Able Masculinities: Jesus, the Son of Man, and the (Sad) Sum of Manhood?" In *New Testament Masculinities*, edited by Stephen D. Moore and Janice Capel Anderson, 93–135. Atlanta, GA: Society of Biblical Literature, 2003.

Lincoln, Andrew T. "Contested Paternity and Contested Readings: Jesus' Conception in Matthew 1:18–25." *Journal for the Study for the New Testament* 34, no. 3 (2012): 211–31.

Lona, Horacio E. *Judas Iskariot. Legende und Wahrheit: Judas in Den Evangelien Und Das Evangelium Des Judas*. Freiburg: Herder, 2007.

Longenecker, Bruce. *Remember the Poor: Paul, Poverty, and the Greco-Roman World*. Grand Rapids, MI: Eerdmans, 2010.

Lopez, Davina C. *Apostle to the Conquered: Reimagining Paul's Mission*. Minneapolis, MN: Fortress Press, 2008.

Louw, J. P., and Eugene Albert Nida, eds. *Greek-English Lexicon of the New Testament Based on Semantic Domains*. New York: United Bible Societies, 1988.

Luz, Ulrich. *Matthew 1–7: A Commentary*. Translated by James E. Crouch, edited by Helmut Koester. Hermeneia. Minneapolis, MN: Fortress Press, 2007.

———. *Matthew 8–20: A Commentary*. Translated by James E. Crouch, edited by Helmut Koester. Hermeneia. Minneapolis, MN: Fortress Press, 2001.

———. *Matthew 21–28: A Commentary*. Translated by James E. Crouch, edited by Helmut Koester. Hermeneia. Minneapolis, MN: Fortress Press, 2005.

———. *Matthew in History: Interpretation, Influence, and Effects*. Minneapolis, MN: Augsburg Fortress, 1994.

Malbon, Elizabeth Struthers. *In the Company of Jesus: Characters in Mark's Gospel*. Louisville, KY: Westminster John Knox Press, 2000.

Markley, John R. "Reassessing Peter's Imperception in Synoptic Tradition." In *Peter in Early Christianity*, edited by Helen K. Bond and Larry W. Hurtado, 99–108. Grand Rapids, MI: Eerdmans, 2015.

Marohl, Matthew J. *Joseph's Dilemma: "Honour Killing" in the Birth Narrative of Matthew*. Cambridge: James Clark, 2010.

Marshak, Adam Kolman. *The Many Faces of Herod the Great*. Grand Rapids, MI: Eerdmans, 2015.

Martial. *Epigrams, Volume I: Spectacles, Books 1–5*. Edited and translated by D. R. Shackleton Bailey. Loeb Classical Library 94. Cambridge, MA: Harvard University Press, 1993.

McCane, Byron R. "Simply Irresistible: Augustus, Herod, and the Empire." *Journal of Biblical Literature* 127, no. 4 (Winter 2008): 725–35.

McDonnell, Myles. *Roman Manliness: Virtus and the Roman Republic*. New York: Cambridge University Press, 2006.

———. "Roman Men and Greek Virtues." In *Andreia: Studies in Manliness and Courage in Classical Antiquity,* edited by Ralph Mark Rosen and I. Sluiter. Niger: Brill, 2003.

Meggitt, Justin. "Taking the Emperor's Clothes Seriously: The New Testament and the Roman Emperor." In *The Quest for Wisdom: Essays in Honor of Philip Budd,* edited by Christine Joynes, 143–69. Cambridge: Orchard Academic, 2002.

Meyer, Marvin W. *Judas: The Definitive Collection of Gospels and Legends about the Infamous Apostle of Jesus.* New York: HarperOne, 2007.

Miller, Amanda. *Rumors of Resistance: Status Reversal and Hidden Transcripts in the Gospel of Luke.* Minneapolis, MN: Fortress Press, 2014.

Moeser, Annelies. "Joseph's Masculinity in the Synoptic Gospels." Paper presented at the Annual Meeting of the Society of Biblical Literature, Baltimore, MD, November 24, 2013.

Montserrat, Dominic. "Reading Gender in the Roman World." In *Experiencing Rome: Culture, Identity and Power in the Roman Empire*, 3rd ed., edited by Janet Huskinson, 153–82. New York: Routledge, 2009.

———. *Literary Criticism and the Gospels: The Theoretical Challenge.* New Haven, CT: Yale University Press, 1989.

Morales, Helen. *Vision and Narrative in Achilles Tatius' Leucippe and Clitophon.* Cambridge: Cambridge University Press, 2004.

Morgan, Teresa. *Popular Morality in the Early Roman Empire.* New York: Cambridge University Press, 2007.

Motyl, Alexander J. *Imperial Ends: The Decay, Collapse, and Revival of Empires.* New York: Columbia University Press, 2001.

Mowery, Robert L. "God, Lord and Father: The Theology of the Gospel of Matthew." *Biblical Research* 33 (1988): 24–36.

Mudrick, Marvin. *On Culture and Literature.* New York: Horizon, 1970.

Murphy, Catherine. *John the Baptist: Prophet of Purity for a New Age.* Collegeville, PA: Liturgical Press, 2003.

Myles, Robert J. *The Homeless Jesus in the Gospel of Matthew.* Sheffield: Sheffield Phoenix Press, 2014.

Nau, Arlo J. *Peter in Matthew: Discipleship, Diplomacy, and Dispraise.* Collegeville, PA: Liturgical Press, 1992.

Netzer, Ehud. "Herod's Building Program." *Anchor Bible Dictionary,* edited by David Noel Freedman, 3:169–72. New York: Doubleday, 1992.

Neyrey, Jerome. "Jesus, Gender, and the Gospel of Matthew." In *New Testament Masculinities,* edited by Stephen Moore and Janice Capel Anderson, 43–66. Atlanta, GA: Society of Biblical Literature, 2003.

Oakes, Peter. "A State of Tension: Rome in the New Testament." In *The Gospel of Matthew in its Roman Imperial Context,* edited by John Riches and David Sim, 75–90. London: T&T Clark, 2005.

Osiek, Carolyn. "The Women at the Tomb: What Are They Doing There?" In *Feminist Companion to Matthew,* edited by Amy-Jill Levine and M. Blickenstaff, 205–20. Sheffield: Sheffield Academic Press, 2001.

Paffenroth, Kim. *Judas: Images of the Lost Disciple.* Louisville, KY: Westminster John Knox Press, 2001.
Parker, Holt N. "The Teratogenic Grid." In *Roman Sexualities,* edited by Judith P. Hallett and Marilyn B. Skinner, 47–65. Princeton, NJ: Princeton University Press, 1997.
Patte, Daniel. *The Gospel According to Matthew: A Structural Commentary on Matthew's Faith.* Philadelphia: Fortress Press, 1987.
Penner, Todd C., and Caroline Vander Stichele. *Contextualizing Gender in Early Christian Discourse: Thinking Beyond Thecla.* New York: T&T Clark, 2009.
Penner, Todd C., and Caroline Vander Stichele, eds. *Mapping Gender in Ancient Religious Discourse.* Atlanta, GA: Society of Biblical Literature, 2010.
Perkins, Judith. *Roman Imperial Identities in the Early Christian Era.* London: Routledge, 2009.
———. *The Suffering Self: Pain and Narrative Representation in the Early Christian Era.* London: Routledge, 1995.
Perkins, Pheme. *Peter: Apostle for the Whole Church.* Columbia: University of South Carolina Press, 1994.
Petronius, *Satyricon.* Translated by Michael Heseltine, W. H. D. Rouse. Revised by E. H. Warmington. Loeb Classical Library 15. Cambridge, MA: Harvard University Press, 1913.
Philo. *Against Flaccus.* Translated by F. H. Colson. Loeb Classical Library 363. Cambridge, MA: Harvard University Press, 1941.
———. *On the Embassy to Gaius.* Translated by F. H. Colson. Index by J. W. Earp. Loeb Classical Library 379. Cambridge, MA: Harvard University Press, 1962.
Philostratus. *Apollonius of Tyana, Volume II: Life of Apollonius of Tyana, Books 5-8.* Edited and translated by Christopher P. Jones. Loeb Classical Library 17. Cambridge, MA: Harvard University Press, 2005.
Plutarch. *Lives, Volume VII: Demosthenes and Cicero. Alexander and Caesar.* Translated by Bernadotte Perrin. Loeb Classical Library 99. Cambridge, MA: Harvard University Press, 1919.
Powell, Mark Allan. "Literary Approaches and the Gospel of Matthew." In *Methods for Matthew,* edited by Mark Allan Powell, 44–82. Cambridge: Cambridge University Press, 2009.
———. "Narrative Criticism: The Emergence of a Prominent Reading Strategy." In *Mark as Story: Retrospect and Prospect.* Edited by Kelly R. Iverson and Christopher Skinner, 19–43. Atlanta, GA: Society of Biblical Literature, 2011.
Price, S. R. F. "Gods and Emperors: The Greek Language of the Roman Imperial Cult." *The Journal of Hellenistic Studies* 104 (1984): 79–95.
Punt, Jeremy. "Lilly Nortje-Meyer's (En)Gendered New Testament Hermeneutics." *Neotestamentica* 53, no. 2 (2019): 231–48.
Reed, David A. "Saving Judas: A Social-Scientific Approach to Judas's Suicide in Matthew 27:3–10." *Biblical Theology Bulletin* 35, no. 2 (May 2005): 51–59.
Reinhartz, Adele. *Befriending the Beloved Disciple: A Jewish Reading of the Gospel of John.* New York: Continuum, 2001.

Rhoads, David, Joanna Dewey, and Donald Michie. *Mark as Story: An Introduction to the Narrative of a Gospel*, 2nd ed. Minneapolis, MN: Fortress Press, 1999.

Richardson, Peter. *Herod: King of the Jews and Friend of the Romans.* Columbia: University of South Carolina Press, 1996.

Riches, John, and David Sim, eds. *The Gospel of Matthew in its Roman Imperial Context.* London: T&T Clark, 2005.

Richlin, Amy. "Gender and Rhetoric: Producing Manhood in the Schools." In *Sex and Difference in Ancient Greece and Rome*, edited by M. Golden and P. Toohey, 202–20. Edinburgh: Edinburgh University Press, 2003.

Rimmon-Kenan, Shlomith. *Narrative Fiction: Contemporary Poetics,* 2nd ed. London: Routledge, 2002.

Rock, Ian E. *Paul's Letter to the Romans and Roman Imperialism: An Ideological Analysis of the Exordium (Romans 1:1–17).* Eugene, OR: Pickwick, 2012.

Said, Edward. *Orientalism.* New York: Vintage Books, 1979.

Schaberg, Jane. *The Illegitimacy of Jesus: A Feminist Theological Interpretation of the Infancy Narratives.* San Francisco: Harper & Row, 1987.

Schüssler-Fiorenza, Elisabeth. *But She Said: Feminist Practices of Biblical Interpretation.* Boston: Beacon Press, 1992.

———. *Rhetoric and Ethic: The Politics of Biblical Studies.* Minneapolis, MN: Fortress Press, 1999.

Scott, James C. *Domination and the Arts of Resistance: Hidden Transcripts.* New Haven, CT: Yale University Press, 1990.

———. *Moral Economy of the Peasant: Rebellion and Subsistence in Southeast Asia.* New Haven, CT: Yale University Press, 1976.

———. *Weapons of the Weak: Everyday Forms of Peasant Resistance.* New Haven, CT: Yale University Press, 1985.

Segovia, Fernando F. "Postcolonial Criticism and the Gospel of Matthew." In *Methods for Matthew,* edited by Mark Allan Powell, 194–237. Cambridge: Cambridge University Press, 2009.

Seneca. *Apocolocyntosis (divi) Claudii.* Translated by Michael Heseltine, W. H. D. Rouse. Revised by E. H. Warmington. Loeb Classical Library 15. Cambridge, MA: Harvard University Press, 1913.

Shepherd, William H. *The Narrative Function of the Holy Spirit as a Character in Luke-Acts.* Atlanta, GA: Scholars Press, 1994.

Sim, David C. "Rome in Matthew's Eschatology." In *The Gospel of Matthew in its Roman Imperial Context,* edited by John Riches and David C. Sim, 91–106. New York: T&T Clark, 2005.

Sjoberg, Gideon. *The Preindustrial City: Past and Present.* Glencoe, IL: Free Press, 1960.

Skinner, Christopher, ed. *Characters and Characterization in the Gospel of John.* London: Bloomsbury, 2013.

Skinner, Christopher and Matthew R. Hauge, eds. *Character Studies and the Gospel of Mark.* London: Bloomsbury, 2014.

Spivak, Gayatri. *A Critique of Postcolonial Reason: Toward a History of the Vanishing Present.* Cambridge, MA: Harvard University Press, 1999.

Stanford, Peter. *Judas: The Most Hated Name in History.* Berkeley: Counterpoint Press, 2016.

Stanton, Elizabeth Cady. *The Woman's Bible.* Amherst, NY: Prometheus Books, 1999.

Stanton, Graham N. *A Gospel for a New People: Studies in Matthew.* Louisville, KY: Westminster John Knox, 1993.

Strecker, Georg. *Der Weg der Gerechtigkeit.* Forschungen zur Religion und Literatur des Alten und Neuen Testaments 87, 2nd ed. Göttingen: Vandenhoeck & Ruprecht, 1971.

Suetonius. *Lives of the Caesars, Volume II: Claudius. Nero. Galba, Otho, and Vitellius. Vespasian. Titus, Domitian.* Translated by J. C. Rolfe. Loeb Classical Library 38. Cambridge, MA: Harvard University Press, 1914.

Sugirtharajah, R. S. *Exploring Postcolonial Biblical Criticism: History, Method, Practice.* Chichester, West Sussex: Wiley-Blackwell, 2011.

Syreeni, Kari. "Peter as Character and Symbol in the Gospel of Matthew." In *Characterization in the Gospels: Reconceiving Narrative Criticism,* edited by David Rhoads and Kari Syreeni, JSNTSup 184, 106–52. Sheffield: Sheffield Academic, 1999.

Tatum, W. Barnes. *John the Baptist and Jesus: A Report of the Jesus Seminar.* Sonoma, CA: Polebridge Press, 1994.

Taylor, Joan E. *The Immerser: John the Baptist within Second Temple Judaism.* Grand Rapids, MI: Eerdmans, 1997.

Theissen, Gerd. *The Gospels in Context: Social and Political History in the Synoptic Tradition.* Minneapolis, MN: Fortress Press, 1991.

Thurman, Eric. "Looking for a Few Good Men: Mark and Masculinity." In *New Testament Masculinities,* edited by Stephen D. Moore and Janice Capel Anderson, 137–61. Atlanta, GA: Society of Biblical Literature, 2003.

———. "Novel Men: Masculinity and Empire in Mark's Gospel and Xenophon's *An Ephesian Tale.*" In *Mapping Gender in Ancient Religious Discourses,* edited by Todd Penner and Caroline Vander Stichele, 185–229. Leiden: Brill, 2007.

Traister, Bryce. "Academic Viagra: The Rise of American Masculinity Studies." *American Quarterly* 52, no. 2 (June 2000): 274–304.

Turner, David L. *Matthew.* Grand Rapids, MI: Baker, 2008.

Unnik, Willem Cornelis van. "The Death of Judas in Saint Matthew's Gospel." *Anglican Theological Review.* Supplement Series (3 March 1974): 44–57.

Vander Stichele, Caroline. "Herodias Goes Headhunting." In *From the Margins II: Women of the New Testament and Their Afterlives,* edited by Christine Joynes and Christopher Rowland, 164–75. Sheffield: Sheffield Phoenix Press, 2009.

Viljoen, Francois P. "The Significance of Dreams and the Star in Matthew's Infancy Narrative." *HTS Theological Studies* 64, no. 2 (Jun 2008): 845–60.

Virgil. *Aeneid: Books 1–6.* Translated by H. Rushton Fairclough. Revised by G. P. Goold. Loeb Classical Library 63. Cambridge, MA: Harvard University Press, 1916.

———. *Aeneid: Books 7–12.* Translated by H. Rushton Fairclough. Revised by G. P. Goold. Loeb Classical Library 64. Cambridge, MA: Harvard University Press, 1918.

Wainwright, Elaine. "Feminist Criticism and the Gospel of Matthew." In *Methods for Matthew*, edited by Mark Allan Powell, 83–117. New York: Cambridge University Press, 2009.

———. *Shall We Look for Another? A Feminist Rereading of the Matthean Jesus.* Maryknoll, NY: Orbis, 1998.

———. *Towards a Feminist Critical Reading of the Gospel According to Matthew.* BZNW 60. Berlin: deGruyter, 1991.

Walters, Jonathan. "Invading the Roman Body: Manliness and Impenetrability in Roman Thought." In *Roman Sexualities,* edited by Judith Hallett and Marilyn Skinner, 29–43. Princeton, NJ: Princeton University Press, 1997.

Weaver, Dorothy Jean. "Power and Powerlessness: Matthew's Use of Irony in the Portrayal of Political Leaders." In *Society of Biblical Literature 1992 Seminar Papers,* edited by E. H. Lovering, Jr, 454–66. Atlanta, GA: Scholars Press, 1992.

———. "'Thus You Will Know Them By Their Fruits': The Roman Characters of the Gospel of Matthew." In *The Gospel of Matthew in its Roman Imperial Context,* edited by John Riches and David Sim, 107–27. London: T&T Clark, 2005.

Webb, Robert L. *John the Baptizer and Prophet: A Socio-Historical Study.* Sheffield: Sheffield Academic Press, 1991.

Whittaker, C. R. "The Poor." In *The Romans,* edited by Andrea Giardina, 272–99. Chicago: University of Chicago Press, 1993.

Wiarda, Timothy. *Peter in the Gospels: Pattern, Personality, and Relationship.* WUNT 2, no. 127. Tübingen: Mohr Siebeck, 2000.

Williams, Craig. *Roman Homosexuality: Ideologies of Masculinity in Classical Antiquity*, 2nd ed. Oxford: Oxford University Press, 2010.

Wilson, Brittany E. *Unmanly Men: Refigurations of Masculinity in Luke-Acts.* New York: Oxford University Press, 2015.

Wilson, Carol. *For I Was Hungry and You Gave Me Food: Pragmatics of Food Access in the Gospel of Matthew.* Eugene, OR: Pickwick, 2014.

Wink, Walter. *John the Baptist and the Gospel Tradition.* New York: Cambridge University Press, 1968.

Wittfogel, Karl. *Oriental Despotism: A Comparative Study of Total Power.* New Haven, CT: Yale University Press, 1957.

Wollstonecraft, Mary. *A Vindication of the Rights of Woman.* London: Farnborough, Gregg, 1970.

Yamasaki, Gary. *John the Baptist in Life and Death: Audience-Oriented Criticism of Matthew's Narrative.* Sheffield: Sheffield Academic Press, 1998.

Zanker, Paul. *The Power of Images in the Age of Augustus.* Translated by Alan Shapiro. Ann Arbor: University of Michigan Press, 1990.

Index

Abraham, 50, 51
Acts, 29, 128
adoption, of Jesus, 63, 64, 83n73
adultery, 36n56; divorce for, 68; honor killings for, 68, 69, 71, 85nn113–14; of Mary, 68, 70, 71, 85n114
agency: of Herodias, 122n80; of Jesus, 175; of John the Baptist, 106–7, 109; of Joseph, 52–53, 59, 61; of Judas, 169, 174, 176, 179; of women, 105
Ahab, 119n31
Ahaziah, 119n31
Albright, W. F., 70
Alföldy, Géza, 20
Allison, Dale C.: on John the Baptist, 93–94, 97; on Joseph and King Herod, 49–50, 54, 58, 68, 72, 86n135; on Judas, 170, 176, 185, 190, 195n9, 198n47; on Peter, 132, 141, 154
ambiguity: of John the Baptist, 100, 109; of Joseph, 53, 73; of Judas, 171, 181; of Peter, 128, 140–43, 156
ambivalence, 1, 8, 22; of John the Baptist, 99–100, 106–7, 108; of Joseph, 53, 56, 61, 64, 66, 73, 76; masculinity and, 32; of Peter, 155, 158; with virtue and power, 36n56

Anderson, Janice Capel, 4, 30–31, 65, 66, 106; on androcentrism, 24; on genealogy, 29
Andrew, 130, 137; as fisherman, 154
androcentrism, 24, 31, 65
angel, Joseph and, 57–59, 60, 61, 63, 69, 71, 81n57
angelophanies, 58
anger: control of self and others and, 57; of John the Baptist, 103; of King Herod, 53, 58, 62; masculinity and, 15; of Peter, 166n100
aorists, 118n14
Apocolocyntosis (divi) Claudii ("Gourdification of the divine Claudius") (Seneca), 74
apostasy, 170
apotheosis, 73–74
Archelaus, 60, 62; Joseph's dream on, 71
Aristobolus, 79n32
asceticism, of John the Baptist, 107–8, 206
Asikainen, Susanna, 4, 5, 28–29
audience-oriented narrative criticism, 43n166
Augustus, 36n59, 80n37, 131; on adultery, 36n56; piety of, 73–74

223

Baal, prophets of, 119n31
baptism, 94; of Jesus, 95, 98, 99, 108, 118n20, 120n48
beheading, of John the Baptist, 1, 109, 124n97
Bethlehem, 62, 82n62
Boaz, 78n7; Jesus and, 51
Bockmuehl, M. N. A., 68, 161n14
body: of Joseph, 59–61; of Mary, 60
body-reflexive practice, 23–24, 42n151
Bosworth, Brian, 73
Brown, Raymond, 65, 66–67, 70, 162n28; on Judas, 196n18, 200n89; on Peter, 135–36
Butler, Judith, 5, 23

Caesar, Julius, 131
Caesarea Philippi, 158
Caligula, 131
Carey, Holly J., 189
Carter, Warren, 20, 21–22, 31; on forgiveness, 164n53; on John the Baptist, 90, 94, 97, 105, 112; on Joseph and King Herod, 51, 54, 59, 62, 73, 79n33; on Judas, 175–76, 185, 190, 192, 197n24; on Peter, 135, 139, 146, 154
Cassidy, Richard J., 130, 161n10
Casson, Lionel, 52
Cato the Elder, 85n111
Chatman, Seymour, 26, 27
Chronicles, 180
Claudius, 74
confession: of Judas, 192; of Peter, 134, 189; women and, 31
Connell, R. W., 4–5, 23–24, 31, 42n151, 61
control of self and others: anger and, 57; by Herod Antipas, 102–11; in ideal masculinity, 103; by John the Baptist, 102–11; by Joseph, 73, 74–75; by Judas, 170–83; in masculinity, 57–66; by Peter, 145–53. *See also* agency

Conway, Colleen, 4, 6, 17, 19, 25, 28, 34n24, 36n51; on Jesus, 98, 101; on Otho, 180; on Peter, 146, 150–51
Cornelius, 29
Cotter, Wendy, 73–74
courage, 80n47
Crossan, Oscar, 21
crucifixion, 124n96, 136; of Jesus, 141, 151, 192, 205

Daly, Mary, 1
D'Angelo, Mary Rose, 75, 82n65, 87n152
Daniel, 72
David, 50, 51, 55, 63, 66–77
Davies, W. D.: on John the Baptist, 93–94, 97; on Joseph and King Herod, 49–50, 54, 58, 72, 86n135; on Judas, 170, 176, 185, 190, 195n9, 198n47; on Peter, 132, 141, 154
de-centering, of masculinity, 23
Demetriou, Demetrakis, 4–5
Deuteronomy, 55, 185–86, 192, 193; adultery, 69; on divorce, 67, 68
Deutsch, Celia, 24
Dionysius of Halicarnassus, 119n32
discipleship: false, 190; feminist theory on, 159–60; forgiveness and, 205–6; imperial masculinity and, 194; to Jesus, 99, 134, 141, 142; to John the Baptist, 99, 109; masculinity and, 32; wealth and, 205. *See also* Judas; Peter
divine service: of Jesus, 101; of John the Baptist, 90–102, *91–93*; of Joseph, 66–75; of Judas, 188–93; masculinity and, 3, 32n5, 37n66, 135, 144, 205–6; of Peter, 129–45
divorce, 67–68; contemplated by Joseph, 57, 60, 67, 85n107
Doane, Sébastien, 29, 78, 82n65
Dodson, Derek S., 71–72
Domitian, 131
Donfried, Karl, 135–36, 162n28
Doyle, Michael, 20

dreams, of Joseph, 58–59, 61–62, 71–72, 75, 86nn124–25
Droge, Arthur J., 202n117
Dube, Musa, 24, 30

Edwards, Catherine, 16, 124n97, 124n100; on Judas, 171
Egypt, flight to, 52–53, 55, 62, 82n62
Eilberg-Schwartz, Howard, 75, 82n65, 208
Eisenstadt, S. N., 20
Elijah, 96–97, 99, 106, 118n22, 119n23, 119n28, 119n30, 123n88, 148, 151; in Kings, 119n31; in Transfiguration, 137, 138, 151, 156
Elisha, 119n31
elites: of Greeks, 51; hegemonic masculinity of, 31; ideal masculinity of, 34n27, 56; masculinity and, 17–19, 34n24, 39n109, 76, 105; power of, 51–52, 109; in Roman Empire, 51–52; wealth of, 51–52, 78n15, 124n100. *See also specific individuals*
Elliot, Neil, 21
Engelhardt, Jillian, 124n104
Exodus, 72, 97, 185
Ezekiel, 85n111

false discipleship, 190
fasting: hunger and, 117n8; by John the Baptist, 99, 102, 112, 117n3, 120n45
Favorinus, 105
fear: Jesus on, 143; Joseph and, 57–59; of King Herod, 58–59, 73; masculinity and, 15, 57–59; of Peter, 151
femininity: as equal of gender, 22, 23; ideal masculinity and, 8; internal and external dynamics of, 4–5; social construction of, 207
feminist theory: on discipleship, 159–60; on Mary, 65; on masculinity, 4, 6, 22–25, 30–31, 41n146; on power, 24
Fiorenza, Elisabeth Schüssler, 24

Flavorinus, 17–18
Flessen, Bonnie, 29
food: hunger and, 117n8; of John the Baptist, 90, 102–3
forgiveness, 164n53; discipleship and, 205–6; Jesus and, 149–50, 156; Peter and, 132, 139–40, 149–50, 156; power and, 149–50; wealth and, 156
Forster, 27
Foucault, Michel, 5, 23
Friesen, Steven J., 39n109, 51, 60

Gainj women, 181
Galilee, 59, 62, 130, 144, 182
Galinsky, Karl, 73
gender: femininity in, 22, 23; narrative criticism on, 27; one-sex model of, 34n27; in Roman Empire, 59–60; social construction of, 24, 35n43; studies, 4. *See also* women
genealogy, of Jesus and Joseph, 29, 31, 50–51, 63, 83n77
Gethsemane, 142, 176
Glancy, Jennifer, 31, 105–6, 122n80
Gleason, Maude, 16–17, 19, 34n27, 38n95, 105
Goffman, Ervin, 67
golden mean of masculinity, 104
Gospel of John, 21, 131, 196n21
Gospel of Mark, 28, 29, 118n19, 131, 137
Gospel of Matthew. *See specific topics*
"Gourdification of the divine Claudius" (*Apocolocyntosis (divi) Claudii*) (Seneca), 74
Greeks: elites of, 51; literature of, 71–72
Grisé, Yolande, 199n61
Gubar, Susan, 185, 195n4
Guest, Deryn, 23
Gunderson, Erik, 16
Gundry, Robert, 165n74; on Judas, 170; on Peter, 128, 130

Hanson, K. C., 20, 154
Harvey, W. J., 26

hegemonic masculinity, 2; defined, 4; of elites, 31; internal and external dynamics of, 4–5; of Judas, 174; passion in, 150–51; power and, 5; sexuality and, 5–6; women and, 5
Hengel, Martin, 161n14
Herod (Kiing), 1, 29, 31, 79nn30–32; anger of, 53, 58, 62; control of self and others by, 57–66; death of, 73; fear of, 58–59, 73; ideal masculinity of, 80n45; Jesus and, 50, 62, 81n53, 86n135; Joseph and, 49–77, 203–4; narrative criticism on, 28; patronage of, 53; power of, 53–54; wealth and, 50–56
Herod Antipas, 1, 29, 31; control of self and others by, 102–11; John the Baptist and, 89–116, 118n19, 122n80, 124n104, 204; narrative criticism on, 28; power of, 108; wealth and, 89, 108, 111–14
Herodias, 31, 95, 106; agency of, 122n80
Hezekiah, 51
Hezser, Catherine, 52
Hochman, Baruch, 27
Holy Spirit, 60
homelessness, 42–53
homosexuality, 5
honor killings, for adultery, 68, 69, 71, 85nn113–14
Hooff, Anton J. L. van, 199n61
Horsley, Richard, 21
Hosea, 85n111
hostels (*mutationes*), 52
hunger: fasting and, 117n8; masculinity and, 15

ideal masculinity, 7; control of self and others in, 103; of elites, 34n27, 56; femininity and, 8; of Jesus, 29, 98; of King Herod, 80n45; patriarchal dividend and, 8; public speaking and, 13; unavailability of, 208; wealth and, 11

imperial masculinity, 5, 20–22; discipleship and, 194; of Jesus, 101; Judas and, 181; Peter and, 129, 146, 157
inns (*mansiones/stationes*), 52
Isaiah, 90, 93, 97
Israel, 51

James, 137, 142, 148
Jehoshaphat, 51
Jeremiah, 96, 186
Jesus: adoption of, 63, 64, 66, 67, 83n73; agency of, 175; anointing of, 173, 183, 189; arrest of, 130, 141, 142, 151, 178; baptism of, 95, 98, 99, 108, 118n20, 120n48; birth of, 54–55; as carpenter's son, 49; crucifixion of, 141, 151, 192, 205; discipleship to, 99, 134, 141, 142; divine service of, 101; on divorce, 67–68; in Egypt, 52; fasting by, 99, 117n3, 120n45; on fear, 143; forgiveness and, 149–50, 156; genealogy of, 29, 31, 50–51, 63, 83n77; as God's son, 97, 137; healing by, 130–31, 145–46; ideal masculinity of, 29, 98; identity of, 63; imperial masculinity of, 101; John the Baptist and, 94–102, 106–8, 114, 115, 118nn20–21, 120n48, 121n55, 130; Joseph and, 50–51, 63, 203; Joseph's control of, 61–62; Judas and, 1, 169–94, 198n47, 201n108, 205; King Herod and, 50, 62, 81n53, 86n135; low birth of, 67; masculinity of, 3, 28, 29, 67; as Messiah, 50, 99, 134; narrative criticism on, 28; patriarchy and, 87n152; Peter and, 1, 45n181, 129–45, 163n43, 164nn69–70, 165n81, 204–5; power of, 100, 145–46, 165n82; prediction of, 135, 141, 146, 151, 164n69, 178; public speaking by, 121n72, 175; resurrection of, 141, 151; Revelation and, 21; Roman

Empire and, 148; Sermon on the Mount of, 207; as Son of God, 132, 162n28; suffering and death of, 136, 147; taxes and, 148, 157; in Transfiguration, 136–38, 147, 148, 151, 156; walking on water, 131, 146, 151; on wealth, 112–13, 140; Wisdom and, 24; women and, 30

Jewish Antiquities (Josephus), 79n32

Jezebel, 119n31

Job, 55

John (disciple), 148; weeping of, 167n101

John, Gospel of, 21, 131, 196n21

John the Baptist, 1, 29, 31; agency of, 106–7, 109; ambiguity of, 100, 109; ambivalence of, 99–100, 106–7, 108; anger of, 103; asceticism of, 107–8, 206; beheading of, 1, 109, 124n97; control of self and others by, 102–11; credibility of, 117n10; death of, 95–96, 101, 105–10, 122n80, 124n104; discipleship to, 99, 109; divine service of, 90–102, *91–93*; Elijah and, 96–97, 99, 106, 118n22, 119n23, 119n28, 119n30, 123n88; fasting by, 99, 112, 117n3, 120n45; food of, 90, 102–3; Herod Antipas and, 89–116, 118n19, 122n80, 124n104, 204; imprisonment of, 102, 105, 112, 113; Jesus and, 94–102, 106–8, 118nn20–21, 120n48, 121n55, 130; Joseph and, 121n68; Judas and, 174; martyrdom of, 90, 95–96, 101; narrative criticism on, 28; Peter and, 133; power of, 105, 109–10; as prophet, 93–94, 96, 97–98, 100–101, 118n22; public speaking by, 105, 107; repentance and, 123n86; righteousness of, 96; scholarship on, 116n2; sexuality and, 104, 121n64; wealth and, 89, 111–14, 154; in wilderness, 90–91, 104–5, 108, 117n7, 123n88

Joseph: agency of, 52–53, 59, 61; ambiguity of, 53, 73; ambivalence of, 53, 56, 61, 64, 66, 73, 76; angel and, 57–59, 60, 61, 63, 69, 71, 81n57; body of, 59–61; contemplated divorce by, 57, 60, 67, 68–69, 85n107; control of self and others by, 57–66, 73, 74–75; dilemma of, 55; divine service of, 66–75; dreams of, 58–59, 61–62, 71–72, 75, 86nn124–25; in Egypt, 52, 55, 62; genealogy of, 29, 31, 50–51, 63, 83n77; as husband of Mary, 63; as ideal man, 65; Jesus' adoption by, 63, 64, 66, 67, 83n73; Jesus and, 50–51, 63, 203; John the Baptist and, 121n68; Judas and, 174; kindness and gentleness of, 70; King Herod and, 49–77, 203–4; masculinity of, 55–56; narrative criticism on, 28; obedience of, 53, 55, 56, 63, 66, 70–73, 75, 76, 83n79, 205; poverty of, 51–52; righteousness of, 53, 56, 63, 66–69, 72–73, 76, 84n98, 85n112, 85n114, 86n117; stigma of, 67; virtue of, 53, 57, 72; wealth and, 50–56, 154

"Joseph's Masculinity in the Synoptic Gospels" (Moeser), 83n77

Josephus, 85n111; on Jon the Baptist, 108–9, 123n91; on King Herod, 58, 79n32; on obedience, 70

Jubilees, 85n111

Judas, 29, 31; agency of, 169, 174, 176, 179; ambiguity of, 171, 181; confession of, 192; control of self and others by, 170–83; divine service of, 188–93; hegemonic masculinity of, 174; imperial masculinity and, 181; Jesus and, 1, 169–94, 198n47, 201n108, 205; as last disciple, 170–71, 172; narrative criticism on, 28; as non-elites, 182–83; Peter and, 170–71, 173, 195n9; regret of, 179, 182, 192, 200n82; repentance of, 192, 200n94, 201n111; suicide of,

179–82, 193, 199n61; wealth and, 179, 183–87, 199n69
Judas Maccabeus, 90
Judges, 85n111

Kautsky, John, 20
Keener, Craig, 202n117
Kelhoffer, James A., 90
kindness and gentleness, of Joseph, 70
King, Helen, 34n27
Kings, 119n31
Klassen, William, 170, 171, 174, 178, 185, 192, 196n15
Knapp, Robert, 18–19, 20
Kuefler, Matthew, 36n51

Laqueur, Thomas, 34n27
Last Supper, 174–75
Lenski, Gerhard, 20, 39n109
Levine, Amy-Jill, 31
Leviticus, 192–93
Liew, Tat-siong Benny, 4, 28, 105–6, 124n104
literalness, 27
Livy, 85n111
Longenecker, Bruce, 20, 40n127
Lopez, Davina, 21, 80n37
Louw, J. P., 77n2
Luke, Gospel of, 66, 72, 82n62, 83n77, 119n26
Luz, Ulrich: on John the Baptist, 94, 97, 99; on Joseph and King Herod, 51, 54, 63, 67, 68, 70, 71, 81n53; on Judas, 174, 180, 184–85, 186, 189, 197n25, 199n61; on Peter, 131, 133, 140, 141, 142, 145, 163n43, 164n70, 165n81; on suicide, 202n117; on walking on water, 161n18, 161n20

Maccabees, 180
magi, 79n33; gifts of, 54–55
Malachi, 97
male privilege, 5
Mann, C. S., 70
mansiones (inns), 52

Mark, Gospel of, 28, 29, 118n19, 131, 137
Markley, John R., 162n26, 162n29
Marohl, Matthew J., 55, 68, 69, 85n111, 85n114
Marshak, Adam Kolman, 79nn30–31
martyrdom: of John the Baptist, 90, 95–96, 101; of Otho, 180
Mary: adultery of, 68, 70, 71, 85n114; body of, 60; contemplated divorce by Joseph, 57, 60, 67, 68–69, 85n107; in Egypt, 52, 55, 62; feminist theory on, 65; Holy Spirit and, 60; Jesus and, 51; Joseph as husband of, 63, 203; Joseph's control of, 61–62, 64, 66; legal status of, 82n66; passivity of, 59; pregnancy of, 60–61, 69, 82n65, 83n79; righteousness of, 55; sexuality of, 64; shame of, 69, 70; as virgin, 72
masculinity: ambivalence and, 32; anger and, 15; apotheosis and, 73–74; control of self and others in, 57–66; de-centering of, 23; discipleship and, 32; divine service and, 3, 32n5, 37n66, 135, 144, 205–6; elites and, 17–19, 34n24, 39n109, 76, 105; fear and, 15, 57–59; feminist theory on, 4, 6, 22–25, 30–31, 41n146; golden mean of, 104; hunger and, 15; of Jesus, 3, 28, 29, 67; narrative criticism on, 25–28, 43nn165–66, 45n182; negative expectations of, 32n3; of non-elites, 18–19, 22, 30, 40n127, 65, 76; one-sex model of gender and, 34n27; in popular culture, 18; power and, 3, 22–25, 58, 65, 73–74, 207–8; in Roman Empire, 2, 17–19, 20–22, 30, 76, 101, 104, 105, 113; sexuality and, 34n19; social construction of, 207; studies of, 4–16; wealth and, 50–56, 113, 114, 124n102, 154; women and, 32n3. *See also* hegemonic masculinity; ideal masculinity;

imperial masculinity; *specific individuals*
Matthew, Gospel of. *See specific topics*
McDonnell, Myles, 35n50
Meggitt, Justin, 20
Men's Movement, 42n162
Men's Rights Movement, 42n162
mercy, righteousness and, 85n112
Messiah, Jesus as, 50, 99, 134
military service, 38n95, 38n100
Mishnah, 85n111
Moeser, Annelies, 67, 83n77, 84n97, 86n124
Montserrat, Dominic, 59, 60–61
Moore, Stephen, 4, 25, 29
Morgan, Teresa, 18
Moses, 137, 138; in Transfiguration, 148, 151, 156
Motyl, Alexander J., 20
Mount of Olives, 191
Murphy, Catherine, 96, 105, 119n26
mutationes (hostels), 52
Myles, Robert, 42–53

narrative criticism, on masculinity, 25–28, 43nn165–66, 45n182
Nathan, 66
Nau, Arlo, 128
Nazareth, 55, 82n62, 86n124
Nero, 36n59, 74
New Testament. *See specific topics*
Neyrey, Jerome, 28, 121n72
Nida, Albert, 77n2
non-elites: Judas as, 182–83; masculinity of, 18–19, 22, 30, 40n127, 65, 76; Peter as, 148, 158
normification, 67
Nortje, Lilly, 41n146

Oakes, Peter, 21
Oakman, Douglas, 20, 154
obedience: of Joseph, 53, 55, 56, 63, 66, 70–73, 75, 76, 83n79, 205; patriarchal dividend and, 15, 144
Ordinary Romans (Knapp), 18–19

Orientalism, 54
Osiek, Carolyn, 31
Otho, 180
Oxyrynchus papyri, 59

paradigm of traits, 26
passion, of Peter, 150–52, 164n69
patriarchal dividend, 15, 61, 144; ideal masculinity and, 8
patriarchy: Jesus and, 87n152; phallus in, 106
patronage, of King Herod, 53
Patte, Daniel, 161n9
Paul, 21
Perkins, Judith, 130
Peter, 29, 31, 127–60; ambiguity of, 128, 140–43, 156; ambivalence of, 155, 158; anger of, 166n100; confession of, 134, 189; control of self and others by, 145–53; denial by, 143, 147, 148, 151–52, 164n70, 176; divine service of, 129–45; fear of, 151; firstness of, 129, 130, 133–34, 145, 155–56, 170–71; as fisherman, 154; forgiveness and, 132, 139–40, 149–50, 156; imperial masculinity and, 129, 146, 157; Jesus and, 1, 45n181, 129–45, 163n43, 164nn69–70, 165n81, 204–5; John the Baptist and, 133; Judas and, 170–71, 173, 195n9; limitations of, 133; narrative criticism on, 27, 28; as non-elites, 148, 158; passion of, 150–52, 164n69; power of, 128, 145–46, 155; public speech by, 147–48; Satan and, 130; sleep of, 142, 151; as spokesperson, 132–33, 139; taxes and, 148, 157; as tempter, 135; in Transfiguration, 136–38, 147, 148, 151, 156; walking on water, 129, 130, 131, 132, 133–34, 146, 151; wealth and, 153–58; weeping by, 143, 152
Petronius, 78n8
phallocentricity, 60–61

Index

phallus, in patriarchy, 106
Pharisees, 94, 99, 120n44, 175, 189
Philo, 85n111
Pilate, 20, 178–79, 181, 186, 191–92, 198n47
Polemo, 105
popular culture, masculinity in, 18
poverty, 22; of Joseph, 51–52; scales for, 20, 39n109
Powell, Mark Allan, 43nn165–66
power: apotheosis and, 73–74; of elites, 51–52, 109; feminist theory on, 24; forgiveness and, 149–50; hegemonic masculinity and, 5; of Herod Antipas, 108; of Jesus, 100, 118n21, 145–46, 165n82; of John the Baptist, 105, 109–10; of King Herod, 53–54; masculinity and, 3, 22–25, 58, 65, 73–74, 207–8; patriarchal dividend and, 15, 144; of Peter, 128, 145–46, 155; phallus and, 106; virtue and, 36n56; wealth and, 51–52. *See also* control of self and others
Promise Keepers, 42n162
prophets, 123n86; of Baal, 119n31; John the Baptist as, 93–94, 96, 97–98, 100–101, 118n22
public speaking: ideal masculinity and, 13; by Jesus, 121n72, 175; by John the Baptist, 105, 107; by Peter, 147–48
purity codes, for women, 31

reader-oriented narrative criticism, 43n166
Reed, David A., 21, 180, 181, 198n54, 202n117
repentance: John the Baptist and, 123n86; of Judas, 192, 200n94, 201n111
Res Gestae (Augustus), 73
resurrection, of Jesus, 141, 151
Reumann, John, 135–36, 162n28
Revelation, 21
Richlin, Amy, 16

righteousness: of John the Baptist, 96; of Joseph, 53, 56, 63, 66–70, 72–73, 76, 84n98, 85n112, 85n114, 86n117; of Mary, 55; mercy and, 85n112
The Roman Antiquities (Dionysius of Halicarnassus), 119n32
Roman Empire: elites in, 51–52; gender in, 59–60; gifts in, 54–55, 80n42; Jesus and, 148; literature of, 71–72; masculinity in, 2, 17–22, 30, 76, 101, 104, 105, 113; taxes of, 148, 157, 166n91; virtue in, 36n51, 36n56; wealth in, 50–56. *See also specific individuals and topics*; *specific topics and individuals*
Ruth, 78n7; Jesus and, 51

Sadducees, 94
Said, Edward, 54
Samson, 180, 181
Samuel, 66
Satan, Peter and, 130
Satyricon (Petronius), 78n8
Schaberg, Jane, 31, 63, 65, 69, 82n66, 85nn112–13, 86n117
Scott, James, 20, 22, 83n71, 124n104
Seneca, 180
Sermon on the Mount, 207
sexuality: hegemonic masculinity and, 5–6; John the Baptist and, 104, 121n64; of Mary, 64; masculinity and, 34n19
Sim, David, 20
Simon. *See* Peter
Sirach, 63, 83
Sjoberg, Gideon, 20
slavery/slaves, 31, 78n8; forgiveness and, 149–50; Peter and, 148; torture or killing of, 38n102
sleep, of Peter, 142, 151
social construction, of gender, 24, 35n43
Solomon, 51
Stanton, Graham, 28, 49, 89
stationes (inns), 52
stigma: defined, 84n97; of Joseph, 67

stylization, 27
Suetonius, 74, 85n111, 167n110, 198n54; on Judas, 180
suicide, 179–81, 193, 198n54, 199n61, 202n117
Susanna, 85n111
synkrisis, 28, 49, 89
Synoptics, 29
Syreeni, Kari, 128, 139, 165n77, 167n103

Tabor, James D., 202n117
taxes, 148, 157, 166n91
Testament of Zebulon (Luz), 186
text-oriented narrative criticism, 43n166
Thurman, Eric, 4, 25, 29
Tiberius, 131
Titus, 131
Traister, Bryce, 35n43
traits, paradigm of, 26
Transfiguration, 136–38, 147, 148, 151, 156
transgenders, 42n152
Trimalchio, 78n8

Uzziah, 51

Vespasian, 74, 131, 167n110
Viljoen, Francois P., 72
virtue: of Joseph, 53, 57, 72; power and, 36n56; in Roman Empire, 36n51, 36n56. *See also* righteousness
virtus, 35n50, 80n47
A Voice for Men, 42n162

Wainwright, Elaine, 24, 25, 31
walking on water, 129, 130, 131, 132, 133–34, 146, 151, 161n18, 161n20
Walters, Jonathan, 16, 38n100

wealth: discipleship and, 205; of elites, 51–52, 78n15, 124n100; forgiveness and, 156; Herod Antipas and, 89, 108, 111–14; ideal masculinity and, 11; Jesus on, 112–13, 140; John the Baptist and, 89, 111–14, 154; Joseph and, 50–56, 154; Judas and, 179, 183–87, 199n69; King Herod and, 50–56; masculinity and, 50–56, 113, 114, 124n102, 154; Peter and, 153–58; power and, 51–52; in Roman Empire, 50–56; of women, 78n15
Weaver, Dorothy, 20
Whittaker, C. R., 20
Williams, Craig, 16, 38nn99–100, 104
Wilson, Brittany, 4, 5, 29
Wilson, Carol, 20
Wink, Walter, 98, 119n23, 119n30, 120n54
Wisdom, Jesus and, 24
Wisdom of Solomon, 63, 83n74
Wittfogel, Karl, 20
women: agency of, 105; anger of, 166n100; confession and, 31; devaluation of, 1; as equal of gender, 22; Gainj, 181; hegemonic masculinity and, 5; Jesus and, 30; masculinity and, 32n3; materiality of, 43n151; one-sex model of gender and, 34n27; Peter and, 148; purity codes for, 31; suicide of, 181; wealth of, 78n15. *See also* feminist theory

Yamasaki, Gary, on John the Baptist, 94, 97, 99, 117n10, 118n14, 118n20, 120n40, 120n43

Zebedee, 142
Zechariah, 185, 186

About the Author

Kendra A. Mohn (PhD, Brite Divinity School) is lead pastor of Trinity Lutheran Church in Fort Worth, Texas.